Class and Gender in British Labour History

CLASS AND GENDER IN BRITISH LABOUR HISTORY

Renewing the Debate (or Starting It?)

Edited by Mary Davis

MERLIN PRESS

© this collection, Merlin Press 2011

Published in the UK in 2011
by The Merlin Press Ltd.
6 Crane Street Chambers
Crane Street
Pontypool
NP4 6ND
Wales

www.merlinpress.co.uk

ISBN. 978-0-85036-668-6

British Library Cataloguing in Publication Data
is available from the British Library

All rights reserved. No part of this publication may be
reproduced, stored in a retrieval system, or transmitted,
in any form or by any means, electronic, mechanical,
photocopying, recording or otherwise, without the
prior permission of the publisher.

Printed in the UK by Imprint Digital, Exeter

Contents

Contributors	vii
Glossary	ix

Introduction and theoretical framework

Mary Davis	Introduction	1
Mary Davis	*The Making of the English Working Class* revisited: labour history and Marxist theory	12

Women and work

Sian Moore	Gender and class consciousness in industrialisation: the Bradford worsted industry, 1820-1845	30
Katrina Honeyman	Sweat and sweating: women workers and trade unionists in the Leeds clothing trade, 1880-1980	55
Sheila C. Blackburn	'The inspector can check a workroom is insanitary by means of his own eyes and nose': rethinking the sweatshop in Victorian and Edwardian Britain	76
Linda Clarke & Christine Wall	Skilled versus qualified labour: the exclusion of women from the construction industry	96
Caroline Bressey	Black women and work in England, 1880-1920	117
Gerry Holloway	United we stand: class issues in the early British women's trade union movement	133

Louise Raw	Striking a light: Bryant & May revisited	150
Cathy Hunt	The fragility of the union: the work of the National Federation of Women Workers in the regions of Britain, 1906-1914	171

Women and politics

Sheila Rowbotham	Alice Wheeldon revisited	190
Annmarie Hughes	Scottish socialist women in the inter-war years	205

Contributors

Professor Mary Davis, Professor of Labour History. Formerly Head of Centre for Trade Union Studies & Deputy Director Working Lives Research Institute, London Metropolitan University

Dr Sheila Blackburn, Honorary Senior Fellow, School of History, Liverpool University.

Dr Caroline Bressey, Lecturer, Department of Geography, University College, London.

Professor Linda Clarke , Director Centre for the Study of the Production of the Built Environment (ProBE), University of Westminster

Dr Gerry Holloway, Senior Lecturer in Life History and Women's Studies, University of Sussex

Professor Katrina Honeyman, Professor of Social and Economic History, School of History University of Leeds

Dr Cathy Hunt, Senior Lecturer, History, Faculty of Business, Environment and Society, Coventry University

Dr Annmarie Hughes, Lecturer in Economic and Social History, School of Social and Political Sciences,University of Glasgow

Dr Sian Moore, Senior Research Fellow, Working Lives Research Institute, London Metropolitan University

Dr Louise Raw, a Labour historian with a background in the trade union movement and political campaigning.

Professor Sheila Rowbotham, Professor of Gender and Labour History, University of Manchester

Dr Chris Wall, Senior Research Fellow, ProBE School of Architecture and the Built Environment, University of Westminster

Glossary

ASW	Amalgamated Society of Woodworkers
AUCO	Associated Union of Clothing Operatives
BATC	Building Apprenticeship and Training Council
CMF	Clothing Manufacturers' Federation
DLO	Direct Labour Organisation
EOC	Equal Opportunities Commission
FE	Further Education
GLHA	Glasgow Labour Housing Association
ILP	Independent Labour Party
IWW	Industrial Workers of the World
LNMCA	Leeds and Northern Clothing Manufacturers' Association
LTC	London Trades Council
LTU	Leeds Tailoresses' Union
MP	Member of Parliament
NASL	National Anti Sweating League
NCO	Non Commissioned Officer
NCF	No Conscription Fellowship
NFBTO	National Federation of Building Trade Operatives
NFWW	National Federation of Women Workers
NHS	National Health Service
NUTGW	National Union of Tailors and Garment Workers
PBR	Payment by Results
PP	Parliamentary Papers
PRO	Public Record Office
SCH	Select Committee on Homework
SCSS	Select Committee on Sweating System
SLP	Socialist Labour Party
SPEW	Society for the Promotion of the Employment of Women
STUC	Scottish Trade Union Congress
TOPS	Training Opportunity Programme
TGWU	Tailors and Garment Workers' Union
TUC	Trades' Union Congress

VET	Vocational Education and Training
WIC	Women's Industrial Council
WPPL	Women's Protective and Provident League
WTUA	Women's Trade Union Association
WTUL	Women's Trade Union League
UCATT	Union of Construction and Allied Technical Trades
UDC	Union of Democratic Control

Introduction

Mary Davis

This book is concerned with the locus of women in the making and remaking of the working class and the labour movement in Britain. However, it will be noted that the title of the book is *Class and Gender in British Labour History*. Why doesn't the word 'women' appear in the title if this is what the book is really about? It is not because we think that 'gender', as a somewhat neutral term, is more acceptable in 'scholarly' circles than the clearly feminist assertion connoted by 'women and class'. Rather we accept the way in which Joan Scott[1] has framed her partiality for the use of the concept of gender in history. As she puts it:

> The realisation of the radical potential of women's history comes in the writing of histories that focus on women's experiences *and* analyse the ways in which politics constructs gender and gender constructs politics.[2]

This is as true of economics as it is of politics.

Katrina Honeyman[3] distinguishes between women's history, gender history and feminist history; although, in her view, some of the differences are subtle and not always understood by historians. She makes the very salient point that not all feminist history is concerned with women and not all women's history is feminist. The contributors to this book hope that in our attempt to write about women in British labour history from a feminist perspective, we have managed to transcend the frequent mismatch between subject and method. In tracing the historiography of women's history, Honeyman notes that now gender is increasingly used as an analytical tool, thus establishing a framework within which women can, at last, be analysed as active historical participants, rather than as victims of historical events. This is in sharp contrast to previous practices of either adding women to history or separating women's history from 'mainstream' history.

This book shares this gendered approach to history but, as is explored in

Chapter 1, it also seeks to weave together the intricate relationship between class and gender. This is because we see both gender *and* class as central to the continual restructuring and renegotiation of capitalist relations of production in Britain over the past two centuries. Older histories of industrialisation in Britain[4], with the exception of Pinchbeck (1930)[5], have barely mentioned women workers, despite the fact that they were among the first factory workers in the mechanised textile industries. Within the last five years, however, there has been a reversal of this trend and much closer attention has been paid to the role of women in the labour force. Most of these works, because they deal with industrialisation, concentrate on the most visible aspects of women's paid labour, especially their role as weavers in the factory-based cotton industry. Janet Greenlees (2008)[6] looks at the involvement of women in the cotton industry in the early stages of industrialisation in Britain and America and argues that these women factory workers, being the first, set the standard for subsequent generations of women's waged labour. She also challenges the conventionally accepted view that women were passive players in the workplace. Jutta Schwarzkopf (2004)[7] too explores the theme of women in the cotton industry; notably their role as weavers in the later period from 1880 to 1914. Beth Harris (2005)[8] is unusual in that she concentrates on a more hidden, yet very prevalent form of women's work in the 19th century: that of needlewomen. Following the tradition of Angela John (1986)[9] and Jane Lewis (1986)[10], Kirsta Cowman and Louise Jackson (2005)[11], in their edited collection, take a broader view of women's paid work and investigate a number of thematic issues and a range of occupations based around the underlying premise that work is a cultural activity as well as an economic one.

It is our view that for working-class women, whilst the prime imperative for paid labour was an economic one (given the palpable myth of the male breadwinner), the cultural aspects of women's work, especially in respect of political and trade union activity, has been neglected. However, most of the above-mentioned recent publications concentrate in the main on women and paid work and say comparatively little about women's involvement in the labour movement. Apart from suffrage history, there have been some, but not many, works covering aspects of women's involvement in socialist politics. Christine Colette (1989)[12] looks at the changing nature of socialist feminism as it unfolded in the Women's Labour League and the see-sawing relationship of the League with the Labour Party. June Hannam and Karen Hunt's book (2002)[13] offers a very useful analysis of the Independent Labour Party and the Social Democratic Federation. It re-examines the traditional presumptions that the former was more pro feminist than the latter. It also examines the link between the socialist movement and the suffrage campaign and the particular areas of tension arising for working-class women over the issue of adult suffrage (vis á vis the traditional women's suffrage demand[14]) and the question of rights for married women. However, since the publication of the second edition of Sarah Boston's book in 1987[15] there have been no recent publications dealing specifically with women's trade union history.

It is our contention that because the class/gender relationship has either been ignored or misunderstood it has been possible to write general histories of the labour movement in which women are hardly mentioned. This is true of older works like Pelling (1963)[16], Clegg, Fox and Thompson (1964)[17] and Briggs and Saville (1971)[18]. But it is also true of more recent books. For example Hunt (1981)[19], Price (1986)[20], Pimlott and Cook (1991)[21], Laybourn (1992)[22] and Cohen (2006)[23] all say little or nothing about women's role in the labour movement.

This book will thus attempt to address such lacunae. It will examine the 'making' of the other half of the working class – women – as workers, as trade unionists and as political activists. It aims to situate the inter-relationship between women and class firmly within the context of the major shifts in the development of industrial capitalism and to examine the political expression of this relationship. This will be set within a framework of understanding that the antagonism between the private nature of reproduction and the social nature of production has had and continues to have a major impact on women's working lives.

The chapters of this volume are written by women historians who have been irritated by the fact that the steady progress made by feminist scholars and activists over the years in uncovering working women's social reality, continues to be marginalised or ignored in standard accounts of working-class and labour history. Hence part of the title of this book reflects our uncertainty about whether we are really renewing a debate on class and gender or starting it. Whatever the answer to this somewhat rhetorical question, we do not imagine that our book is the last word on the subject. Rather we hope that it will mark the beginning of a new integrative discourse among labour historians on the gender and race dimensions of class and vice versa.

The book is divided into three interconnected sections, each dealing with an aspect of the particular way black and white women workers experienced exploitation and oppression at work, the way in which women workers were either marginalised or excluded from the trade union movement and the elimination of women from mainstream political life. But whilst acknowledging and analysing exclusionary practices, the authors also show that women were not passive victims of such patriarchal prejudice. Indeed, the remarkable discovery of feminist labour historians is the growing body of evidence to show that, against all the odds, women played an important part in class formation, trade union struggle and political action throughout the 19th and 20th centuries. The fact that they have been airbrushed out of mainstream accounts is a product of the failure to comprehend the intersections between class and gender: an approach which this book seeks to rectify. Thus while not presenting either a complete or a chronological survey of women's role in class formation and the labour movement, these original and analytical essays will, nonetheless (re)visit some of the terrain vacated by standard labour histories and will reflect different aspects of the main theme of the book outlined above and expanded more fully in Chapter 1; *The Making Of The English Working Class Re-Visited: Labour History & Marxist Theory.*

1. Women and Work

The first section of the book deals with the place of black and white women in the labour force. It throws light on their central role in textile production, in this case the Bradford worsted industry in the early years of industrialisation, a highly visible factory based industry. However, this section also looks at the less visible aspects of women's work; their role in the 'sweated trades'. Taken together, both types of employment were seen as offshoots of women's domestic labour and could thus be seen as typical 'women's work'. In fact in the 19th century domestic service itself accounts for the greatest percentage of women's employment outside the home. But what about atypical work, such as the building industry and the printing trades? Women were systematically excluded from such work and their exclusion from atypical work (in this case the building trades – explored in the chapter by Clarke and Wall), helped to establish, retain and reinforce a pattern of job segregation which in itself was (and remains) a product of women's role in the family. There were exceptions to this general pattern, for example women chain makers and women coal miners, (after the 1842 Mines Act, women miners were prohibited from working underground), but in general the restricted and segregated nature of women's employment prevailed throughout the 19th and 20th centuries – except, of course, during the First and Second World Wars when women were deemed capable of substituting for men in all branches of industry. The experience of black women seeking to find employment was mediated by the double oppression of sexism and racism. This is explored in the chapter on black women's employment in London.

Sian Moore's *Gender and class consciousness in industrialisation – the Bradford Worsted Industry, 1780-1845* explores the relationship between gender and class consciousness during industrialisation. It is based upon a case study of Bradford, West Yorkshire and the renegotiation of social and gender relations within worsted production. It assesses the extent to which industrial transition reinforced the sexual division of labour and the extent to which existing gender relations were undermined and challenged. It explores women's consciousness of themselves as wage earners and the way they resisted at both an individual and collective level the imposition of industrial capitalist relations.

Katrina Honeyman contributes a chapter on *Sweated Labour: Sweat and sweating: women workers and trade unionists in the Leeds clothing trade 1890-1980* in which she explores the intersection of class exploitation and women's oppression through the example of sweated labour in the Leeds tailoring industry from the early years of its expansion in the later nineteenth century until its late-twentieth-century demise. It explains the persistence of sweating beyond the 'classic' period ending in 1914 with reference to the gender division of labour and the gendered distribution of skill, and by examining the involvement of sweated labour in trade union action. Using evidence from trade union records and oral accounts, three episodes of strike action – in the late 1880s, in the inter-war years, and in 1970 – are analysed to identify the key components of gender and class relationships. The conclusions drawn in this chapter are that gender divisions in tailoring production perpetuated a system of low pay and poor conditions for the majority of women workers; and that exploitation, sweating and intensification of female labour were each the outcome of employer action, from which the female dominated trade unions ultimately offered little protection. Throughout the history of the industry, the women operatives revealed characteristics of unity, solidarity and co-operation, positioning themselves firmly within their class situation, while also recognising their particular gender concerns.

The second chapter on the sweated trades by Sheila Blackburn, *'The inspector can check a workroom is insanitary by means of his own eyes and nose': Re-Thinking the Sweatshop in Victorian and Edwardian Britain*, argues that if we are to understand the mechanism of sweating, a class-gender approach is essential. The two main aims of Blackburn's chapter are to locate the causes of sweating, and to establish why, by the late nineteenth century, sweating became virtually synonymous with female homeworkers. A class-gender perspective exposes the procedures whereby the employment of wives and daughters was frequently exploited by capitalists seeking competitive labour market advantage. Only when sweating is viewed in this wider ambit can its true nature and extent be revealed.

Chris Wall and Linda Clarke contribute a chapter, *Women in the Building Trades in England: skills, training and union barriers to entry*, on what may be considered as atypical work for women. This chapter is about the ways in which women have been excluded from the building trades in England, in particular through the apprenticeship system. Through denying women access to craft apprenticeship, the building trades from the sixteenth century onwards remained almost exclusively male. So too, consequently, did the craft unions from their formation in the nineteenth century. The chapter explores the implications of this, in particular the fact that 'skill' as an ideological construct remained a male property and craft unions a male preserve. It also examines those periods and areas where women succeeded in entering the building trade, such as into 'semi-skilled' work in periods of war and into training schemes from the 1970s.

Caroline Bressey's chapter on *Black Women & Work in London 1880-1920* attempts to recover Black women's experience of work and consider how race and racism impacted upon their everyday experiences. The chapter seeks to explore what these experiences of work and discrimination were and what they tell us about networks between workers throughout the period. The empirical focus of the chapter is on Black women who advertised themselves in newspapers as domestic workers between 1880 and 1920. The chapter ends with the case of Grace Stevenson, who worked as a domestic servant in the 1920s but committed suicide. Her friends believed she was driven to her death by the racist taunts she faced on the streets of London. Her death will be placed in the context of the racial hostility which Black women faced in the 1910s and 1920s, and ask if the labour movement failed to support the Black community as they faced increasingly violent discrimination.

2. Women and Trade Unions

The second section of the book contains three chapters devoted to different aspects of re-interpreting or re-discovering women's role in the trade union movement. It starts with a chapter by Gerry Holloway on *Class Issues in the Women's Trade Union Movement before the First World War* in which she examines the ways that both class and gender shaped the development of the women's trade union movement. She goes on to suggest that some of the problems of the movement were sown in its very early years. The chapter traces and analyses the organisational structures and practices of the

Women's Protective and Provident League and its daughter organisations the Women's Trade Union League and National Federation of Women Workers. In so doing, questions are raised about how the organisations represented the membership in their decision-making processes and how they reflected or challenged dominant notions of women's roles in the workplace held by many male trade unionists at this time.

The case of the Bryant and May Strike in 1888 prompts Louise Raw to re-assess the conventional interpretation of the beginnings of new unionism. In her chapter *The Beginnings of New Unionism reconsidered: the Bryant & May Matchworkers Strike 1888* she discovers serious flaws in the conventional story of the strike which, once exposed, revolutionise the traditional view of the strike and its main players. There is extensive and conclusive proof that Annie Besant did not lead, and indeed could not have led, the strike. Bryant & May, whilst eager to publicly endorse the Besant-led version of events, privately identified five matchwomen as the true 'ringleaders' of the strike. This chapter goes some way towards restoring to the matchwomen their own voice and agency, serving both as a re-writing of the beginnings of a new phase in British labour history, and as a tribute to the women whose courage and determination made possible the 'wonderful harvest' of New Unionism.

The very important, but under-researched, National Federation of Women Workers is the subject of Cathy Hunt's chapter. Under the leadership of Mary McArthur the NFWW claimed to have 15,000 members and stated that as many as 74 branches had been established across the regions of Britain. The aim of this chapter, *The fragility of the union: the work of the National Federation of Women Workers in the regions of Britain 1906-14*, is to view branch life within the National Federation of Women Workers from as close quarters as possible. Instead of dwelling on national leadership, as seems too often to be the case in labour history, it seeks to find out more about local organisation in order to build a picture of what it meant to be a Federation member in the years before the First World War. The chapter seeks to answer two broad, linked questions. Firstly, is it possible to identify what, if any, common features made for a successful branch of the National Federation of Women Workers? Secondly, why were some branches, including ones that experienced high profile victories and attracted high membership numbers, unable to remain strong?

3. Women and Politics

The third section of the book is concerned with women and politics. Working women played an active part in socialist politics, although far too little is known about their role, eclipsed as they often were by male leaders. In writing about the fissured history of the socialist movement, Barbara Taylor expresses eloquently the faltering connection between women and the labour movement:

> No aspect of the socialist tradition more clearly reveals this uneven, fractured history than its relationship to feminism. Women have always played an important part in socialist organisations, but only at particular points have the independent aspirations of women – their aspirations to overturn their status as the 'second sex' – found a central place within socialist strategy. The woman question moved in and out of socialist politics, leaving in its wake a host of unmet demands and unresolved questions – questions not only about present and potential relations between the sexes, but about the nature of the socialist enterprise itself.[24]

In *Alice Wheeldon revisited*, Sheila Rowbotham looks at the case of the socialist and feminist Alice Wheeldon, who was accused on the evidence of an agent provocateur during the First World War of conspiring to assassinate Lloyd George. The trial, which resulted in her conviction, brings to the surface an unusual amount of material about local activists in the socialist and feminist movements. It shows the resilience of memory when 'history' is not looking, and gives a glimpse of a fluid radical movement which cannot be comprehended simply in terms of organisational affiliations.

Annmarie Hughes, concentrating primarily on Scotland, has written a chapter on *Socialist Women in the Inter War years*, a period which is often portrayed as a bleak one for working-class women's politics, despite women having won the first stage of the franchise in 1918 (women over 30 with a small property qualification) and full franchise (over 21) in 1928. In contrast to the period before and during the First World War, it is generally assumed that women's political agency in the Independent Labour Party, the Labour Party, the Co-operative Women's Guild and the labour movement was, by and large, quite barren. The challenges women had mounted against the sexual division of labour, like their interests in general, were apparently sidelined, constrained by the reformulation of traditional gender ideals, the economic climate and the need for class unity in the face of reactionary Conservative or Conservative-dominated governments. In addition, it has been argued that women's political agency was confined largely to the sphere of local government with the implication that it was less significant than that of their male counterparts operating in national politics. Scottish socialist women did face many of these impediments. However, it is also true that the labour movement was not a uniform experience for women. A considerable number of female activists proved capable of advancing the interests of those who were identified and accepted as their constituents: working-class women. In doing so, they developed a range of strategies to challenge the sexual division of labour and the male-dominance of the labour movement. The strategies that women adopted were not always highly visible or vocal, but they were effective forms of resistance that were both class and gender based. 'Socialist women' used subversion and defiance and they were not adverse to crossing party lines to achieve their aims. These women were at one and the same time reactionary, revolutionary and prudent in their protests on behalf of working-class women. Many of these strategies do not fall into male-centric norms of political activity, thus socialist women's agency has been neglected in labour historiography that evaluates success either in electoral terms or by engagement in national issues.

The three sections of this book – the experience of women as workers, as trade unionists and as political activists – are connected but also heavily circumscribed by the enormous issue, not dealt with specifically, but underlying the totality of working women's lives; namely their role in the home and the family. The double burden thus faced by working-class women inevitably limited their ability to engage in politics and trade union activity on the same terms as men. And yet paradoxically it was the very fact of their entry into social production outside the home that offered women the possibility of engaging in collective action as women and as workers. The dominant notion (still prevalent) of 'women's proper place', while having little resonance for working women, served to marginalise their concerns among male workers, but this did not prevent women's self activity, although at times (especially from the 1850s to the 1870s) it was in danger of stifling it altogether.

Whether or not this book starts or renews debate, it is to be hoped that it will stimulate much more historical scholarship and creative thinking about the class/gender relationship, but not just within a framework that is content with a 'her-story' approach. Within the field of labour history, we *have* to write about class because we are concerned with workers. Thus the issue of women has to be theorised in the context of class. In other words we have to reclaim labour history for women and in so doing we will reclaim it for the working class as a whole.

Notes

1. Scott, J. *Gender and the Politics of History*, New York: Columbia University Press, 1998.
2. Ibid., p. 27.
3. Honeyman, K. *Women, Gender & Industrialisation in England, 1700-1870*, Basingstoke: Macmillan, 2000.
4. For example:
   Ashton, T.S. *An Economic History of England - the 18th Century*, London: Methuen, 1966.
   Deane, P. *The First Industrial Revolution*, Cambridge: Cambridge University Press, 1965.
   Flinn, M.W. *Origins of the Industrial Revolution*, London: Longman, 1966.
5. Pinchbeck, I. *Women Workers and the Industrial Revolution*, London: Cass, 1969 (first published 1930).
6. Greenlees, J. *Female labour power: women workers' influence on business practices in the British and American cotton industries, 1780-1860*, Aldershot: Ashgate, 2008.
7. Schwarzkopf, J. *Unpicking Gender: The Social Construction Of Gender In the Lancashire cotton industry 1880-1914*, Aldershot: Ashgate 2004.
8. Harris, B. *Famine and Fashion: Needlewomen In The Nineteenth Century*, Aldershot: Ashgate, 2005.
9. John, A. *Unequal Opportunities: Women's Employment in England 1800-1918*, Oxford: Blackwell, 1986.
10. Lewis, J. *Women in England 1870-1950*, Brighton: Wheatsheaf, 1986.
11. Cowman, K. and Jackson, L. (eds.) *Women and Work Culture: Britain c1850-1950*, Aldershot: Ashgate, 2005.
12. Colette, C. *For Labour and for Women: the Women's Labour League 1906-19*, Manchester: Manchester University Press, 1989.
13. Hannam, J. & Hunt, K. *Socialist Women; Britain, 1880s to 1920s*, London: Routledge, 2002.
14. That women obtain the vote 'on the same terms as that agreed or may be accorded to men' – this, of course meant according to many women trade unionists, a class and property franchise.
15. Boston, S. *Women workers and the trade unions*, London: Lawrence & Wishart 1987.
16. Pelling, H. *A History of British Trade Unionism*, London, Macmillan, 1963
17. Clegg, H.A, Fox, A &.Thompson, A.F. *A History of British Trade Unions since 1889*, Oxford: OUP 1964
18. Briggs, A. & .Saville, J. (eds.) *Essays in Labour History 1886-1923*, London: Macmillan 1971. Women do not even merit an entry in the index although it should be noted that Hinton's chapter on Dilution is by its nature about women workers in the First World War.
19. Hunt, E.H. *British Labour History*, London: Weidenfeld & Nicholson, 1981. Hunt opines that women's unequal pay was 'not entirely a matter of custom and prejudice' (p.103), it was due to the fact that men were naturally stronger, were able to take better care of their machines and were hence not delayed by

minor breakdowns.
20   Price, R *Labour in British Society*, London: Routledge, 1986.
21   Pimlott, B & Cook, C (eds.) *Trade Unions in British Politics: the First 250 years*, London: Longman, 1991 (2nd edn.) Again, amazingly neither women workers nor women trade unionists merit an index entry, let alone any serious consideration.
22   Laybourn, K. *A History of British Trade Unionism*, Stroud: Allan Sutton, 1992.
23   Cohen, S. *Ramparts of Resistance*, London: Pluto, 2006. This history of US and British workers since 1968 looks at grassroots struggles. Hence it is particularly surprising that there is scant acknowledgment of women's role and in particular only two brief mentions of the fight for equal pay.
24   Taylor, B. *Eve and the New Jerusalem*, London: Virago, 1991 p. x.

The Making of the English Working Class revisited: labour history and Marxist theory

Mary Davis

Introduction

Whilst accepting a Marxist definition of class, this chapter will suggest that a gender and colour-blind misapplication of Marxist theory has resulted in a partial understanding of class which has had profound repercussions in labour historiography and labour movement practice. It will offer a definition of class which is predicated upon an understanding of the relationship between class exploitation and oppression. It will suggest that an ability in theory and practice to connect the hitherto separate spheres of class, race and gender in a manner that comprehends both their distinctiveness and inter-relationships is long overdue. However, it will be argued that it is only through understanding the primacy of class as an economic relationship to the dominant mode of production that the connections between class, race and gender can be correctly understood. This will be explored in the context of the shaping of the English working class within an old and established labour movement which has had a strong but partial understanding of 'class' but a more limited perception of race and gender.

The renegotiation of the gender division of labour was central to the process of industrialisation in Britain – the first industrial nation – and to the formation of a working class. Since women were amongst the first factory workers, they led early industrial action, whether on an informal or formal basis, and were amongst the first trade unionists. Gender remains central to the continual restructuring and renegotiation of capitalist relations over the past two centuries. This is also true of the history of black people; however, this chapter will concentrate on gender.

The fact that such an obvious point has had so few repercussions for the study of mainstream working-class and labour history requires both an explanation and a remedy. One of the explanations lies in the positivist rejection of theory which has characterised so much of the English historical tradition. In offering an antidote to this trend, this chapter will seek to renew the theoretical foundations underlying the project begun by what Harvey Kaye (1984) called the British Marxist historians. In so doing it will attempt to lay the basis of a non-gender-blind understanding of class in British history by examining the meaning and unravelling the relationship between oppression and exploitation.

Historiography

Historians have got a lot to answer for: our knowledge of the past is filtered through their collective lens. The repercussions of this are felt more acutely in our own era given the fact that until the 20th century historical writing concerned itself in the main with statecraft and the relations between states. However, thanks largely to the efforts of von Ranke and his school, history was established as an academic discipline (even though it was a positivist and constitutionalist one) in the 19th century. It began thereafter, albeit slowly, to undergo great changes reflecting the transformation of European society wrought by the extension of the franchise and the corresponding enlargement of the ideological apparatus of the state. The 'age of the masses' thrust 'the common people' onto centre stage as performers rather than subservient spectators and hence they too became historical subjects. Thus it was that the late 19th and early 20th century witnessed the beginnings of social, working-class and labour history, pioneered by, among others, S and B Webb, J.L and B Hammond, R.H.Tawney, G.D.H. Cole, Wanda Neff and, later, Ivy Pinchbeck among others.[1]

However, beginning in the inter-war period, but gaining ground steadily and, remarkably, at the height of the Cold War, a new kind of history emerged. This school of history – subsequently identified as that of the English Marxist historians, (a product of the History Group of the Communist Party), exercised a profound intellectual influence in both subject matter (this included works on classical antiquity, feudalism, the English Revolution, economic history, imperialism, labour history) and method (historical materialism). The group included at various times E.J. Hobsbawm, V. Gordon Childe, Edward and Dorothy Thompson, Dona Torr, John Saville, Christopher Hill, Victor Kiernan, A.L. Morton and others.[2] Historical materialism was attacked by the positivist and empiricist school led by Karl Popper and his later disciples leading to dry but sometimes very illuminating debates such as that which raged in the 1960s in the pages of *The Economic History Review* over the British standard of living in the early years of industrialisation.

Nonetheless, at long last there was an antidote to the constitutional history presented to us as revealed truth by positivist 'scientists' concerned only with 'the facts'. As E.H.Carr[3] noted, partisanship is always evident in the selection 'the facts'. Partisanship, however, is rarely acknowledged the closer the historian is to the prevailing orthodoxy. The further away from this the more prone historians are to accusations of 'bias'. But the Marxist historians, through their sheer scholarly force, broke through the stigma usually accorded to those with radical anti-establishment views, and refreshingly managed to gain an open acknowledgement that privileging historical materialism in both subject and method was not only credible but also intellectually superior.

From the 1970s onwards the tradition of writing working-class and labour history was continued by the 'history from below' school. Its theoretical foundations were less rigorous than the Marxist historians, but nonetheless their research was often pioneering and through the medium of their most well known publication, *History Workshop Journal*, gave rise to valuable insights into hitherto ignored aspects of social reality. Thus in subject although not always in method there was a point of continuity and an over-riding point of agreement: notably the acceptance of the centrality of the conception of class, class relations and class struggle as the motor of social change – a conception shared by all the contributors to this book.

Class and the Making of the English Working Class

However, despite the enormous contribution made by these historians, there are failings within the Marxist tradition. I want to examine the repercussions of the most important error committed by what I term the mainly manly Marxist greats: namely their gender blindness, which in turn, despite their pre-occupation with class has, paradoxically, led them to an incomplete understanding of the very essence of the nature of the working class and class relations in capitalist society.

Probably the most glaringly obvious example of this of this is E.P. Thompson's seminal work *The Making of the English Working Class* (1963). This book, in Thompson's words is 'a biography of the English working class from its adolescence until its early manhood' in which he 'seeks to rescue the poor stockinger, the Luddite cropper, the "obsolete" handloom weaver…from the enormous condescension of posterity'.[4]

Of course, this is a wonderful book, beautifully written and meticulously researched, uncovering a treasure trove of new material – all labour historians cut their teeth on it. It would seem churlish to offer any criticism of a book that is generally regarded as a masterpiece. However, it is clear that there is a major lacuna in this book; notably any substantial examination of the female half of the English working class, let alone an analysis of its place in the relations of production. In the over 800 pages of Thompson's magnum opus women make an appearance as individuals and sometimes as groups, but not as part of a class, much less as part of the 'making' of the English working class. The contemporary evidence can rebut the charge of feminist historicism in this respect. Thompson uses primary sources which could have rendered his account more complete. For example he quotes Dr Andrew Ure who in his *Philosophy of Manufactures* (1835) estimated from the reports of the Factory Inspectors in 1834 that the total adult labour force employed in textile mills in the United Kingdom in 1834 was 191,671, of whom 102,812 were women (88,859 men)[5] – that is, over half of all mill workers were women. This figure does not account for the high numbers of women employed in less visible occupations – domestic service, lace making, straw plaiting, dressmaking (and a host of others), nor in more visible occupations such as chain making, jute making and coal mining.

There is much other contemporary and secondary evidence Thompson and others could have used to show how important women were to the making of the English working class. Marx himself, who Thompson doubtless read, fully appreciated this point. Marx argued in volume one of *Capital* that the use of machinery in the new factory-based industries laid the pre-condition for the greater use of the labour of women and children. This is because, according to Marx, machinery dispenses with muscular power:

> it therefore becomes a means of employing labourers of slight muscular strength…The labour of women and children was, therefore, *the first thing sought by capitalists who used machinery*. (my emphasis).[6]

Hence he is unsurprised by the testimony of 'Mr E', a cotton manufacturer who took full advantage of his ability to use women's labour and gave an additional reason for employing them:

> [He] gives a decided preference to married females especially those who have families at home dependent on them for support: they are attentive, docile, more so than unmarried females, and are compelled to use their utmost exertions to procure the necessities of life.

Frederick Engels, writing in 1844[7], cited figures used by Lord Ashley when he introduced the Ten Hours Bill in the House of Commons in 1844. Of 419,000 factory operatives in employment, over half (242,296) were women.[8] Engels then quoted the testimony of Dr Hawkins in the Report of the Factories Inquiry Commission to show that in cotton factories 56.25 per cent of the operatives were women, in woollen mills women accounted for 69.5 per cent of the workforce and in flax spinning the figure was 70.5 per cent. Engels was at pains to show the number of women employed in textile factories was very high – it supported his theory that, contrary to Victorian morality, industrialisation led to role reversal in the home, and was responsible for alarmingly high rates of infant mortality. However, whatever his motives, Engels' figures have not been shown to be inaccurate. Indeed both Ivy Pinchbeck[9] and Wanda Neff[10], writing thirty years before Thompson, made the point that after the First Factory Act of 1833, which limited child labour, the proportion of women working in factories increased: in cotton, worsted, silk and flax women continued to outnumber men. Hence there is ample evidence, both contemporary and secondary, to show that women not only played a major role in the labour force of 'the dark satanic mills', but that they were among the first to enter factory production.

Such well documented evidence should have had profound repercussions for the study of working-class and labour history. It should have deepened our understanding of the role of women workers in the formation of an industrial proletariat and their important part in the formation of the first trade unions. Unfortunately, this level of perception has been absent from mainstream and even Marxist labour historians.

Labour history has always been a male preserve. The best labour historians, even when they explicitly write about Marxism and history, make only passing reference to women and black people. R.S.Neale's otherwise excellent *Class in English History* (1981) starts off tantalisingly well with a (misleadingly titled) chapter on 'Women & Class Consciousness', but the chapter is concerned only with women and property relations with relevance to middle and upper class women. A similar problem arises in his next book *Writing Marxist History*[11]. Despite the fact that this book was written in 1985 and thus, unlike Thompson, the author had the benefit of 20 years of feminist theory and feminist history, there is little evidence that those who, like Neale, wrote Marxist history felt moved by the need to integrate the experiences of the other half of the working class into their own work. Interestingly, however, Neale was aware of this lacuna. He acknowledged the fact that 'work on women and women's consciousness has proceeded outside the mainstream of urban and class history'.[12] Eric Hobsbawm made an even more frank confession in 1978 when he wrote:

> Women have often pointed out that male historians in the past including Marxists have grossly neglected the female half of the human race. The criticism is just, the present writer accepts that it applies to his own work.[13]

Unfortunately most male labour historians have not taken up the challenge implicit in Hobsbawm's self-critical statement written 30 years ago. Hence the charge still applies today and simply cannot be written off as predictable or even unfair criticism from a carping feminist. The omission betokens something much more fundamental than a tirade against gender blindness. It is only when we pose the question (albeit rhetorically) as to whether it matters if the working class is perceived as white and male; that is, whether it matters if we only half understand what class really is, that we can begin to appreciate that the issue goes beyond the issue of historical scholarship and into the domain of Marxist-feminist epistemology.

The consequences of a partial view of class

As in life so in history, the story of the super exploited and oppressed (those who in Sheila Rowbotham's phrase have been 'hidden from history') is told separately. However, unlike 40 years ago, women's history and the history of black people is now being studied, but these histories, although they have acquired an academic importance and have accomplished much in constructing women's historical reality, still occupy separate spheres. This poses a problem insofar as despite the huge contribution made by socialist feminist historians, their work has resulted in a separate discipline which has had little impact on 'mainstream' labour history. This has resulted often in a de-classed approach to women's history and the continuation of an imperfectly understood notion of class among labour historians. As Joan Scott notes, women's history does not have a long-standing historiographical tradition and because there was (and is) an incomplete theorisation of the place of women in class formation, 'the subject of women has been either grafted on to other traditions or studied in isolation from them'.[14] Women write women's history and men write about the labour movement. The problem is not resolved through the new discipline of intersectionality which seeks to incorporate class, race and gender in a non-hierarchical relationship, but fails to understand the crucial relationship between exploitation and oppression underlying such relationships.

I shall argue that it is precisely because the connection between class exploitation and oppression has been imperfectly understood that intellectual enquiry has been forced into separate spheres. On the one hand 'mainstream' socialist literature still unconsciously constructs the history and development of the working class and labour movement through a white and male lens, and on the other hand the literature of the oppressed ploughs its own furrow as a separate entity filling the intellectual space and in some cases making important and creative discoveries. This is not to suggest that the latter should be subsumed in the former, but rather that at the level of theory it is now imperative for some degree of integration to prevail within an historical materialist framework. This eschews the well meaning moral relativism of intersectionality and places the problem within a Marxist perspective.

Without this labour and working-class history will become yet another academic discipline/heritage project- removed from the inheritors of that history – the working class and the labour movement. At best, dealt with by committed friends of the movement it will provide useful specialist monographs, but at worst it gives rise to a positivist revival already happening since 1970s, bolstered now, since the 1990s by post-modernist 'end of grand theory' school. For the post-modernists the rejection of the 'meta narrative' is coupled with a welcome rejection of empiricism, but this, as Mary Fulbrook[15] notes poses:

> a fundamental challenge to the very possibility of doing history at all... accompanied as it is by a widespread scepticism about being able to know and/or say anything about the real past which was not in some sense fictional.[16]

This challenge to history itself has provoked a response among academic historians of a revival of empiricism – of history without theory, heralding a shift away from the analytical to the descriptive method. Historians have retreated into their myriad specialisms and in so doing will have failed to build upon the rich heritage bequeathed by those like Thompson and others who began to open up the field of 'history from below' and to make such history accessible. They will have also failed to understand some remarkable historical moments in which the separate spheres of class, gender and race politics cohered, for example in the work of Sylvia Pankhurst – a socialist feminist and anti-racist pioneer.

Historical materialism and the renewal of Marxist theory

Having identified the problem, it would appear that the solution is simple: all we need to do is connect the separate spheres and ensure that standard working-class and labour histories have something to say about women and black people. However, this is not good enough. It leads to the accustomed equal opportunities approach transmuted to history – the oppressed are seen as victims – social forces linked to but tangential to class- they are 'add-ons'. We thus need to look again at the meaning of class and in particular to understand how and why class relations are produced and reproduced.

Class exploitation itself cannot be understood without an understanding of capitalist relations of production in a much wider sense. This entails looking further than the point of production itself, vital though this is. It necessitates an understanding of the way in which such relations operate in their economic, political and ideological/cultural settings and looking at how class rule is both maintained and reproduced. The concept of oppression is a key factor in this. Oppression is the most important means of maintaining the class relations which support class exploitation and as such oppression is both a function of class society and a product of it.

Towards a Marxist theory of oppression

So, what is oppression? Is it the same as inequality, discrimination or disadvantage? At one level of course, the search for a more precise use of abstract nouns is nothing more than a semantic quibble, but for our purposes these terms reveal important theoretical differences and are not interchangeable. It will be demonstrated that the language and the concept of inequality does not fully express the nature of the relationship between class, race and sex. The term 'oppression' more accurately describes this relationship.

The notion of equality has a long pedigree linked with the development of capitalist society. In the struggle to end feudal and/or aristocratic domination, liberal constitutionalists advocated the notion of equality. Starting in 17th century England, bolstered by the Enlightenment and the French Revolution at the end of the 18th century, the notion of equality became an unquestioned article of faith in the 19th and 20th centuries. Initially it was a notion embracing men only, since only white men were perceived as citizens. 'Equality' began to embrace women and black people in the twentieth century. However, as Juliet Mitchell[17] has pointed out, under capitalism the concept of equality has a very limited meaning – it can only refer to equality under the law: it is an abstract concept, saying nothing about the inherent and pre-existing inequalities of those who are subject to its writ. Juridical equality 'does not apply to the economic inequities it is there to mask'.[18] This is not to deny the importance of the battles to obtain equality – without them women would still be voteless and all but the sons of rich white males would be entitled to educational and countless other opportunities.

Inequality, discrimination or disadvantage is experienced by many groups in society because of the difficulties they experience at some or all points of their lives to fit in with the dominant norm. In this sense almost everybody experiences disadvantage – because they are too young or too old, because they are not 'handsome' or 'pretty', because they are too fat or too thin, etc. For others, like those with a disability, the discrimination is an ever-present feature of their lives. However, discrimination itself is not a function of class society even though it is an almost inevitable by-product of the inherent inequalities within all forms of class society.

Oppression, on the other hand, although it may take the form of discriminating against the oppressed, stands in a different relationship to class society. It is the most important means of maintaining the class relations which support class exploitation and as such oppression is a function of class society as well as being a product of it. This is because oppression, unlike discrimination, is linked materially to the process of class exploitation as well as operating at 'superstructural' level through oppressive ideologies which serve to maintain class rule by dividing the exploited. This is particularly clear in the case of capitalism, which will henceforth be used as the 'exemplar' of class society. Such ideologies are not simply explained by 'false consciousness' operating as an invented infecting agent. They are themselves so rooted in the material world of production that they have become integral to it.

Let us now look at the way in which oppression operates at these two levels.

i) class exploitation

Firstly, at the material level the historic subjugation of women and black people explains their augmented exploitation (super-exploitation) at the point of production. Historically an inbuilt inequality within the labour force, expressing itself through low wages and job segregation, has reproduced itself as the normal process when workers sell their labour power. Its victims are the most easily identifiable workers – black people and women. At the level of sociological observation this fact – super-exploitation and job segregation based on gender and race is not in doubt. All indices of wage rates nationally and internationally show that the wages of women[19] and black people are lower than that of white males. From the mid 19th century onwards the widespread acceptance of the notion of the 'family wage' to be won by the male breadwinner was internalised into the very fabric of the labour movement. Hence, not only was unequal pay accepted as a norm, but women's work was only tolerated if not threatening to the man. In any case, it was seen as a mark of shame if a man permitted his wife to work, hence the general practice, hardly contested by the unions until the twentieth century, of barring married women from employment altogether. The fact is, though, that contrary to the accepted ideology, married women continued to work because the family wage was a myth and was rarely enough to support dependents. Such attitudes and practices help to explain women's increasing job segregation and the fact that so much female labour was literally hidden. It is not surprising therefore that the unions until the mid 20th century demonstrated a studied indifference if not downright hostility to women workers. This fact operated to the material advantage of the owners of the means of production – the capitalists for whom any increase in profit is dependent on an increase in the rate of exploitation. It is hence no accident that despite conventional morality about the sanctity of family life and the key role of women within it, the labour of women is often preferred to that of men because it 'attracts', as Marx pointed out, lower wages.[20] Similarly the transfer of production to the low wage economies of the ex-colonies in Africa and Asia performs the same function for capitalism in its relentless pursuit of profit. Indeed the function of slavery in establishing the conditions for the take off of industrial capitalism in Britain in the late 18th century provides the most telling example of the historic de-humanisation of black people who became commodities in themselves.[21] Slavery which even today, long after its abolition, together with the aggressive imperialism of the late 19th century, has laid the foundations for the continued super-exploitation of black people *within* the imperialist nations as well as in the neo-colonial world.

Hence there is a material basis historically and at present for our suggestion that women and black people have been used for different reasons and are still used as a source of cheap labour, and that this fact has been integral to the operation of class exploitation. Women in particular are historic victims of job segregation and have continuously performed undervalued and sometimes unnoticed jobs outside the home. It is simply not the case that they have been used as a 'reserve army' of labour, their presence within the labour force has been constant. Very similar patterns of women's paid work established in the 19th century still persist today. Some feminist historians pointed this out 20 years ago:

> the sexual division of labour is basic to an understanding of the way in which capitalism has maintained itself, for it has allowed capitalism to divide the workforce, to secure lower wages…and to ensure cheap maintenance and reproduction of the labour force.[22]

Thus whilst the fact of super-exploitation is not controversial, the significance we attach to it is more so and 'raises' the status of women and black people beyond that of discrimination. Their role within capitalist relations of production as super-exploited workers is woven into the very fabric of these relations and is not a chance or transitory phenomenon and it is here that we must extend the analysis founded on historical materialism to more fully understand it.

The *fact* of class exploitation (and super exploitation) as the central pillar of the capitalist mode of production does not in itself explain how the relations of production are maintained and reproduced. This can only be understood by examining factors which exist outside the economic relations of production, through the operations of ideologies, whose function it is to maintain (whether consciously or not) class relations in a more general sense. There is a huge range of literature on the meaning of ideology attempting to interpret the already voluminous writings of Marx and Engels on the subject.[23] The interesting point about the theoretical discussion of ideology is just that, it is entirely theoretical with only rare references to a specific ideology and the way that it functions. What concerns us here though is something specific, namely the identification of ideologies which maintain the historic subservience of women and black people – in other words, the ideologies of oppression. But first it is necessary to say something about the role of ideology in general.

ii) Ideologies of oppression

We have already noted the particular and super-exploited place of women and black workers within class society. It seems that the specific ideologies supporting this – racism and sexism – have operated so insidiously and so successfully over centuries in the concealment of contradictions[24] that the ideologies have passed unnamed and unnoticed until the mid 20th century. Indeed a gender blind and colour blind approach to class politics has, until relatively recently, permeated even the most class-conscious sections of the labour movement.

As ideologies, racism and sexism can be seen to have a direct material connection to the maintenance of capitalist relations of production in two important ways. Firstly, because they are related to the very real need of capital to maintain profit by pushing the value of labour power to its lowest possible limit. Secondly, the ideologies of racism and sexism are the chief non-coercive means of preventing the unity of the working class and thereby facilitating the perpetuation of the domination of the minority class over the majority. Hence these ideologies, unlike for example liberalism or nationalism, appear as an almost pure reflection of the material needs of the exploiting class. They perform a very obvious function in the maintenance of the existing relations of production. This may seem to be a very crude and deterministic interpretation of ideology, failing to do justice to the sophistication of its lived form. Other ideologies such as religion are much harder to analyse from a historical materialist standpoint. They seem to have a life and history of their own unrelated to the mode of production and this has given rise to a major debate among western Marxists who get round this problem by one of two means. Firstly, by suggesting that ideology is in itself a material force giving rise to its separate study as a means of representation which interacts with the economic base. Or secondly, in an attempt to avoid economic determinism, the suggestion is made that ideology has a 'relative autonomy' within the superstructure but is connected to the economic base by being determined by it 'in the last instance'. We do not appear to need the 'relative autonomy' waiver clause when analysing racism and sexism. That is not to say that as ideologies they do not have their own histories or that their form is at all times strictly determined by the economic base. It is clear, however, that their form and function as ideologies have a very direct relationship with the economic base, more so than most other ideologies (other than economic ideologies themselves, especially that of the 'free' market and the 'free' sale of labour). It is perhaps for this very reason that the ideological form of oppression has remained hidden. The subjugation of women and black people has been historically connected with class society for so long that it has become the accepted natural order of things. The oppressive ideologies sustaining subservience is so culturally rooted that it has passed beyond naked statements of class rule and entered into the very fabric of our lives including language itself.[25] As such these ideologies have become universalised and hence disembodied from their class origins. They have thus fulfilled the ultimate goal of ideology – namely to represent the interests of the dominant class as the interests of society as a whole. How else are we to explain the permeation of racist and sexist ideas within the working class and even within the socialist movement? Perhaps the same could be said of all ideologies, but this misses the very direct function of oppressive ideologies, the force of which in the capitalist epoch is dependent on their ability to disunite the working class. It is of course true that women and black people do not constitute a class, but this fact, while explaining that not all women and black people are exploited, should not obscure the fact of their oppression based on race and gender. This is the real meaning of the oft-quoted statement that all oppression is based on class exploitation.

Racism and sexism as material and ideological facts are central to the maintenance of capitalist and pre-capitalist class relations. However, this is not to put a narrow economistic interpretation on their force. These are not simply mechanisms for keeping black and women workers in a subordinate position since, as oppressive ideologies, they cut across class boundaries and depend as all ideologies do on their universalism. Hence they impinge on the lives of all black people and women regardless of class and determine society's perception of race and gender. They operate historically in varying degrees and forms through both the coercive and ideological apparatuses of the state. It is not my place here to examine the ways in which these ideologies are produced and reproduced – there is a vast literature on this. I only want to re-state the critical importance of one aspect of oppressive ideologies and oppression in general for us today. That is its specific function in relation to the definition of the working class.

Class

The point made earlier about women and black people not constituting a class has often obscured the relationship of these two huge groups to the class structure. Seen as non-class entities, male labour historians and socialist and labour movement politicians have either ignored women and black people altogether (along with other groups) or they have, as Thompson seems to imply, assumed that 'class' is a universal term, embodying both male and female workers, or they have assigned them to the newly invented category of 'new social forces'.[26] At best this latter has been a well meaning attempt to avoid class reductionism and to respect the autonomy of black and women's liberation groups, but at worse it represents a failure of Marxist theoreticians to confront reality. In practice such a failure has meant that no credible alternative has been posited to that of 'identity politics'. After all, if the oppressed and disadvantaged exist outside classes, that is outside society, then the logic must be an increasingly atomised self-organisation based on self-identity. This is not to deny the importance of autonomy and self organisation as a necessary complement to class politics. 'Identity politics', however, is a founded upon conscious rejection of class and is seen by its post-modernist advocates as a substitute for it. Although 'analytical Marxists' like Erik Wright[27] eschew post-modernist identity politics, their comprehension of women's oppression is surprisingly detached from class analysis. Wright is one of the few male Marxists of today who engages with, let alone mentions, feminism. He regards both Marxism and feminism as emancipatory theories 'built around the critical analysis of oppression – class oppression and gender oppression'[28] although in his view feminists, unlike socialists are silent on the emancipatory project. This displays confusion as to the relationship between oppression and class exploitation and in so doing misses the critical point as to the role of oppression and oppressive ideologies as a material force in maintaining capitalist relation of production. In his attempt to 'distinguish class and gender as two dimensions of social relations which interact'[29], Wright falls into the idealist trap of presuming that gender is only tangentially related to class. He makes no mention of race.

The debates during the 1980s about the composition of the working class missed a crucial point, namely that the working class is *not* and never has been all white and male. This is not simply a rhetorical point. If we take the so-called 'broad' definition of the working class, that is to say all who sell their labour power for a wage (as opposed to the narrower definition: those who are *directly* engaged in the production of surplus value), then it is clear that the vast mass of women and black people are workers. [30] Indeed all projections show that the proportion of 'economically active' women is set to rise despite the often high rates of male unemployment. Indeed women in the UK already account for 50 per cent of the labour force. Hence the relationship between class exploitation and oppression has become in our day a very tangible issue for class politics provided we jettison traditional gender and race-blind preconceptions about the nature of the working class. This does not mean that oppression is thus subsumed by class exploitation but it does mean that the traditional call by socialists for the unity of the working class has to be understood in a different way. Unity cannot be built by refusing to recognise differences. The argument here is that the most crucial divisions within the working class are based on race and gender oppression and that these have to be recognised as ideological practices in themselves if they are to be overcome. It is the *fact* of oppression which determines the super-exploitation of women and black people as *workers* as well as their inequality as citizens.

A class analysis of the two major oppressed groups is thus vital for the understanding of the nature of the working class historically and today. This avoids the twin problem of either not assigning half of the population of this country (and the majority of the population of the world) to any class whatsoever and of failing to notice the realities of today's class structure and the specific status of oppressed groups within it. This is not a class reductionist argument – it does not mean that the oppressed form a class, rather that they belong to a class and the overwhelming majority of them are workers – an especially important point when we see that women were integral to the making of the first factory proletariat and today constitute over half of the working class, defined as those who sell their labour power for a wage.

Whilst it is true that class interests may divide the oppressed, this is probably less important now than in the 19th century because of the relentless tendency of capital to sweep intermediate strata, small producers and the petty bourgeoisie into the ranks of wage/salary earners. This 'broadening' of the working class creates its own problems for socialists, namely the existence of strata *within* the working class and the consequent lack of perception of class consciousness among those whose exploitation is more masked, or who have less access to collective struggle and organisation – the very stuff of labour history. But lack of class consciousness should not be confused with an objective analysis of class position.

Conclusion

A more fully worked out conception of historical materialism based on a clearer understanding of the nature of the working class and the relationship between exploitation and oppression would have had (and can still have) significant implications for writing labour history in a non colour or gender blind fashion.

This chapter has tried to show that there is an important connection between Marxist theory and practice, whether such practice involves historical scholarship or labour movement activism. The consequences of an inability to appreciate the role of women in the making and re-making of the working class have resulted in, until recently, the exclusion of oppressed groups from the mainstream of the labour movement. In this respect labour historians who ignore women are reflecting the innate sexism and patriarchy that has been the hallmark of the mainstream of the British labour movement for much of its history. However, as feminist historians, including the contributors to this book, have shown, this did not mean that women played no part in working-class politics or trade union activity and certainly their role in the labour process itself was and continues to be vitally important. The exclusion of women from working-class and labour history compounds the misunderstanding of class and class formation and has reinforced the theoretical confusion over such invented ideological constructs of the 'family wage' and the 'male breadwinner' which has insinuated itself into labour movement thinking since the mid 19th century. Such confusion explains the persistence even today of women's unequal pay and the fact that many trade unions either opposed equal pay or failed to accord it a priority in their campaigning.

This is not to write off the entire labour movement over its 200 year history as a misogynistic backwater. Working-class organisations do not proceed in a linear onward and upward fashion. They are always marked by peaks and troughs in activity, effectiveness, membership and ideological clarity. These ups and downs are not always crudely determined by economic circumstances but have a great deal to do with the prevailing level of political class consciousness. The fact that this elusive construct escapes causal explanation does not invalidate its existence. At key moments its presence determines the defiant rather than the defensive aspect of the movement when it consciously seeks to break the ideological yoke chaining it to capitalist society, its norms, practices and values. However, if class consciousness does not explicitly embrace the female half of the working class, such consciousness is but a chimera. The development of the British Labour movement throughout its history is a product of the tension between rival ideologies – between the vision of harmonious accommodation within the capitalist system and the vision of a different system altogether. Variously the ideologies inspiring these visions and the practices which they inspired could be called, in their pure and most polarised forms, left or right, radical or reactionary, socialist or capitalist, revolutionary or reformist. Rarely are the complex battles which shape a movement played out in their starkest forms, but nonetheless the underlying tension was often there. In Britain the infinite capacity of the first industrial nation to accommodate dissent led ultimately to the defeat of the early revolutionary tone of the movement – a movement which, because it challenged the dominant values of industrial capitalism, created a space for an early flowering of feminism expressed in the early general unions, Chartism and female reform societies. Ultimately and gradually a dominant labourist[31] consensus triumphed which, while offering at times the possibility of hope and change, accepted the parameters of the existing social order and sought defence of its interests within it. Women were the victims of this consensus. On the other hand those whose consciousness of class led them to challenge consensus and collaboration bequeathed to us the legacy of defiance and this legacy because of its hostility to and rejection of the settled values of capitalist society, began to encompass, albeit in halting measure, the wider cause of the struggle to end oppression as an integral part of the fight to eradicate class exploitation.

Notes

1   Webb, S. & B. *History of Trade Unionism*, London: Longmans Green, 1894.
    Hammond, J.L. and B. *The Village Labourer*, London: Longmans Green, 1911.
    The Town Labourer, London: Longmans Green, 1917.
    The Skilled Labourer, London: Longmans Green, 1927.

The Age of the Chartists, London: Longmans Green, 1930
Cole, G.D.H. *A Short History of the British Working Class Movement*: George Allen and Unwin, 1925.
Tawney, R.H. *Religion and the Rise of Capitalism*, London: Murray, 1926.
Neff, W. *Victorian Working Women*, London: Allen & Unwin, 1929.
Pinchbeck, I. *Women Workers in the Industrial Revolution*, London: Routledge, 1930.

2. The contribution of these historians is discussed in Kaye, H. *The British Marxist Historian*, Cambridge: Polity, 1984, and more recently in Blackledge, P. *Reflections on the Marxist Theory of History*, Manchester: MUP, 2006.
3. Carr, E.H. *What is History?* Harmondsworth: Penguin, 1964.
4. Thompson, E.P. *The Making of the English Working Class*, London: Gollancz, 1963, p. 12.
5. Thompson, E.P. p. 305
6. Marx, K. *Capital* vol.1, London: Lawrence and Wishart, 1970, p. 394.
7. Engels, F. *The Condition of the Working Class in England in 1844* in *Marx & Engels On Britain*, Moscow: Progress Publishers, 1962.
8. Ibid., p. 175.
9. Pinchbeck, I. *Women Workers & the Industrial Revolution*, op.cit.
10. Neff, W. *Victorian Working Women*, op.cit.
11. In fairness, however, R.F. Neale does point out in 'The Poverty of Positivism: from Standard of Living to 'Quality of Life, 1780-1850' in *Writing Marxist History*, Oxford: Basil Blackwell, 1985, p.112, that the standard of living debate, referred to earlier in this chapter, excluded wage indices for all women workers.
12. Neale, *Writing Marxist History*, op cit., p. 156.
13. Hobsbawm, E.J. 'Man & Woman: Images on the left' in Hobsbawm, E.J, *Worlds of Labour*, London: Weidenfeld & Nicholson, 1984, p. 82.
14. Scott, J. 'Towards a Feminist History' in *Gender and the Politics of History*, New York: Columbia University Press, 1988, p. 16.
15. Fulbrook, M. *Historical Theory*, London: Routledge, 2002.
16. Ibid., p. 18.
17. Mitchell, J. 'Women and Equality' in *Feminism & Equality* ed. A. Phillips, Oxford: Basil Blackwell, 1987.
18. Ibid.
19. See for example the Equal Opportunities Commission (EOC) report on *The Gender Pay Gap*, 2001, which shows that the gap between men's and women's earnings in Britain is the widest of all EU member states.
20. See Marx, K. *Capital*, vol. 1, ibid., for useful insights from early 19th century millowners on why they preferred to use the labour of married women with dependent children.
21. For a fuller elaboration of this point see Williams, E. *Capitalism and Slavery*, London: Deutsch, 1964 and Davis, M. *Comrade or Brother? A History of the British Labour Movement*, London: Pluto Press, 2009.
22. Newton, J., Ryan, M. and Walkowitz, J. eds. *Class and Sex in Women's History*, London: Routledge & Kegan Paul, 1983 editors' introduction pp. 2-3.

23 The following is a selection of some of the most useful (and comprehensible!) contributions which have informed my analysis.
Marx, K. & Engels, F. *The German Ideology*, London: Lawrence & Wishart, 1965.
Althusser, L. *Lenin & Philosophy & Other Essays*, London: NLB, 1971.
Althusser, L. *For Marx*, London: Allen Lane, 1965.
Barrett, M *Women's Oppression Today*, London: Verso, 1986.
Eagleton, T. *Ideology*, London: Verso, 1991.
Korsch, K. *Marxism & Philosophy*, London: NLB, 1970.
Larrain, J. *Marxism & Ideology*, London, Macmillan, 1983.
McCarney, J. *The Real World of Ideology*, London: Gregg Revivals, 1980.
Parekh, B. *Marx's Theory of Ideology*, London: Croom Helm, 1982.
24 Larrain, op cit.
25 For an excellent discussion of this point see Barrett, M. *Women's Oppression Today*, London: Verso, 1986.
26 This is classically expressed in the Communist Party programme, *The British Road to Socialism*, 5th edition, 1977.
27 Wright, E. *Interrogating Inequality*, especially the chapter on 'Explanation & Emancipation in Marxism and Feminism', London: Verso 1994.
28 Ibid., p. 212.
29 Ibid., p. 220.
30 This is not to underestimate the difficulties involved in the 'broad' definition – most notably the managerial strata, who whilst selling their labour power for a wage (salary), are functionally linked to the maintenance of the process of exploitation.
31 A term first used by Rothstein, T. *From Chartism to Labourism*, London: Lawrence, ,1929 and subsequently taken up by Miliband, R. *Parliamentary Socialism*, London: Merlin Press, 1973 (reprinted 2009).

Gender and class consciousness in industrialisation: the Bradford worsted industry 1820-1845

Sian Moore

This chapter explores the expression of gender and class interests at a political level in the context of the industrialisation of worsted production in Bradford and Keighley, West Yorkshire. These interests were defined by the renegotiation of social and gender relations, which characterised the transition to industrial capitalism. The study is based upon one location and labour market, and is thus able to capture the range of coexisting and conflicting forms of protest and political response during a period of changing class and gender relations. It looks at the way working-class women responded to and resisted, at both an individual and collective level, the imposition of industrial capitalist relations.

For labour historians this period has generated a number of studies and debates over the definition and existence of class consciousness, foremost E.P. Thompson's *The Making of the English Working Class*[1], which documents the active 'making' of the working class as a social and cultural formation, based upon the agency of working people and nurtured by a continuous radical, dissenting artisanal legacy. In Foster's study of Oldham[2] the period is marked by a transition from a labour or trade union consciousness to mass political struggle against the system itself, based upon male workers asserting themselves as a class led by a vanguard group. Calhoun[3] argues that Thompson defines class as a cultural and political category, which leads him to impose class struggle upon moments when class structure was not yet fully formed. He focuses upon the social foundations of collective action and argues that the most radical social mobilisations of at least the earlier period had their material basis, not in class, but in traditional communities of craft and locality. They were thus populist and cannot be characterised as class struggle, although their potency should not be devalued because of this. At least until the 1830s working people were engaged in defensive struggles against their proletarianisation. Calhoun's analysis generally distinguishes two distinct communities, one of older craftworkers and labourers mobilising on the basis of more radical and populist goals and the other of newer urban industrial workers. A critique of exploitation within industrial capitalism, emphasising class, emerged in the 1820s appealing to the latter group, but suggesting more reformist objectives.

These debates on the formation of class and the possibility and definition of class consciousness are generally marked by the absence of any substantial consideration of gender. Yet as the history of Bradford in this period demonstrates the restructuring of the gender division of labour was integral to the renegotiation of capitalist relations. Working women were crucial to the formation of the working class and gender was central to its political expression. The chapter highlights episodes in the earlier, but also later period, in which familial and communal ties were central to mobilisations against the impact of industrial capitalism upon the labour process. Industrial militancy continued to be based upon alliances between skilled male labour and the female and juvenile industrial workforce. These two groups did not form distinct communities, but one community based upon different but clear social relations to industrial capitalism. Familial, communal and class relations mediated and accommodated possible tensions.

As Calhoun concedes, whilst mobilisations based upon community can be radical, they are often defensive and can also be reactionary. Throughout the period working women in Bradford participated in community-based informal protest and the chapter considers the ability of such protest to address non-economic issues and women's specific grievances. The discussion suggests that such protest was often based upon 'traditional' gender relations and unable to challenge the existing social and gender system. Marx and Engels argued that it was the increased organisation of workers in the workplace that would provide the social basis of class activity. Sarah Eisenstein[4] (in her study of working-class women's consciousness in the US between 1890 and the First World War) has suggested that it is only when women began to work outside the home that recognition of their shared social situation could emerge. Prior to this the position of women within working class communities defined women in a familial context and this precluded 'the experience of structured interaction which might be a basis for perceiving their common situation in social terms'. In Bradford it was women and children who formed the first factory proletariat (although they were not necessarily the first to experience proletarianisation, which cannot be equated with the transfer of production outside of the household); this chapter explores women's consciousness of themselves as wage earners and as women and the different forms that consciousness took. It describes a number of episodes throughout the period, within Bradford, in which working-class women take some sort of action, whether individual or collective, formal or informal. The episodes are not necessarily recounted in chronological order, since it is important to emphasise how different forms of activity co-existed and had continuity, as well as identifying transitions. If class consciousness is difficult to define and identify, then the relationship between class and gender consciousness is even more elusive. As Barbara Taylor, in her study of Owenite Socialism and Feminism in the nineteenth century, puts it, 'what is harder to unravel, however, is how women's involvement in the emergent labour movement related to their experience and consciousness of themselves as women, as members not only of an exploited class, but also of an oppressed sex'[5]. The first part of the chapter looks at the familial and communal context of protest, which was momentary and informal, as well as linked to formal industrial struggle, exploring how this defined working women's roles and consciousness. The second part moves on to examine the shift in the location of women's wage-earning and its impact on women's consciousness of themselves as women and as workers. The third part of the chapter looks at the emergence of political movements based upon fears of the subversion of gender relations and opposition to female and juvenile factory labour and the reassertion of working-class male interests. The chapter ends by exploring both Chartism and Owenite Socialism in Bradford as movements capable of articulating both class and gender consciousness.

1. FAMILIAL AND COMMUNAL SOLIDARITIES

The 1825 Bradford Combers and Weavers' Strike

In Bradford, industrialisation was characterised by the diversity and range of capitalist forms of production. It did not give rise to separate communities of workers and the experiences and interests of handloom weavers and combers, who increasingly did not own the means of production, cannot be counterposed to a new industrial workforce[6]. It is clear that during the course of their lifecycles men, but more especially women, continually moved between 'domestic' (but more often workshop) and factory settings. The familial context of work persisted throughout the period and this is illustrated by the 1825 Bradford Combers and Weavers' Strike. This dispute has been characterised as a response to the transformation of the labour process and of the relationship between technology and work[7]. The mechanization of worsted spinning in the last years of the eighteenth century and first two decades of the nineteenth century facilitated an increased demand for woolcombing. Apprenticeship regulations were increasingly disregarded, suspended every year from 1802 and finally abolished in 1809. The 1825 Strike (or turn-out) lasted several months and involved all domestic and factory workers employed in the worsted industry in Bradford, although it was reported that unrest spread to all workers in the town, whilst funds to support the striking workers were donated from all parts of the country. It was provoked by the refusal of the employers to respond to the Weavers and Combers union's demand for an advance in wages and the equalisation of wages between employers. The combers demanded concessions due to changes in the conditions of woolcombing, particularly the introduction of superior wools. The strike was a response by the combers to the early signs of the decay of their trade. They were gradually losing control of the labour process with the concentration of capital amongst a few who owned the means of production – the combs. In a similar process, by the end of the period the handloom weaver had essentially lost the battle for control over the labour process, with the transfer of the instruments of production into the hands of the capitalist who hired out looms and parts of looms to their employees on credit.

The technological development of the worsted spinning process contrasts with that of the cotton and woollen industries where expansion and the gender specificity of technological development generally meant shifts in the sexual division of labour. In worsted the centralisation and mechanism of spinning did not entail the displacement of female labour. The shift in the division of labour was as much by age as sex; the new factory labour force comprised children of both genders and young women, depending upon the specific process.

Yet as well as representing a battle over the labour process, the strike also illuminates gender relations during the period, and the extent to which gender and familial solidarity overcame a potential conflict between factory workers employed in worsted spinning – largely young workers, children and women – and artisan values. The strength of the strike lay in its community and familial base and the fact that it affected all worsted workers.

The union struck against three firms who were amongst those paying the lowest wages. The employers reacted by meeting to defend those firms involved and effectively outlawed the union by resolving not to employ any comber or weaver belonging to it. The union consequently extended its strike to all mills in the town. The employers required all workers to sign a declaration renouncing the union and then resolved to dismiss any combers and weavers found to contribute to the funds of the union, whether or not they were a member. The employers then declared: 'That the workpeople in the mills belonging to the union and the children in the mills whose fathers belong to the union shall be discharged at the end of the current week'[8]. As the second address of the Combers and Weavers committee stated of the employers: 'In a word they struck against the whole town'[9].

The employers reinforced the alliance between factory operatives and handworkers, which was largely built upon family ties. The union had already discussed whether children working for the firms against which they were taking action should be withdrawn from the factories, but there had been some objection because of the money that would be required to support the children. Community and familial solidarity facilitated the survival of the strike, with children put out of work because their parents belonged to the union sent to live with other workers. Women were automatically drawn into the conflict, firstly as wage earners and secondly as wives and mothers supporting male workers on strike and ensuring the survival of their households. It was reported that girls were turned away from the mills because their mothers and grandmothers would not sign papers renouncing the union[10]. In one instance women were amongst those committed to hard labour for attacking a former union member who had returned to work, on their release crowds greeted them[11]. A record of expenditure during the strike shows that of the 6,036 to whom money was paid by the Union Committee 2,900 were men, 213 women and 2,923 children. The women supported by union funds were weavers who had entered the occupation prior to the strike[12]. The mass production of yarn facilitated by the mechanisation of spinning between the late eighteenth century and 1820 created a demand for weavers. The more recent introduction of the worsted trade meant the type of apprenticeship regulations which governed the woollen industry had never been strictly enforced in worsted and thus there were fewer obstacles to the influx of labour into handloom weaving which occurred in the first decades of the nineteenth century – a substantial proportion women and children, some of whom had been deprived of employment through the mechanization of spinning. In addition it was reported that in the later part of the turn-out 800 women were given relief[13], probably factory operatives rendered unemployed by the closure of the mills.

The strike in its objectives and organisation reflected and reinforced existing gender relations. The employers, in their attempts to crush the turn-out, exploited the familial context of waged work and what they perceived as the gender divisions of labour and power entrenched in the working-class family. They demanded that

> The father, if living, and if not the mother of every spinner, drawer, reeler, rover, warper and other child in the mills under the age of 18

years shall sign a declaration that such parent does not belong to the Weavers and Combers union before the children shall be allowed to begin their work next Monday morning and that all workpeople of the description before mentioned who are above 18 years old shall sign a similar declaration, except married women of that age, whose husbands shall give a like disavowal.[14]

During the course of the strike a debate ensued between employers and the union about the level of weaving wages, which involved a discussion about women's wages, with both sides acknowledging the wage differential between the genders. The union expressed concern about the low rates, which female weavers were earning. Yet, the demands of the Combers and Weavers reflected existing differentials and definitions of skill and assumed the existence of a family wage economy[15] in which women were secondary wage earners. The newspapers commented that the prevailing male wage did not have to support a family since children were sent to the mills and young women also contributed; 'the wages of the husband taken singly was thus no criterion of the state of the combers generally. These statements will all apply to the weavers as well as the combers…'[16]. The allocation of funds by the union supported this notion of the family wage and the perception of women as secondary wage earners, even though prior to the strike women had paid the same contributions to the union as men. For the first 15 weeks female members received the same allowance as men, but 'were then reduced to something less'. The additional 800 women 'were relieved at a rate of 1s each a week during the latter part of the turn-outs or rather as they were married women their husbands received 8s a week instead of 7s'[17]. The rhetoric of the union acknowledged men as primary wage earners, yet in asking higher rates for female handloom weavers they were recognizing the importance of the female contribution to the family income.

The turn-out ended after 23 weeks, with trade depressed and union funds increasingly unable to support the 6,036 unemployed because of the strike. The combers and weavers failed to secure an increase in wages but gained recognition for their union. The strike suggests the importance of familial and communal solidarity to mobilisation and could be described as defensive, since it was resisting changes to the labour process; yet it also suggests a clear trade union or labour consciousness (and national support meant it went beyond the local) shared by both male and female workers.

Informal community protest

The strength of community-based protest appeared to endure throughout the period. Working-class women were often the instigating force behind informal popular protest, which could address areas which formal working-class politics increasingly chose to ignore, including the sexual division of labour. This has been characterized as 'female' as opposed to 'feminist' consciousness[18]. Reddy[19] asserts that non-market grievances remained central motives of working-class protest and evidence for Bradford suggests that these found expression in informal, popular protest and actions to which women were integral. In some of these protests women acted independently; others were mixed, but reports usually indicate women's active role. Some of these actions concerned issues surrounding consumption and could be regarded in the tradition of the food riot. One challenge to the authorities involved rescuing friends or relatives when overseers attempted to remove the poor to the workhouse. A proportion of informal popular protests confronted, in some way, gender relations within the community, for example domestic violence or incest. In one sense these actions can be seen as stemming from traditional plebeian culture and ritual, the charivari or rough music whereby an individual or individuals who had violated a community's sexual or moral code were punished. Traditionally some charivari were provoked by second marriages. The limitations of available sources mean that most of the instances in question are from the 1830s and 1840s, but these show that traditional forms of popular protest survived changes in social relations and not just in the 'traditional' manufacturing communities or industrial villages which comprised Bradford parish. Many of the examples are from central Bradford where factory industry was concentrated, where the substantial number of migrants to the area had settled and where one might expect social dislocation to be most acute. E.P. Thompson[20] stressed that older forms of popular expression can take on new meanings in different social contexts. Where one of the major targets of the charivari was the wife who opposed the values of a patriarchal society by dominating her husband and, indeed, the husband who had failed to uphold patriarchal authority; by the nineteenth century it was the husband who abused his wife who became the standard victim. There is some evidence for this view in the Bradford area, with examples of action against men committing adultery and domestic violence. In 1845 a coroner's jury sat on the case of Mary Ann Greenwood, who actually died from typhus, but amidst rumours that her death was the result of injuries inflicted by her husband, George Greenwood:

Greenwood who had been in custody in the room during the proceedings was then removed to the courthouse. The same ill feeling was manifested towards him on going down as had been when he came up. Along Manchester Road groups mostly composed of women had collected at various parts and altogether could not be fewer than a thousand people congregated to learn the result of the inquest and, loud was the disapprobation manifested when the likelihood of a verdict of acquittal was announced.[21]

Underdown[22] suggests that the enhancement of women's roles with the growth of the market economy may have given women a greater independence, which men found threatening. E.P. Thompson[23] has perceived the increasing focus of rough music on to men who mistreated their wives as reflecting changes in the definition of sexual roles. Such informal, often spontaneous community protest, could allow women and men to confront sexual relations in a way that, as Reddy[24] has shown, structured working-class politics increasingly did not. These actions made public what was increasingly confined to the private and exposed the boundaries imposed between the two spheres. The survival and vitality of these forms of protest indicate the inadequacy of formal political language to deal with issues central to the lives of both women and men. Popular mobilisations survived throughout the period in question and beyond. The ability of popular, informal politics to address the issue of sexual relations within the community should not be seen as a remnant of traditional plebeian culture, but as a means through which contemporary conflicts in gender relations could be expressed, arising from the failure of the language prevailing in the public realm to acknowledge these issues.

However, to perceive of informal community protest as a substitute for a politics that challenged industrial capitalist relations and gender relations is to ignore the ability of such actions to confirm and reinforce prevailing social relations and ideologies. For example, in Bradford there is evidence that working-class women were central to popular movements directed against the Irish community. Kaplan[25] suggests female consciousness can bring women into conflict with male political authorities and have potentially revolutionary consequences. She asserts that traditional values and consciousness can shift during struggle, yet it must also be acknowledged that women were assuming roles accorded them by the prevailing gender division of labour, and were acting to defend and enforce gender relations. Bradford court records contain instances of women prosecuting their husbands for neglect and indicate women's anger at their husbands' inability to provide for them – reflecting the material realities of their position. Outrage at wife-beating served to punish those who overstepped the accepted boundaries of relations between the sexes. It is questionable how far women taking on traditional roles in popular politics were able or chose to transform those roles, and we are faced with the paradox of women both challenging and upholding the prevailing sexual hierarchy, sometimes in the same moment.

2. WOMEN AS WAGE EARNERS

In the early Bradford worsted industry rural production co-existed and was interdependent with more centralized urban-artisan production. A study of changes within handcombing following the 1825 strike demonstrates the diverse forms proletarianisation took. Whereas in spinning this meant a shift from a domestic basis, in combing the opposite occurred. Transition entailed the destruction of urban male artisan production and the emergence of handcombing as a domestic outwork industry, to which the use of familial and juvenile labour was fundamental. There was then no unilinear progression to factory industry.

Steam engines were introduced into the Bradford area from the turn of the eighteenth century, but it was not until the 1830s that steam became more important than water. Subsequently expansion was rapid: between 1835 and 1850 the number of power looms in the West Riding worsted industry multiplied ten times, and this involved the redistribution of industry from a dispersed to a concentrated form within central Bradford. By the end of the period the mechanisation of weaving and implicit shift in the gender division of labour meant the displacement of the large predominantly male weaving labour force by a class of young female industrial workers. The competition between hand and power loom undermined the wages of both groups of weavers. By 1841, almost one quarter of the entire population of Bradford Borough was engaged in factory work and of these five sixths were female; by 1845 there were 12,000 female factory workers in Bradford.[26]

The establishment of factory industry meant the further sexual segregation of the workforce in some processes of worsted production. Eisenstein[27] draws upon Mannheim's emphasis on the importance of the factory in providing the conditions for the development of a collective identity amongst working-class women. In Bradford it was women and children who were the first to contest industrial discipline in this new environment, both individually and collectively, but drawing upon modes of protest characteristic of the domestic industry.

Women and industrial discipline

In Bradford the tradition of resistance to industrial discipline established in the domestic industry shaped the responses of female factory workers. Industrial discipline was not something new to early factory workers, although the pace of machinery and the authority of the capitalist may have been. Resistance to capitalist control over the labour process transcended the shifts in the location of production processes. Women had a history of challenging industrial discipline in the domestic industry and were central in challenging labour discipline in the factory. Continuity between the forms which protest took is striking, challenging the notion that centralized and supervised production eradicated the irregularity of the working day and illegal appropriation by the domestic workforce. Embezzlement, a feature of domestic worsted production, survived the transition to the factory and indeed the shift in location provided new opportunities for both factory and domestic workers to smuggle materials from their employers' premises. Reddy[28] sees pilfering from the early textile mills as a continuation of the tradition of 'taxation populaire' whose success depended upon communal accord, as an informal tactic for imposing equity if rates of pay were reduced. Evidence from Bradford suggests that capitalist control of the factory was never total and industrial discipline was continually contested. Factory workers often broke their contracts and changed jobs (in one factory 44 per cent of workers under 18 lasted under 6 months and 58 per cent under 12 months)[29].

Between 1836 and 1842 the local newspaper and the courts were expressing concern at the frequency with which female powerloom weavers were leaving their work in an unfinished state. Women prosecuted for this under the Master and Servant Act generally attributed their actions to the 'bad' state of the warps which made it impossible to complete the pieces which they were weaving, since they were paid by the piece their wages consequently suffered. In one example Hannah Hardisty and Martha Wood had been convicted in July 1839 for leaving their work unfinished; they went further in August of that year when, with Alice Wilkinson, they were charged with damaging their work:

> It appeared that they had all left their employers' work without finishing their warps and had in consequence been summoned and each had been ordered to go back and finish their warps. Whilst finishing, they had, through willful carelessness or otherwise damaged a piece in process of weaving.[30]

Such actions reveal that women were aware of their labour as a commodity, which they could take elsewhere if necessary. As Charlotte Watson, a powerloom weaver, told her overlooker after she had been repeatedly kept waiting for a warp and then found there were no bobbins for her: 'This won't do for me, I'll see if I cannot get work elsewhere'[31].

Informal collective protest

Women workers also organised collectively. Their actions in defending or advancing their rights as wage earners tended to be informal and spontaneous and independent of existing trade union organisation, which characterized strikes by Bradfords's shoemakers, tailors, weavers and combers from the beginning of the period. Women's action appeared to take the form of simply leaving the workplace in protest, as distinct from withholding labour over a sustained period:

> In consequence of Messrs Horsfalls attempting to reduce the wages of their hands engaged in the superintending of the powerlooms on Monday morning they refused to work; and in lieu thereof took a mornings walk, to enjoy the fragrance of a summer breeze out of the rattle of shuttles and din of machinery. About 250 of them struck.[32]

Yet women workers also led sustained strike action. These often included some sort of parade or procession, drawing upon older customs and symbols that could mobilize the wider community:

> For the last two weeks there was rather an extensive strike of the powerloom weavers in Shipley and its neighbourhood. The hands of four firms had struck for an advance of sixpence per piece. We have not heard whether the employers and their workpeople have come to an understanding since Tuesday week. On that day one of the Masters was paraded in effigy through the village and then shot and burned.[33]

These struggles were over the wage, as distinct from the labour process,[34] suggesting women workers were organising to gain concessions from the employer over the conditions of their employment at the same time as they were engaged in more defensive actions resisting the imposition of a new industrial regime. This questions any unilinear transition from actions designed to resist industrial capitalist relations to offensive actions based upon class. It shows that working women developed a labour consciousness independently of men, yet this was also informed by cultural inheritances from domestic industry and did not simply reflect the experience of factory work. The formal collective organisation of the powerloom weavers as a trade union was not, however, an autonomous process.

The Powerloom Weavers Protective Society

In 1845 a meeting of the powerloom weavers was held to consider the necessity of forming a protective society; 'the first meeting of females on this subject, it was stated, in the kingdom'[35]. At this time male trade unionists were critical of female powerloom weavers for what was seen as a disinclination to organise, although 'various strikes'[36] were acknowledged. It appears that there were between 150 and 200 women present, but what is striking is the extent to which the meeting and process was dominated and controlled by men and the instigation for the establishment of the union was said to be the Woolcombers Protective Society. The meeting was chaired by one of the minority of male powerloom weavers and all speakers and those putting resolutions were male, with the exception of the adoption of a letter to the Trades Conference, moved and seconded by two female weavers. At the end of the meeting a committee was elected and it appears that it comprised a disproportionate number of men[37]. In its structure and constitution the Powerloom Weavers Protective Society was in many ways a duplication of the Woolcombers Protective Society.

At a further meeting in May it was reported that the Powerloom Weavers Protective Society had 800 members[38]. Female trade unionists appear to have perceived themselves as a secondary and auxiliary force in the battle between labour and capital and in reports (in the bourgeois media) they constantly apologise for transgressing sexually defined roles, even if these were imposed from above. Miss Rothwell, treasurer of the Powerloom Weavers Society, told a public meeting of woolcombers and other trades:

> She hoped the meeting would not view her in the light of one wishing to depart from the usual reserve and modesty of her sex and trusted they would excuse in her the want of that eloquence which had been so ably displayed by the preceding speakers. In addressing a meeting composed of hundreds of thinking men, she keenly felt her situation and was aware that among the ranks of the middle and upper class she would obtain the unenviable epithet of a bold and forward girl but should that be the case they who would thus charge her should remember that the blame lay at their own door. While she had a tongue to proclaim the wrongs of sisters in slavery, while a drop of British blood flowed in her veins she would strive for the emancipation of her class and ere long they would find that the female workers in Bradford

would be a powerful auxiliary in the onward march to a fair days wage for a fair days work.[39]

We are faced with the dilemma of women on the one hand proclaiming themselves to be a powerful, industrial force and on the other subordinating themselves to the men of their class. There is no evidence that the female powerloom workers' alliance with male workers was based upon the confirmation of male power in the family, in the form of support for the primacy of the male breadwinner. The provision of waged work for women in Bradford meant that such demands were not realistic.

This determination by male trade unionists to organise the female powerloom weavers was part of a wider drive, by the combers in particular, to amalgamate the Bradford trades with the proposed Association of United Trades of Great Britain, which they expected the forthcoming Conference of Trades delegates to facilitate. In placing their faith in unity between trades and in mutual protection, the combers were forced to acknowledge the potential power of the powerloom weavers and the right of women to sell their labour outside the household in return for a fair wage. It was when skilled male workers were at their most defensive that solidarity between workplaces and genders was possible. As attempts to establish a branch of the Owenite Consolidated Union of Trades Confederation in the 1840s show, Bradford trades unionism was at this time based upon a combination of older unions and newer industrial unions with female and juvenile membership. This prevented or delayed the dominance of skilled male exclusionist trades unions. Industrial action continued to embrace large sections of the working-class community. Yet women workers' spontaneous mobilisations continued into the 1840s and did not die with the establishment of the Bradford Weavers Protective Society. Informal workplace protest, whether on an individual or collective level, cannot then be counterposed to union organisation. It is likely that the same women were, at different moments, involved in both.

3. THE CHALLENGE TO GENDER RELATIONS

Bourgeois ideology

The period in question was one in which gender and class relations were fluid, but by the 1840s prevailing values and ideas were to some extent founded upon a series of perceptions of women and children's waged work informed by male fears of social and, to a greater degree, sexual upheaval. Amongst the bourgeoisie such fears drew upon and reinforced existing ideas about separate spheres and female domesticity. In Bradford evangelical ideas incorporating domestic ideology were embodied in such figures as the Reverend G.S. Bull and the town's major worsted manufacturer, John Wood – both Anglican Tories involved in radical reformist but socially conservative movements. Contemporary observers identified a threat to the primacy of the male bread-winner and consequently to his authority within the household. With increasing numbers of females and juveniles employed in factories and the simultaneous decline of the male-dominated handloom weaving and combing trades, alongside recurrent cyclical depression, it was asserted that in some cases men were contributing less and women and children more to household incomes and in certain circumstances could support the household. In 1841 two Bradford factory owners wrote to an MP that male handloom weavers were unable to get work, but their daughters were employed in factories, girls as spinners and young women on the powerlooms[40]. The necessity of female wage earning lead to the possibility of a reversal in a traditional sexual division of labour with women going out to the powerloom and men taking up domestic work. For middle-class observers this renegotiation of social relations was perceived as a threat to existing gender relations and consequently as a challenge to the stability of the social system. With regard to the maintenance of parents by children, G.S. Bull asserted, '[i]t inverts the order of society in that respect'.[41]

In objecting to the employment of married women, William Walker (John Wood's partner) argued that:'[t]he practice of husbands depending on the wages of their wives is an inversion of family order and ought to be put down by every means reasonably available for that end'.[42] From the 1830s fears of the subversion of social and sexual relations began to coalesce into overt hostility to female and juvenile waged labour outside the home. Opposition was expressed to a large extent through the Factory Movement, focused upon the perceived inconsistency of the employment of girls with the acquisition of domestic skills. In 1840 Wood and Walker ruled that no married women should be allowed to work in their mills – 'they are expected to remain at home'[43].

Yet these Anglican manufacturers could not survive economically without juvenile and female labour and in particular without the labour of young women. Their resolution was the attempted imposition of paternalist relations upon the factory workforce – a source of social control mediating bourgeois sexual ideology. One manufacturer established a school within his factory educating girls in domestic skills, sewing and knitting[44]. Similarly, during periods of female unemployment G.S.Bull established schools of industry wherein women were supplied with needlework[45]. Evangelical ideology was based upon a stringent sexual morality and the supposed immorality of the female factory worker was continually referred to. Employers increasingly sought ways to control the sexuality of female factory workers. At one mill 'Any single women known to conduct herself improperly must instantly quit her employment'[46]. By 1845 a committee of manufacturers proposed that manufacturers require young unmarried female operatives not residing with their parents to live in approved boarding or lodging houses under supervision and with 'evening instruction in domestic matters and in religious and mental improvement'[47].

The working-class response

How far did the Bradford working classes share increasingly prevalent notions of female dependency and domesticity? Thomas Laquer's[48] study of the Sunday School Movement has argued that the period witnessed the birth of a working-class culture rooted in the ethic of education, religion and respectability embodied in the Sunday School Movement – a largely autonomous and indigenous institution of the working-class community. Working-class politics was largely 'the creation of a people steeped in religion and the Bible'[49] and this is underlined in Bradford by the existence of radical, Owenite and Chartist Sunday schools. Records of Methodist and Baptist chapels in Bradford, where the predominantly female congregation were mill workers, reveal exclusion for transgressions of sexual morality[50]. What Lacquer describes as the puritan ethic was not an imposition of the bourgeoisie, although such ideas might be confined to skilled sections of the working class. The 1830s and 1840s saw the spread of the Temperance Movement in Bradford and both the Socialists and the Chartists established their own Temperance Societies.

The Factory Movement was based upon a Tory-Radical alliance, which cut across class, although evidence suggests that the short-time committees were largely working class. Sources imply that certain sections of the working class shared the middle-class concern with the balance of sexual power within the household. A meeting at Keighley, supporting Ashley's Ten Hours Bill, heard a resolution moved and seconded by operatives, which argued that the long hours of labour in factories:

> deprive families of time and opportunity for attending to those domestic duties for which they are by nature adapted and subverts some of the most valuable institutions and customs of English society'[51].

It appears that a section of the (probably skilled) working class, drawing upon 'traditional' artisanal culture, retained a belief in distinct familial roles and the primacy of the male breadwinner. However, the Bradford working population also reflected the traditions of the substantial number of rural immigrants and of the Irish community, informed by different customary expectations. It is likely that a process of negotiation took place between different values.

The 1830s and 1840s saw Bradford male working-class fears of the subversion of sexual relations and their consequent opposition to female and juvenile labour increasingly expressed in political terms. Evidence suggests that working-class men identified machinery and the employment of female and juvenile labour as responsible for undermining skilled male labour. Meetings of handloom weavers in and around Bradford adopted resolutions attributing the depressed state of the working class to amongst other causes, '[t]he adoption of machines and every improvement to children and youth, and women, to the exclusion of those who ought to work – THE MEN'[52] A pamphlet produced by the Central Committee of the Handloom worsted weavers of the West Riding argued, 'When our labour was protected by "fettering competition" Britain increased in wealth, prosperity and happiness; we could then earn a living without dragging our wives and infants into the market of labour'[53].

The possibility of tension between the largely male skilled sector and an industrial workforce dominated by women and young people increased throughout the period. The Bradford Chartist rising of 1840 involved plans to destroy powerlooms, and competition between the two groups of workers is suggested by a strike in 1844 by powerloom weavers. This was reported to have ended with an increase in the price paid for different pieces, but in order to offset some of his loss the employer reduced the wages of the woolcombers he employed[54]. Another incident suggests that tension could lead to conflict, in this case arising from a strike by woolcombers employed by a major Bradford manufacturer:

> An Irish lad named Andrew Macdonald was charged with having so threatened a girl named Anne Bateman that she was afraid of him doing some grievous bodily harm. The complainant is in the employ of Messrs Rand as the defendant recently has been and it was alleged that this threatening occurred in consequence of her refusal to 'turn-out'. Macdonald was also charged with assaulting two children employed at Rands. Jabez Althusan, an officer of the Woolcombers Protective Society was also charged with assaulting one Sarah Steel, in a row occasioned by the turn-out at Rands.[55]

The Plug Riots or General Strike of 1842 saw an attempt by handworkers to stop machinery in the mills and to force factory operatives to leave their work. Some female millworkers testified against those men charged following an attack on Slubbing House Mill, Keighley, one witness said she had known one defendant had known since he was a boy;[56] further implying that the interests of the working class and community were not always shared.

Accommodation?

Thus there is evidence of social and economic dislocation and a suggestion that a perceived threat to skilled male labour provoked sexual antagonism and a working-class politics and culture divided along gender lines. Yet the continuing familial context of work and evidence of considerable movement and interaction between those working in factory and 'domestic' or workshop settings suggests that tensions were also accommodated within 'the family', 'community' and through class-based industrial and political organisation. Potential divisions were often overcome since handworkers and factory operatives were related or at least part of the same communities. In 1843 during a strike of woolcombers working for a major mill a subscription of two shillings and sixpence towards the support of the men was announced, 'a shilling of it given by the women'[57]. In 1845 weavers at one mill struck against a reduction of wages; the United Trades Mutual Protective society was able to draw out all factory hands, but the woolcombers also struck and thus the operatives of the whole firm (between 400 and 800 people) were out for nearly a month[58]. The centrality of familial ties meant that industrial militancy could be based upon the family wage economy. In one example woolcombers withdrew their children from the mill in support of their own demands, but continued to work themselves – they did not strike because the masters could purchase tops ready combed – and the children were paid the equivalent of their wage by the combers[59]. Women were also out on strike, but were paid the same rate as children by the Woolcombers Protective Society[60] – class action was based upon familial relationships, but consequently reflected gender inequality.

Communal ties among working-class women were rooted in the material realities of the gender division of labour – for the majority of women class and gender were not counterposed. Communal and neighbourhood networks were vital to the formation of working-class consciousness, door-to-door collections in support of political causes were common. Existing networks facilitated spontaneous protest in support of political movements. Certain working-class political movements to which women were central entailed a defence of the working-class family against the threat of industrial capitalism. One of the focal points of opposition to the New Poor Law was the separation of husbands and wives in the workhouses.

Evidence points to the involvement of working-class women in the Factory Movement, which clearly identified the destruction of family life as the foremost evil of the factory system. Opposition to female exploitation was based upon a conception of women's roles, that underlined the demarcation between male and female spheres and female subordination. Yet in 1839 a public meeting of women in Bradford resolved to support Joseph Rayner Stephens, leader of opposition to the New Poor Law, who preached about the disruptive impact that the factory system had upon marriage and the family and argued in favour of the abolition of female factory labour, resolving to:

> pledge itself to assist the friend of the ill-treated poor of this country in pecuniary aid against his coming trial and if necessary to go with their husbands, fathers and sons and brothers to defend with their arms that friend of the factory child the Reverend J. R.Stephens.[61]

Chartism

Women's participation in political action could thus be an extension of familial roles, for example in the continuation of older traditions such as exclusive dealing. One newspaper described a procession of 600 female chartists from the Bradford district: 'At the head of the procession there was carried by a woman a large printed board with the words 'exclusive dealing'[62].

Bradford Chartism was of the 'physical force' variety, culminating in the rising of 1840. There is no doubt of Bradford women's support for Chartism, with a number of Female Radical Associations in existence in the area in the late 1830s and a Female Chartist Association established in 1841. As Dorothy Thompson has put it, 'the presence of women in Chartism would seem to indicate that divisions of sex and gender did not any more than division of religious adhesion and ethnicity, inhibit prevailing class loyalties'[63]. Chartism allowed women to act in the public sphere – at least one Chartist woman lectured in Bradford and female Chartists recognised and asserted their rights as women. However, more generally the language of Chartism failed to challenge the gender division of labour or the existing sexual hierarchy and female Chartism reflected traditional sexual and familial roles. In this it reflects the establishment of the Bradford Powerloom Weavers' Protective

Society and it is probable that links between the powerloom weavers and Chartism were close, with the Powerloom Weavers Committee meeting to enrol members in the Chartist rooms. Women were encouraged by men to establish female Chartist Associations and such associations were often addressed by men, while it was generally only in segregated organisations that women held office. Many of the statements issued by women Chartists suggest that they allotted themselves a subordinate, but nonetheless crucial, role in the struggle, but that their prime motivations were the support and encouragement of male kin, with such statements playing upon the moral influence which women supposedly held over them. It is not possible to ascertain how far Chartist women accepted the reassertion of male sexual power that Chartism often implied or sometimes specifically embodied. Bradford Chartism was not the politics of a dying artisanate, the support of the Bradford factory workers was significant. Yet for many working-class women class solidarity generally overcame the specific interests and demands of women.

Owenite Socialism

Yet Chartism was not the only working-class political response to industrialisation. For Barbara Taylor[64], Owenite Socialism gave rise to a vision of society to which women's emancipation was integral. Most accounts of Owenite Socialism in Bradford concur that it was never as important or as popular as Chartism. Yet, reports suggest that it did have a significant following; a Social Institution was opened in 1837, a subsequent lecture attracted an audience of 800 and the New Moral World commented that it 'will shortly be one of our most useful and flourishing branches'. In 1838 Owen lectured to 1200. In the 1830s Bradford fell under the influence of Owenite trade unionism, which crucially advocated an alliance between the older male 'skilled' and newer female 'unskilled' occupational unions. Evidence suggests considerable support for Owenite Socialism amongst women; the last of the series of four meetings held when Owen visited Bradford in 1838 was described thus:

> Upon the concluding evening, Thursday, the Hall was literally crammed and the attendance of females, for whom the large orchestra was then, as it had been every previous night been reserved, was uncommonly numerous. The platform was nearly wholly occupied by females.[65]

Women's participation was never defined in terms of their familial roles as was the case with Chartism. Rather Owenism appealed to women on issues specifically affecting them as women. Possibly for these reasons evidence for Bradford gives the impression that Socialism attracted younger, often single women – those whom changes in productive relations had given a measure of economic independence. Working-class women and men in Bradford were exposed to Socialist ideas advocating the transformation of sexual and marital relations and women's emancipation. In 1839 a series of lectures against the marriage system took place in Bradford, with 'the attendance of females particularly requested', and it was reported that between 300 and 400 attended[66]. During one meeting a Socialist male responded to attacks launched on them:

> I should like to know if marriages of their system (i.e. the Christian system) be well-regulated marriages? Is it a good regulation which treats the wife as a slave? Does not the Christian marriage ceremony require the female to promise to obey? Is it therefore neither more nor less than a system of slavery?[67]

Although nationally the character of Owenism was distinct from Chartism, never having the same focus upon political change, in Bradford it appears that the Owenite's relationships with the Chartists was a close one, with the two movements overlapping. Since Chartism could incorporate a wide range of ideas[68] it is unlikely that popular support for the two movements was mutually exclusive. At certain moments Chartism directly addressed itself to Bradford women, including their right to suffrage (excluded as a demand in The Charter and by the Chartist movement in general). The Northern Star reports a lecture given by Chartist leader Jonathan Bairstow in the Working Men's Hall, Keighley, on 'the Principles of Radicalism', including a survey of Females in Society, entailing an 'eloquent address on behalf of their rights to the suffrage along with the males, requesting them to unite along with the men in assisting in the good cause'.[69] Such evidence suggests the possibility that working-class women in Bradford were exposed to dynamic debates about the relationship between gender and class.

Conclusions

How far did industrialisation provide the material conditions for the emergence of feminist consciousness as a political current seeking to transform social and gender relations? Evidence for Bradford shows that the experience of factory work provided the socio-economic base for women's identity as waged workers and for collective action and that this did to some extent liberate them from traditional roles. Women therefore played a vital part in the formation of labour and trade union consciousness, since they comprised, with children, the first factory workforce and resisted the imposition of the industrial capitalist labour process as well as challenging the wage relation in this new setting. Individual and collective resistance was often informal and independent of male organization. Later in the period Owenite Socialism may have allowed them to express some political consciousness of themselves as women workers, but this movement coexisted with Chartism, a largely sexually conservative movement, reflecting the material conditions of Bradford's industrialization. Class consciousness, as it emerged during the period, was gendered. Working-class politics reflected fears of the subversion of existing social and sexual relations and the reassertion of male power. Taylor[70] argues that political movements of the 1830s and 1840s were 'explicitly preoccupied with sexual/familial relations and their dislocation'.

The political articulation of consciousness is often momentary. The episodes described in this chapter suggest that consciousness is a continuum, ranging from the existence of class and gender, to the expression of consciousness at an individual, informal and/or collective level, to its organized political articulation. There is no unilinear progression from one to another, but women and men move between different forms at different times. As well as acting independently as workers, women in Bradford acted alongside men in the defence of family, community and class. Experiences of factory, workshop and domestic production and of different processes of worsted production were embodied and accommodated within the family and/or household. Even when tensions developed, these inter-relationships mitigated against the existence of separate communities of workers and accommodated tensions between a largely male 'skilled' workforce experiencing the degradation of work and the early female and child factory labour force subject to appalling abuses and conditions. Women's roles in movements based on community and class were generally an extension of their domestic role and reinforced rather than challenged the gender division of labour.

Throughout the period, industrial militancy could be based upon alliances between declining skilled male labour and the female and juvenile industrial workforce. This found political expression in Bradford in the form of Owenite trade unionism, which aimed to unite skilled and unskilled trade unions. In Bradford men were engaged in defensive struggles and this to some extent forced them to accept women's participation and to promote women's trade union organisation. Both Dorothy Thompson[71] and Barbara Taylor[72] have suggested that this political alliance was short-lived. They have illustrated the subsequent growth of exclusionist trade unions; that is the strengthening of economic organisation among newly skilled male workers with largely economic objectives and with demands based upon the assumption of a male breadwinner.[73] This is part of a wider separation of economics and politics and a move away from the mass politics of the earlier period. It is based upon the increasing rationalization and formalisation of political structures in the 1840s. Dorothy Thompson[74] dates the withdrawal from public activity by working-class women from this period.

The industrialization of Bradford suggests that unless the concept of feminism is redefined in class terms one cannot look for a pure feminist consciousness amongst women workers. As Anna Pollert's[75] study of women factory workers in twentieth century Bristol concludes, 'for the working-class majority of women it makes no sense to fight their oppression as women in isolation from their exploitation as workers'. Consciousness is rarely a pure expression of either gender or class interests, since gender and class are not experienced separately, but are intertwined. Women's consciousness reflects the dynamic between productive, familial and communal relations and the diversity of social relations in which they engaged over the course of their lives.

Notes

1 Thompson, E.P. *The Making of the English Working Class,* Harmondsworth: Penguin, 1972.
2 Foster, J. *Class Struggle and the Industrial Revolution,* London: Methuen, 1974.
3 Calhoun, C. *The Question of Class Struggle,* Chicago: University of Chicago Press, 1982.
4 Eisenstein, S. *Give us Bread but Give us Roses,* London: RKP, 1983.
5 Taylor, B. *Eve and the New Jerusalem,* London: Virago, 1983, p. 89.
6 As Pat Hudson has shown whilst the West Yorkshire woollen industry developed in an artisanal form, worsted was based upon a 'putting-out' system with a greater degree of specialism between different processes of production. 'Proto-Industrialisation: in the case of the West Riding Wool Textile Industry in the Eighteenth and Nineteenth Centuries' in *History Workshop Journal,* No.12, 1981.
7 Smith, J. 'The Strike of 1825', in Wright, D.G. and Jowitt, J.A. (eds) *Victorian Bradford: Essays in Honour of Jack Reynolds,* City of Bradford Metropolitan Council, Libraries Division, Bradford, 1982.
8 *Minute Book of the Meetings of the Associated Masters,* Bradford Central Library.
9 *Leeds Mercury,* 9 July, 1825.
10 *Trades Newspaper,* 2 October, 1825.

11 *Leeds Intelligencer,* 15 September 1825; *Bradford Courier,* 15 September 1825.
12 Tester, J. *The History of the Bradford Strike,* 1826, Bradford Central Library. Tester was Secretary to the union.
13 Tester, J. *The History of the Bradford Strike,* 1826, Bradford Central Library.
14 *Minute Book of the Meetings of Associated Masters,* Bradford Central Library.
15 Maxine Berg has challenged the idea that industrialisation involved a transition from a 'family economy' wherein family members cooperated in production to a 'family wage economy' wherein family members sold their labour power, generally outside the household. Berg, M. 'Political Economy and the Principles of Manufacture 1700-1800', in Berg, M., Hudson, P. and Sonenscher, M. (Eds) *Manufacture in Town and Country before the Factory,* Cambridge: CUP, 1983.
16 *Leeds Intelligencer,* 1 September 1825.
17 John Tester, ibid.
18 Kaplan, T. 'Civic Rituals and Patterns of Resistance in Barcelona, 1890-1930, in Thane, P. Crossick, G. and Floud, R. (Eds) *The Power of the Past,* Cambridge: Cambridge University Press, 1984.
19 Reddy, W. 'Skeins, Scales, Discounts, Steam and other objects of Crowd Justice in Early French Textile Mills', in *Comparative Studies in Society and History,* xxi, 1979.
20 Thompson, E.P. The Moral Economy of the English Crowd in the Eighteenth Century, *Past and Present,* No. 50. February 1971.
21 *Bradford Observer,* 17 February 1842.
22 Underdown, D. 'The Taming of the Scold: the Enforcement of Patriarchal Authority in Early Modern England, in Fletcher, A. and Stevenson, J. (Eds), *Order and Disorder in Early Modern England,* Cambridge: Cambridge University Press, 1985.
23 Thompson op. cit., 1971.
24 Reddy, W. 'The Textile Trade: the Language of Class at Rouen 1752-1871', in *Past and Present,* No. 74, February 1977.
25 Kaplan, op. cit., 1984.
26 *Bradford Observer,* 8 October 1845.
27 Eisenstein op. cit., 1983.
28 Reddy, op. cit., 1979.
29 Business records of *Brigg, Calversyke Mill* in Keighley Library.
30 *Bradford Observer,* 11 July 1839; *Bradford Observer,* 15 August 1839.
31 *Bradford Observer,* 2 May 1839.
32 *Northern Star,* 7 July 1838.
33 *Bradford Observer,* 13 February 1845.
34 Stedman-Jones, G. *Languages of Class: Studies in English Working Class History 1832-1982,* Cambridge: Cambridge University Press, 1983.
35 *Bradford Observer,* 27 March 1845 and *Northern Star,* 22 March 1845.
36 *Bradford Observer,* 27 March 1845.
37 *Northern Star,* 29 March 1845.
38 *Northern Star,* 17 May 1845.
39 *Northern Star,* 3 May 1845.

40 Alfred (pseud. Samuel Kydd). *The History of the Factory Movement from 1802 to the enactment of the Ten Hours Bill in 1847*, 1857.
41 'Minutes of Evidence before the Select Committee on the Poor Law Amendment Act', *Parliamentary Papers 1837-8, xviii.*
42 Alfred, op. cit.
43 Alfred, op. cit.
44 'John Woods Mill' in W. Dodd, *The Factory system*, Cass Library of Industrial Classics, No. 10, 1968.
45 *Bradford Observer*, 19 December 1839.
46 Alfred, op. cit.
47 *Bradford Observer*, 20 November 1845 and 8 October 1845.
48 Laquer, T.W. *Religion and Respectability: Sunday Schools and Working Class Culture 1780-1850*, New Haven: Yale University Press, 1976.
49 Ibid., p. 244.
50 *Bradford Central Library(BCL) Archives*, 17D81/17; 17D81/18; 5D76/21e/4a. C.J. Radcliffe, *'Who were the Prospect Place Baptists?: A Textile Workers' Chapel: A study of membership of a General Baptist Church 1837-1852'*. Unpublished Manuscript in BCL.
51 *Northern Star*, 20 April 1844.
52 *White Slavery*, Volume 9.
53 *White Slavery*, Volume 8. Maxine Berg suggests that the pamphlets were possibly written by Oastler and corrected by G.S. Bull, Berg, M. *The Machinery Question and the Making of Political Economy, 1815-1848*, Cambridge: Cambridge University Press, 1980.
54 *Northern Star*, 27 January 1844.
55 *Bradford Observer*, 8 May 1845. PRO Chancery Lane Assize 45/66.
56 *PRO Chancery Lane Assize* 45/66 20 August 1842.
57 *Bradford Observer*, 20 July 1843.
58 *Northern Star*, 31 May 1845.
59 *Northern Star*, 10 May 1845.
60 *Northern Star*, 31 May 1845.
61 *Northern Star*, 30 March 1839.
62 *Northern Star*, 3 August 1839.
63 Thompson, D. *The Chartists*. Hounslow, Temple Smith, p. 31. 1985.
64 Taylor, op. cit., 1983.
65 *New Moral World*, 12 October 1838.
66 *New Moral World*, 28 December 1839.
67 *New Moral World*, 19 December 1 1839.
68 Taylor, op. cit., p. 265, 1983.
69 *Northern Star*, 19 October 1839.
70 Taylor, op. cit., 1983.
71 Thompson, D. 'Women and Nineteenth-Century Radical Politics: a Lost Dimension', in *Outsiders; Class, Gender and Nation*, London: Verso, 1993.
72 Taylor, op. cit., 1983.

73 In Bradford such developments were reflected in the emergence of the Woolsorters' Societies and in the Bradford Overlookers' Friendly Society – both unions comprising exclusively skilled working class males.
74 Thompson, op. cit, 1993.
75 Pollert, A. *Girls, Wives, Factory Lives*, London: Macmillan, 1981.

Sweat and sweating: women workers and trade unionists in the Leeds clothing trade, 1880 to 1980[1]

Katrina Honeyman

Historical discussion of 'sweating' has commonly focused on the tailoring trade and on the period from the mid nineteenth century until the First World War.[2] The image of impoverished needleworkers sustaining a meagre existence through long, but irregular hours of work in their own homes or in sweatshops, permeated contemporary accounts; and have subsequently dominated historians' interpretations.[3] This chapter explores the subject of sweating[4] by using the example of the Leeds men's tailoring trade throughout the period from its origins in the late nineteenth century until its demise in the 1970s. Firstly, it establishes the persistence of sweated labour beyond the 'classic' period ending in 1914. Sweated conditions of work existed in large factories as well as in workshops, and did not diminish over time.[5] Secondly it introduces an examination of the gender dimension of the industry. The persistence of sweating was facilitated by the pronounced subdivision of tasks and the gendered distribution of work. By developing the notion that sweating was partly, if not mainly, a matter of cheap female labour,[6] it considers the extent to which, if at all, men were associated with low paid tasks within the Leeds tailoring trades. Finally it identifies the relevance of trade union activity to the persistence of sweating as well as the involvement of sweated labour in trade union action. Three episodes of industrial action, namely those of the late 1880s, the inter-war years, and the early 1970s, will be examined.

Sweating in the long term

From the later nineteenth century until the 1970s, the dominant feature of the Leeds economy was its production of men's tailored outerwear. From an insignificant position in the 1860s, its subsequent expansion was such that by the early twentieth century its output had surpassed all other centres except London.⁷ Rapid absolute and relative growth in the Leeds tailoring trade was believed to be partly the result of an early shift to factory production which was less common elsewhere.⁸ But growth was also the result of relatively low wages paid to women workers on which the industry depended throughout the period covered in this chapter.⁹ The persistence of low wages was facilitated by the extensive subdivision of tasks which the larger units of production permitted. The 'deskilling' of labour through the mechanisation of the sewing process and the breaking down of garment making into many small tasks, confirmed the sweated nature of work and facilitated the payment of low wages even in large, 'modern' factories over the long term. Of course not all work was deskilled. In the cutting sector, for example, the bandknife, which enabled the cutting of several layers of cloth at a time, and later the Eastman cutter, which applied power to the process, accelerated the work but did not eradicate its skilled elements. It was not until the late 1970s, with the introduction of computerised cutting, that the skilled position of the cutters finally crumbled.¹⁰

Most of Leeds's production of men's suits took place in large-scale units, but this manufacturing form was not ubiquitous. Indeed the interdependence of factory and workshop, and the practice of subcontracting from large to small factories, characterised the Leeds industry until its demise towards the end of the twentieth century.¹¹ Evidence from the Censuses of Production indicate that throughout the period, productivity varied little across production units of different sizes, indicating that manufacturing was organised similarly irrespective of the number of employees.¹²

Throughout the life of the Leeds clothing trade, few technological changes occurred in the machining sector, with which women were primarily associated, or in the nature of work. The key elements of 'sweating' were maintained through persistent gender divisions of tasks, intensification of labour, and employer strategies of cost containment.¹³ The highly profitable firms of Burton, Prices, Hepworth, notwithstanding, most firms struggled after the 1930s peak, and remained in business only through a combination of very low wages paid to the female machinists and work practices which forced these women to work ever harder.¹⁴

The gender dimension

The gender division of labour, complicated in the early years of the industry by racial distinctions,¹⁵ was central to the organisation of tailoring production in Leeds.¹⁶ At first sight, the division between male and female workers was stark; all machinists were women and all cutters were men. The inequality of pay and conditions between the machinists and the cutters was wide from the outset and subsequently became even more so. The quantitative importance of women in the tailoring workforce and the association of women with less skilled processes, became more pronounced as the subdivision of tasks was extended.[17] Machining formed the bulk of women's work in the industry, but other 'female' tasks included binding, trimming, buttonholing and finishing. Wage levels varied among these tasks and also according to age, but typically most women were paid less – and often considerably less – than most men. The most highly-paid male workers were the cutters, the tailors and the pressers;[18] and throughout the history of the industry these positions were the most protected from the employer strategy of cost containment. However, not all men fitted into this category, and a small number of unskilled male jobs existed such as packing and warehouse work. Nevertheless such work rarely conformed to the 'sweating' pattern because although it might be irregular, men were paid by time rather than piece, so sweating did not reach the level of intensity imposed upon the women who performed machining tasks.[19]

Gender segregation was conspicuous. There was little overlap between men and women either spatially or in terms of the nature of work. Tasks were allocated to men and women hierarchically, and distinctions between them were reinforced through a number of mechanisms: by perceptions of skill, by the way in which monetary reward was calculated, by conditions of work, by access to training, promotion, job control, and workplace power and by status within the unions. The perception of women as unskilled – despite evidence that machining was difficult to do well[20] – was immutable and based more on their sex than on their ability to perform.[21] Equally, the bulk of the tasks performed by men were deemed to be skilled solely on the basis of the gender of the performer, supported, as was the case with women, by custom and practice.[22] Gender, therefore, determined the function to be performed and so the wages earned. Wages in the clothing trade were notoriously low for both men and women, but the average female rate never rose much above 40 per cent of the male level. This differential was institutionalised by the mechanism of wage calculation. Women's pay was determined by a system of piece rates through which employers were able to – and indeed did – influence the degree of work intensity. Employers also exercised control over female workers in a way that did not apply to men, through compulsory working time, irrespective of amount of work required; disciplinary procedures, including routine fines for lateness and for mistakes in their work – all practices that persisted through to the 1970s. Deductions from women's pay were made for the thread that they used, for the power that ran their machines, for the stoves on which they might heat their dinners, for their scissors, and sometimes even for machine parts. Such deductions which continued in some firms into the 1930s despite resistance, could amount to at least ten per cent of gross pay.[23] There is no evidence that men were required to pay for their own materials or implements, nor subject to any other of the controls imposed upon women.[24] Indeed their treatment was generally more generous, and employers accorded them more freedom. The wages of the most highly paid male workers were assessed by the mysterious log system.[25]

The predominance of women in the clothing industry and the low wages paid to them became reinforcing tendencies. Employers, even the largest of them, had little incentive to invest in machinery to reproduce work performed (usually efficiently and at high speed) by cheap women.[26] The high proportion of labour in total costs meant that attempts to raise productivity focused on the intensification of women's work. In the years after the Second World War, female clothing workers in the Leeds industry were subjected to regular and rigorous investigation through Work Study, and Time and Motion Study, which not only intensified the work but also generated complex and poorly specified systems of payment.[27] Payment by Results (PBR), which became the typical method of calculating women's wages from the 1950s, provided employers with a new means of controlling their female labour force and of intensifying their work. Many workers found the system of wage calculation incomprehensible and were unable to check that they had been paid correctly. This was precisely the opposite of the cutters' log system, which the employers were unable to understand, and further confirmed the unequal status of women and men and the differential value placed upon their contribution to production.[28]

Gender inequality and the inability of women to escape the sweated conditions of their work also emanated from differential access to training. The subdivision of work, common throughout the industry nationally but most intense in Leeds because of the larger units of production, ensured that the majority of tasks within the production process, especially in the machining sector, were relatively simple and assumed to be easily learned. The amount of training allocated to a particular task had a gender component. From the early years of the industry, girls and boys were segregated as they entered the industry and acquired their various capabilities and distinct positions on the skill hierarchy. Girls, who typically started work upon leaving school at fourteen, not only received very little training, but were retained on the 'learner' grade for several years despite competence demonstrated through experience.[29] Boys selected to become cutters, received a seven year training, which evidence suggests to have been a little on the generous side.³⁰ Even male labour not destined for a career in cutting was typically provided with a structured training programme. The confirmation of gender divisions through training persisted through the decades after the Second World War.

The gendered construction of skill can be illustrated by an example taken from the period towards the end of the Second World War, when many cutters found themselves short of work and were redeployed to machining tasks. Most men were unable to perform even the simplest of machining jobs. In a statement to the National Union of Tailors and Garment Workers Union (NUTGW) conference of 1943, a female delegate described how a male machinist, earning £6.10/- per week 'sits next to a row of women machinists who were earning from £2.5/- to £2/10- per week', yet the women could 'knock the man into a cocked hat'.³¹ Temporary fluidity in the gender allocation of tasks immediately after the Second World War soon gave way to 'traditional' gender distinctions; as the union continued to protect male status, and as worker training schemes of the 1950s and 1960s reaffirmed the conventional hierarchy. During the mid 1960s consultation between the employers' associations and the NUTGW about the possibility of breaking down traditional divisions of tasks failed to shift union intransigence.³²

From the point of view of employers, the most significant feature of the gendering of work was the creation of a divided labour force which facilitated the control and exploitation of the majority. Women clothing workers were among the lowest paid of all industrial labour, and their relative position deteriorated after the Second World War. This may have benefited individual employers in the short term, but had implications for the industry as a whole. The numerical dominance of women – who employers believed could be easily subordinated – not only confirmed the clothing industry's low wage status but also influenced strategic decisions within it.³³ The maintenance of low wages informed the industry's structure and then compounded its dependence on cheap labour. Productivity gains within the Leeds trade were achieved largely through intensification of work, increased discipline and downward pressure on female wages, rather than through investment in technical and organisational improvements, or through training. The divided labour force facilitated each of these. Low wages for women, however, did not mean high wages for men. Research indicates that the larger the proportion of women in a trade, the less both its male and female workers earn.³⁴ So men were not immune from sweating, when understood as low paid work with poor conditions and prospects, but the majority of men were protected from the worst excesses of the system. The trade union focus on the interests of skilled male workers, however, neglected the less skilled categories of male workers as much as it failed to protect women.

The early profitability and the later survival of the Leeds industry depended on mass ranks of women machinists, for whom 'sweating' shifted from irregular working, low wages and exploitative contracts of employment in the later nineteenth century to later twentieth century equivalents of PBR and Work Study. The imposition of such practices was clearly facilitated by the divisions within the tailoring workforce, mirrored in trade union structures and practices. The activities of the trade unions for much of the period under consideration were apparently directed towards the maintenance of gender segregation.

Trade union representation and action

The existence and persistence of sweating among female labour has often been associated with inadequate trade union representation.[35] The purpose of this section is to explore the role of trade union activity in the Leeds tailoring trade. Its history is complex, reflecting the diverse racial, political and gender composition of the workforce; as well as variations in the level of skill.[36]

Three episodes of trade union activity have been selected to illustrate different aspects of the intersection of gender and class over the course of the industry's 100 year history. The first of these, the later 1880s, illustrates the organised activities of women in response to specifically female concerns. The differential treatment of women, described above, was imposed from the outset; and despite their relatively weak position, women battled against the unfair conditions under which they laboured. This they did without being an integral part of a formal trade union structure.

Women's representation in the tailoring unions was initially poor, not least because, as unskilled workers, they were perceived as a threat to the skilled position of male tailors. The records of the Amalgamated Society of Tailors, for example, contain a series of resolutions in the 1860s and 1870s for the union to 'use its strength against the increasing employment of women in the tailoring trade'.[37] Jewish male tailors, however, were much less driven by gender hostility than by self defence, as their support of the tailoresses in their struggle of 1889 suggests.[38] Unions of women tailoring workers were generally short lived. One of these, the Leeds Tailoresses' Union (LTU), supported by Clementina Black, Isabella Ford and Emma Patterson, was formed specifically to address women's discontent with the gender-specific system of fines and deductions,[39] and the requirement that women, but not men, stayed at the factory even when there was no work to be done.

In October 1889, Isabella Ford organised a public meeting out of which the LTU emerged. A strike ensued almost immediately.[40] Seven hundred women workers from Arthurs' clothing factory left work 'to obtain a reduction in the charge made for power which amounted to one penny in every shilling earned'.[41] Ford organised a strike committee and became its secretary; she produced and circulated evidence of pay and conditions at Arthurs, and established a strike fund. Support for the action derived from both the Liberal-dominated Trades Council and from the Socialist League.[42] Jewish tailors in the town expressed solidarity by refusing to take on work of the striking tailoresses;[43] but although other women in the trade offered moral support, they felt unable, for financial reasons, to participate in the action. Nor did the male cutters at Arthur's factory demonstrate solidarity.[44] The firm's management threatened reprisals and although the strike – and strike pay – continued for two months, the female workers drifted back to work. In the short term it appeared that the stoppage had failed, yet once the dust had settled Arthur's management withdrew some of the charges previously imposed.[45] The strike had also raised public awareness of women's poor conditions of work, and encouraged trade union activity elsewhere in the clothing trade – both among the male skilled workers and the Jewish tailors.[46] However, membership of the LTU declined markedly – from 1000 to 98 – in the aftermath of the strike, and although it recovered slightly following a successful strike in 1892, it fell further, to 61, by 1894.[47] Through the 1890s, Leeds tailoresses engaged in sporadic strike activity, pursuing class concerns as well as challenging gender inequality.[48] Ford devoted time and energy to the process of rapprochement between the LTU and the Associated Union of Clothing Operatives (AUCO). Despite reservations on both sides, amalgamation was achieved in 1900,[49] but it was not until 1909 that membership among tailoresses reached double figures.[50]

This early period of industrial unrest demonstrates women's capacity to challenge inequity through the organisation of strikes and associated fund raising. Low levels of union membership beyond the short term, however, was the result of financial constraints as well as women's preference for single issue disputes over sustained commitment to a union cause.[51] Female engagement may also have been weakened by a gender exclusive approach to trade union structure and action within which women struggled to get their voices heard. Nevertheless, women participated fully in activities that they believed to be in the interest of all workers. The following sections explore the extent to which women trade unionists in the clothing trade co-operated in ventures that served class concerns while not directly in their interests as women workers.[52]

During the inter-war years, women's participation in national union activity rarely served to enhance female working conditions. On the contrary, it can be argued that their relative position – certainly within the Leeds clothing trade – was almost certainly undermined by the priorities and preoccupations of the trade unions. From the beginning of the twentieth century, recognition that union strength was related to size of membership led to a push for amalgamation and for the greater involvement of women and Jewish workers.[53] Union representation among women grew substantially during the First World War, as employment levels increased and as amalgamation appeared to parallel growing support for women's specific concerns. However, by 1923 membership of the Tailor and Garment Workers' Union (TGWU) had fallen to 45,000 from its 1920 peak of 100,000. The gender distribution of those leaving the union, 48,000 women and 9,000 men, can only be partly attributed to post-war labour market restructuring; and was also connected to female disenchantment with the priorities of the male leadership.[54] Although female membership subsequently crept up, oral evidence from the Leeds industry in the inter-war years suggests that although women joined the union, contributed to membership drives, and participated in strikes – even those that served male interests at the expense of their own – the networks formed by women in the machine room were important in supporting their own day to day working interests.[55]

Strike activity in the 1920s and 1930s consisted of a series of disputes in individual firms rather than strikes which affected the whole of the Leeds trade. In this respect, parallels with the late nineteenth century period can be drawn. The disputes focused on threats to 'traditional' gender roles by new technologies and work organisation. The competence of women in performing 'male' tasks, encouraged employers to attempt to substitute cheaper female labour in the longer term.[56] In 1927, for example, Burtons experienced a shortage of skilled tailors and sought to employ a group of tailoresses. The dominant union of the time, the TGWU, resisted this move, insisting that boys – less skilled and competent than the women in question – be taken on instead.[57] In the light of employer resistance, a strike ensued to establish a principle that no female labour be employed in the tailoring section.[58]

Throughout the early 1930s, the NUTGW was even more preoccupied than usual with what it saw as the displacement of male workers by women. In January 1931, for example, the Leeds branch of the union drew attention to, and successfully circumvented, the persistent attempts of Burton to introduce 'women onto men's work'.⁵⁹ Two months later, the Leeds branch reported that there had been two special meetings of cutters to gather 'information on the conditions operating throughout the cutting rooms in Leeds'.⁶⁰ The Executive Board emphasised the importance of resisting the 'introduction of systems contrary to the city's custom and practice, specifically the threatened encroachment of women in the cutting rooms and female employment in pressing'.⁶¹ In April of 1931 the Leeds branch committee was found to be 'tackling the question of trying to persuade some employers to engage a larger number of male workers than they at present employ. The tendency has been for some years to eliminate male workers wherever possible and ...the committee feel that it is time that something was done to stop this gradual decline'.⁶²

It should be emphasised that employer attempts to vary the traditional distribution of jobs were not motivated by the desire to improve women's pay and conditions, but rather to reduce their own costs by replacing expensive men with cheaper women. Union moves to challenge substitution and dilution were thus well founded, but by focusing on this issue the union failed to tackle the matter of female sweating. In this respect they may have neglected an additional route to protecting male working conditions. An equal pay strategy, for example, which might have led to all round improvements, was rarely suggested. Addressing an NUTGW meeting in Leeds in 1935, a male member suggested that 'it was not so much a necessity to get higher wages for men as it was to raise the rates for women. If this could be done there would be some protection for the men'.⁶³ But this was an isolated voice; and the issue of equal pay which exercised the labour movement as whole during the inter-war years, failed to be discussed fully within the NUTGW until it was obliged to reply to a TUC questionnaire in 1945. The union's response to this enquiry concentrated on the disadvantages to men of challenges to the established gender division of labour, and paid little attention to the low pay and poor conditions of women workers. Finally, it contended that 'the employment of men and women at unequal rates of pay has been at the expense of the men, who have been faced with gradual elimination from certain sections of the industry'.⁶⁴

Further disputes in the 1930s – in which women were fully engaged – reflected concern to deflect challenges to the traditional gender division of labour generated by changes to the organisation of production. A major stoppage at the Alexandre factory in 1932 resulted from the attempts of the employers to alter the grading of work in its new coat department. While the General Secretary of the union dwelt upon the importance of custom and practice in determining the employment of male labour on certain processes in the making of coats,⁶⁵ Bernard Lyons, the company's owner and Managing Director, insisted on his right to employ whomsoever he deemed appropriate for the work. The union refused to entertain the employment of female labour in tasks that were regarded as male operations and that 'in the event of the expansion of the business calling for additional employees it would be essential that men should be employed'.⁶⁶

The dominance of women in machining tasks and their very limited representation elsewhere may indicate the effectiveness of union vigilance, not only in cutting processes but also in pressing.⁶⁷ The Leeds branch of the NUTGW remained firm in its resolve to maintain the segregation of women and to enhance the position of male workers. A mass meeting in 1935 of delegates 'representing' 36,000 local clothing workers demanded 'protection for men against female labour'. Mr P Johnson, joint secretary of the Leeds branch, contended 'that for a long time in Leeds it has been felt that in any future agreement there should be a clause protecting male labour against displacement by female labour'.⁶⁸

The threat of displacement, which the NUTGW challenged vigorously, continued throughout the 1930s. In 1938, finally responding as a group to union complaints, the employers confirmed that men would be given priority in such categories of work as cutting, marking up, laying up and chopping out. Nevertheless, they asserted that in the few cases where women were employed in such tasks, they should be paid an equivalent wage, and that 'they had no intention of removing women who are at present employed in cutting operations….but if and when replacements are made they should be as far as practical by the substitution of males'. Trimming and fitting up were generally recognised as jobs on which 'women are and may continue to be employed'.⁶⁹ The NUTGW anticipated that, in the post-war period, the clothing industry might require a higher level of skill from the female labour force. 'This, together with stronger trade union organisation amongst them, should lead to the building up of women's rates'; and, disingenuously, they blamed employer reluctance to train women because of their shorter productive life.⁷⁰

The third episode in the history of tailoring trade unions illustrates the participation of women in a local, but industry-wide dispute, during which workers fought an iniquitous wage agreement and expressed wider concerns about pay and conditions in the industry. As it turned out, the issues which precipitated the strike were also core elements in the industry's demise. Although the locational origin of the strike was a sectional dispute between the cutters and the employers at Colliers' factory, women clothing workers ensured that this escalated into a city-wide struggle.⁷¹ The poor pay of clothing workers, especially the women machinists, on which the industry had long depended, can be identified as the focus of the strikers' grievance. The strike marked the conclusion of a long period in which the low pay of clothing workers of both sexes supported an inefficient industry. Although employers eventually came to acknowledge the justification of the workers' demand for improved remuneration, the industry was considered unable to sustain a higher level of pay for its labour force.[72] The dispute also reflected the strained relationships among workers; and the talent of women for political organisation.

The Leeds clothing strike of 1970 marked a turning point[73] in the history of the industry and in gender relations in the NUTGW. A local dispute, it nevertheless stemmed from national concerns and generated nationwide outcomes. Its significance here is the key role played by women in the both the organisation of the strike and its resolution. Successful in achieving improvements in pay and conditions, especially for the female workforce, the action also marked the beginning of the end of the industry in Leeds, and of continuing tensions between men and women in the workforce. In her obituary of Gertie Roche, one of the leaders of the strike, Diane Gold recalls their first meeting when Gertie 'was dealing with the disintegration of the transient unity between the women tailoresses and the men in the cutting room', in the aftermath of the strike.[74]

From the late 1940s, the NUTGW cooperated with managers in implementing 'scientific' procedures for calculating wages and enhancing productivity. The National Agreement, which came into operation in February 1970, was a poor one for the industry's workforce.[75] Its terms expedited the implementation of PBR, and established a low and discriminatory pay rise of 5 pence per hour to men and 4 pence per hour to women. Clothing workers were thus to receive less than £1 a week rise at a time when workers in other industries were negotiating weekly increases of £2 or £3. As a result of the agreement, therefore, the pay gap between clothing employees and other workers widened, and the already unfair differential between men and women was extended.[76] Not only was this agreement not approved by the membership, but prior to the Executive's acceptance of it, members of all three Leeds branches had voted for a one shilling per hour rise and against the introduction of PBR. Resentment at leadership failure to represent the will of the membership influenced the shape of the strike, which eventually achieved an improved pay award but little change in intra-union relationships.

The particular role of women in the strike and its aftermath was the subject of much contemporary analysis. Although the agreement angered all workers, women were justified in their rage against both the paucity of the rise and its unequal distribution.[77] Efforts by some firms to pre-empt strike action by offering preferential pay deals notwithstanding,[78] the dispute spread rapidly from its origin at Colliers, through the Leeds clothing factories and workshops and then to the satellite factories in south Yorkshire and the north-east of England. The strike, unofficial throughout, was opposed by national and local officials, and reflected a serious rift between the leadership and the membership of the NUTGW.[79] In the absence of organisational support from the union, a strike committee, which ultimately consisted of 150 strikers, half of whom were women, guided the action.[80] Although women were poorly represented in the leadership of the committee,[81] they played a key role in energising the strikers and in encouraging co-operation among its participants.[82] As the strike gathered in scale and momentum, relationships between strikers and union officials deteriorated.

Union leaders were especially belligerent towards the women strikers,[83] whose importance to the visibility and the success of the strike was increasingly recognised. National newspapers referred to the influence of women. According to Vincent Hannah, for example, 'there is no doubt that the strike is inspired and led by the women members';[84] and Celia Haddon referred to women providing the strike committee's 'firepower'.[85] In a letter published in the *Yorkshire Evening Post*, Gertie Roche, herself largely responsible for motivating the women and sustaining their subsequent action, argued that strike action by the women clothing workers was the expression of long-repressed bitterness. 'The revolt is due', she wrote, 'to twenty years of neglect by the employers'.[86] Most of the women reacted against wage agreements and decisions imposed upon them by unknown groups of men through an undemocratic decision-making process. It was firmly believed that unified action was urgently required to counter the large manufacturers' mounting use of PBR and Work Study to control shop floor negotiations and future wage rises.[87] Women's willingness to co-operate with male counterparts in the pursuit of common objectives was in marked contrast to men's own past actions. Men may have achieved short-term gains for themselves by ignoring women's interests, but the strategy had disastrous long-term outcomes. At a mass meeting of the strikers on Woodhouse Moor towards the end of the dispute, Jim Roche, the strike committee's publicity officer, warned the male workers 'that you have to concern yourselves more and more with the women's conditions…it will not be long before the whole industry will be mechanised in such a way that you will be begging for the women to support you in your jobs in the cutting room. If the employers don't reorganise themselves, the women will reorganise the industry for them'.[88]

As the employers' position softened, NUTGW officials agreed to recall the union's general conference. This was viewed by the strikers as a significant victory.[89] The strike was called off; negotiations between the NUTGW and the Clothing Manufacturers' Federation (CMF) began almost immediately, and within days an improved offer found approval. On top of the increases of the original agreement it provided for increases of 10 pence per hour for women and 8 pence per hour for men, amounting to gains of 19 and 11.2 per cent respectively.[90] At the reconvened national delegates' conference the new offer received overwhelming support with only a handful of delegates, mostly from Leeds, demurring. The contribution of the Leeds strikers to the improved agreement was recognised; 'it was the strike rather than the union that had won the increases'.[91] The success of the strike was attributed to the effectiveness of women organisers and the participation of the bulk of the female workforce. Conference agreed that the fight for equal pay, and better conditions for all, should continue.[92]

However, although 'in 1970 the workers of Leeds got an opportunity to get together – men and women – and to transform the undemocratic, unresponsive men's club that was the Leeds Union of Tailors and Garment Workers',[93] the unity engendered during the strike was not maintained. Solidarity between men and women evaporated, as the industry entered a period of terminal decline. Employers sought to concentrate production in areas away from the tradition-bound and strike-prone factories of Leeds.[94] By 1974, as the Leeds clothing industry contracted, women workers were readily made redundant, while those remaining were subject to further discipline and wage pressure. The sweated conditions of work were reasserted with a vengeance. Producers of high quality tailored garments provided conditions of relatively easy discipline and generous piece rates, and these firms achieved some success and stability. But the majority of employers attempted to survive by making clothes cheaply through the implementation of tight wage and disciplinary control through PBR.[95] Although this strategy, or variants of it, had been profitable for almost a century, the days of sweated labour were numbered. Manufacturers of cheap clothes on the basis of cost-containment measures could not compete with the products of really low wage economies, and most ceased trading during the 1970s and 1980s.[96]

The discussion of trade unionism and industrial action has demonstrated that although women in the Leeds clothing trade were perpetually disadvantaged within the labour force, they were not passively exploited. They were proactive. As trade union members, which the majority of women were, they were full participants in serving class interests; but they also recognised that the trade union structure did not always provide a positive framework within which their objectives could be met. Alternative forms of representation and expressions of solidarity were sought; but as the 1970 strike indicates, women also attempted to improve the structure and representation of the NUTGW.

This chapter has explored rather than challenged the significance of the association of sweating with the tailoring trade. It has confirmed that the majority of workers in the trade whose labour and conditions can be described as 'sweated' were, as conventional wisdom suggests, women. Although many men in the Leeds trade were lower paid than men in other contemporary industries, they were almost always better paid than women clothing workers and enjoyed superior conditions of work. It has also suggested that sweating in the Leeds clothing trade was not confined to the 'sorry dog kennels'[97] of the years between 1870 and 1914, but that very similar conditions existed in contemporary factories and persisted, albeit in amended form, until the demise of the industry. The 1970 strike has been seen as hastening the end of the industry, but in truth, warning signs were evident well before this. Employers alleged that the higher wages implemented following the successful strike were unaffordable, and indeed many businesses folded under the weight of rising costs. Until then, costs had been contained to the extent that labour was in short supply. By the late 1960s, female school leavers found better paid work elsewhere – mainly in the service sector – and were reluctant to expose themselves to the long hours and poor wages endured by their mothers and grandmothers. The end of the industry, therefore, was also the result of labour supply constraints generated by the failure of clothing firms to modernise their procedures. Sweating provides an accurate description of the labour of women in the Leeds tailoring trade from its inception to its demise, irrespective of location and organisational form. As far as trade union representation was concerned, undoubtedly the tailoring unions failed to protect the majority of women who worked in exploitative conditions. Where women took action on their own initiative, however, as was the case in the 1889 strike and again in 1970, they demonstrated how fruitful their actions could be.

From the evidence presented in this chapter, it is difficult to avoid the conclusion that gender divisions at work perpetuated a system of low pay and poor conditions for the bulk of women workers and that the unions rarely addressed this issue. The only occasions on which the unions argued for equal pay were during the World Wars. When, during the First World War, for example, women became engaged in tasks that had previously been uniquely male, their pitiful earnings, which had not concerned men before the war, now became viewed as deplorable.[98] The relatively poor pay for women engaged on 'men's tasks' during the war, which exercised male unions in many trades at the time, became a focus of clothing union action. Following strike threats and accusations that employers exploited female labour, agreement about the conditions for substitution was reached. Such agreement protected male pay and conditions, but did nothing to ameliorate women's position in the industry in the longer term. Upon the outbreak of the Second World War, even more strenuous measures were implemented to prevent women encroaching on male preserves, with little attention paid to the remuneration of women workers.

Such an approach may be seen as inappropriately shifting responsibility for women's sweated labour away from the culpable employers to the unions. This has not been the intention. Exploitation, sweating, intensification of labour, were each the outcome of employer action, whether individual or collective. The labour intensity of the production process proved to be an irresistible temptation to employers to contain costs by exploiting the most vulnerable component of its workforce. This they successfully did for a number of decades. Yet these exploited workers enjoyed trade union representation, which did not apply, historically, to all sweated labour. The overwhelming majority of the Leeds female clothing workers became active members of the union, which itself was largely female. So how was it that the NUTGW was not more effective in rectifying the sweated conditions of many female clothing workers? The argument presented here is that the priority of the union was to protect an already privileged group of male workers at the expense of women.

Throughout the history of the Leeds clothing industry from its birth to its effective demise, women operatives had revealed characteristics of unity, solidarity and co-operation, identifying class interests more clearly than male unionists, whose self-interest and lack of concern for the poor pay and conditions of women workers can be seen to have weakened the position of the clothing labour force as a whole.[99]

Notes

1. Many thanks to the participants of the conference in July 2006 and to John Barber for very helpful comments on an earlier version of this chapter.
2. Bythell, D. *The sweated trades. Outwork in nineteenth-century Britain*, London: Batsford, 1978, pp. 65-80; Schmiechen, J. *Sweated industries and sweated labor: a study of industrial disorganisation and worker attitudes in the London clothing trades, 1867-1909*, PhD thesis, University of Illinois, 1975; Morris, J.

Women workers and the sweated trades: the origins of minimum wage legislation, Aldershot: Gower, 1986.

3   Harris, B. (ed) *Famine and fashion. Needlewomen in the nineteenth century*, Aldershot: Ashgate 2005. Although this work does not fundamentally challenge this view, contributions to the collection together offer a more rounded interpretation, with tales of proactive and politically engaged needlewomen supplementing visions of oppression and exploitation.

4   Defined here as a form of work characterised by intense labour conditions and low wages paid by the piece.

5   Morris, J. 'The characteristics of sweating: the late nineteenth-century London and Leeds tailoring trade', John, A.V. (ed) *Unequal opportunities: women's employment in England 1800-1918*, Oxford: Basil Blackwell, 1986, pp. 95 and 117-118, provides evidence for the existence of sweating in a range of organizational forms.

6   Morris, *Women workers and the sweated trades*, p. 67.

7   Chapman, S. 'The innovating entrepreneurs in the British ready-made clothing industry', *Textile History*, 24, 1993, pp. 5-25; Godley, A. 'The development of the UK clothing industry in the long run – 1850-1950: a review of the data. in the censuses of population', University of Reading, Department of Economics discussion paper, 290, 1994, Table 6; Thomas, J. *A history of the Leeds clothing industry*, Hull, 1955, p.12.

8   Morris, 'The characteristics of sweating', pp. 95-121.

9   The proportion of women in the Leeds tailoring labour force, 70-80 percent through most of the period, was greater that in London. Low wage rates, especially compared with London, were part of the explanation for the growth of the Colchester trade. See Phillips, A. 'Women on the shop floor. The Colchester rag trade 1918-1950', *Oral History*, 22, 1994, p. 56.

10 Honeyman, K. 'Gender divisions and industrial divide: the case of the Leeds clothing trade, 1850-1970', *Textile History*, 28, 1997, p. 51.

11 Kershen, A. *Uniting the tailors. Trade unionism among the tailoring workers of London and Leeds, 1870-1939*, Ilford: Frank Cass, 1995, pp. 28-29; Buckman, J. *Immigrants and the class struggle. The Jewish immigrant in Leeds 1880-1914*, Manchester: Manchester University Press, 1983.

12 Report on the census of production: tailoring, Dressmaking etc trade, 1924, 1930, 1935, 1948, 1951, 1954; Men's and boys' tailored outerwear, 1958, 1963, 1968, 1970.

13 Honeyman, K. *Well suited. A history of the Leeds clothing industry 1850-1990*, Oxford: Oxford University Press, 2000, pp. 130-153.

14 The oral testimony of Sammy Wagenhem, cutter at Burtons for 41 years, refers specifically to the harsh conditions endured by women, to the extent that he witnessed the collapse and death of one 'girl' at Burtons. Interview held on 28 June 1993 at the informant's home. Given the pressure on many women to earn a 'subsistence' wage on the basis of piece work, it was not unusual for women to work themselves to death.

15 See Sandler, O. 'Jewish women in the late nineteenth-century Leeds labour market: a study of the influence of race and gender', MA Thesis, University of

Leeds, 1991.
16. The pattern was similar elsewhere. See Phillips, 'Women on the shop floor', on the Colchester trade.
17. In London, where the craft sector had been less diluted, the proportion of women workers was only 59 per cent. Morris, 'The characteristics of sweating', p. 106.
18. Some women became pressers but only on sufferance, and they always constituted a minority
19. Jenny Morris shows that at least before the First World War many men earned below the level required for family subsistence. Morris, 'Characteristics of sweating', p. 100. Honeyman, *Well suited*, p. 173.
20. At the end of the Second World War, for example, a number of cutters for whom there was temporarily no work, were allocated machining tasks. Despite being paid several times the rate of the women they sat alongside, their productivity and the quality of the work that they performed was substantially inferior. Oral testimony of Joe Ratchford, former cutter and shop steward at Burtons, interviewed 12 May 1993 at the informant's residence.
21. Such association of women with lack of skill was of long standing. See, for example, Berg, M. *Age of Manufactures: industry, innovation and work 1700-1820*, London: Fontana, 1985, chapter 6; Busfield, D. 'Tailoring the millions: the women workers of the Leeds clothing industry, 1880-1914', *Textile History*, 16, 1985.
22. Busfield, D. 'Skill and the sexual division of labour in the West Riding textile industry, c1850-1914', in. Jowitt, J. A and McIvor, A. J. (eds) *Employers and labour in the English textile industries, 1850-1939*, London: Routledge, 1988, p. 154.
23. Kershen, *Uniting the tailors*, p. 73.
24. Dobbs, S. P. *The clothing workers of Great Britain*, London: Routledge, 1928, pp. 122-124.
25. This system of calculating wages was understood only by the male cutters themselves.
26. Coyle, A. *Redundant Women*, London: Women's Press, 1984, pp. 7-10.
27. Discussed in Gospel, H.F. 'The management of labour', in Wrigley, C. (ed) *A history of British industrial relations 1939-1979; industrial relations in a declining economy*, Cheltenham: Edward Elgar, 1996, p. 92. Despite the opposition of the membership to such methods, the leadership of the National Union of Tailors and Garment Workers consistently co-operated with employers. NUTGW Circulars to the Executive Board, 1959 and 1965.
28. Honeyman, 'Gender divisions', p. 49.
29. The oral testimony of a large number of former women workers in the Leeds tailoring trade emphasizes that their 'training' consisted of watching others work sometimes for as little as a few hours.
30. The importance of the initial cutting to the success of the finished garment should not be underestimated; yet women were able to perform this task satisfactorily during war time shortages of male labour. The length of the period of instruction which was much longer in men's tailoring than other

sectors suggests the importance of custom and practice in training. Cutting in the rainwear and waterproof sectors for example, was allocated little more than two months training. Belbin, E. and Sergean, R. *Training in the clothing industry: a study of recruitment, training and education*, London: Twentieth Century Press, 1963, p. 64.

31 Report of the NUTGW conference of 1943 in *Men's Wear*, 14 August 1943. This was confirmed by oral testimony. Joe Ratchford, for example, recalls his own relative incompetence as a machinist while continuing to collect his cutter's wage.

32 Honeyman, *Well suited*, pp. 190-191; report of the Joint Consultative Committee of the CMF and the NUTGW, 13 June 1966.

33 See Rainnie, A. F. 'Combined and uneven development in the clothing industry: the effects of competition on accumulation', *Capital and Class*, 22, 1984.

34 Reskin, B.and Padavic, I., *Women and men at work*, Thousand Oaks, California: Pine Forge Press, 1994, p. 9.

35 Blackburn, S. 'Between the devil of cheap labour competition and the deep sea of family poverty?: Sweated labour in time and place, 1840-1914', *Labour History Review*, 71, 2006, pp. 109-111.

36 See Kershen, *Uniting the tailors*; Honeyman, *Well suited*, especially chapters 7 and 10.

37 Drake, B. *Women in trade unions*, London: Virago, 1984, p. 21.

38 Kershen, *Uniting the tailors*, p. 61.

39 Women were required to pay for their own thread, scissors and sometimes even power; and were fined excessively for mistakes and lateness. See Kershen, *Uniting the tailors*, p. 73. Such activity continued well into the 1930s in many firms. Fines and deductions were common in other 'sweated' trades. See, for example, Blackburn, 'Between the devil of cheap labour competition', p. 104.

40 Hendricks, J. 'The tailoresses in the ready-made clothing industry in Leeds 1889-1899', M.A. thesis, University of Warwick, 1970.

41 Hannam, J. *Isabella Ford*, Oxford: Basil Blackwell, 1989, p. 38.

42 Hannam, ibid. p. 39.

43 Kershen, *Uniting the tailors*, p. 73.

44 Hannam, op.cit., p. 39; Kershen *Uniting the tailors*, pp. 73-74.

45 Kershen, op.cit., p. 74, argues that such a change resulted in an increase in the tailoresses' take-home pay.

46 Hannam, op. cit., p. 41.

47 Kershen, op. cit, p. 80; Hendricks, 'The tailoresses', Hannam, *Isabella Ford*, p. 56.

48 Honeyman, 'Gender divisions', p. 58.

49 Hannam, *Isabella Ford*, p. 76; Honeyman, 'Gender divisions', p. 52. Shortly prior to the amalgamation and possibly a catalyst, the *Yorkshire Factory Times* published its discovery that 10,000 of the 16,000 male tailoring workers in Leeds had female relatives employed in the trade, but that only 200 women in the whole of the Leeds industry were unionised *Yorkshire Factory Times* 27 October 1899.

50 Kershen, op. cit., p. 80.
51 See the example provided by Steve Tolliday, 'Militancy and organisation: women workers and trade unions in the motor trades in the 1930s', *Oral History*, 11, 1983.
52 For men, there was less tension between class issues and gender concerns. Cynthia Cockburn, in her analysis of gender and trade unions in the printing trade, highlights the difficulty for historians of examining class issues and those of gender at the same time. See *Brothers. Male dominance and technological change*, London: Pluto, 1983, pp. 191-194.
53 Honeyman, *Well suited*, pp. 158-166; Stewart, M. and Hunter, L. *The needle is threaded. The history of an industry*, London: Heinemann/Newman Neame, 1964, pp. 132-172. Kershen, A. 'Trade unionism amongst the Jewish tailoring workers of London and Leeds, 1872-1915', in Cesarani, D. (ed) *The making of modern Anglo-Jewry*, Oxford: Basil Blackwell, 1990, pp. 35-44.
54 *Men's Wear*, 10 April 1920; Dobbs, *Clothing workers*, p. 133; Honeyman, 'Gender divisions', p. 58.
55 Honeyman, 'Gender divisions', p. 58, n 75 and 76.
56 Employers had been impressed with women's capacity to perform skilled 'male' tasks during the First World War, for example, and sought to continue this.
57 *Men's Wear*, 26 November 1927.
58 *Men's Wear*, 3 December 1927.
59 *Garment Worker*, January 1931.
60 NUTGW Executive Board minutes, 22 March 1931.
61 Ibid.
62 *Garment Worker*, April 1931.
63 *Men's Wear*, 26 January 1935, carried a detailed report of the meeting.
64 NUTGW reply to TUC questionnaire, 20 February 1945.
65 Letter from Andrew Conley to the Wholesale Clothiers and Manufacturers' Federation (WCMF), considered at a meeting of the WCMF executive committee, 18 January 1932.
66 WCMF, Minutes of the Executive Committee meeting 4 February 1932.
67 NUTGW Minutes of the Executive Board meeting, 13 December 1931. However, more women were employed in pressing than in cutting, and by 1938, union investigation found that 2000 women were employed nationally on pressing processes; rather more than was desired. *Tailor and Garment Worker*, June 1938.
68 *Men's Wear*, 26 January 1935. This edition carried a detailed report of the meeting.
69 WCMF Minutes of the Executive Committee meeting, 2 March 1938.
70 NUTGW reply to TUC questionnaire, 20 February 1945.
71 Gold, D. 'Collective action among women workers in the Leeds clothing industry', B.A. Dissertation, Radcliffe College, 1973, p. 204.
72 This position was expressed, for example, by George Little, Chairman of the Leeds and Northern Clothing Manufacturers' Association (LNCMA) at the time of the strike, in an interview with Olav Arnold, 26 November 1995.

73 This was the view of George Little, clothing manufacturer and federation leader at the time of the strike.
74 Gold, D. 'Obituary: Gertie Roche 1912-1997', *History Workshop Journal*, 45, 1998, p. 313.
75 It constituted the first productivity agreement negotiated nationally by the union, and was described by Jim Roche as the worst productivity agreement he had ever read. 'The Leeds clothing strike', in Topham, T. and Barratt Brown, M. (eds) *Trade Union Register*, London: Merlin Press, 1970.
76 This was particularly iniquitous as it took place in the context of a general move in government and other industries towards a position of equal pay.
77 Gold, 'Collective action', p. 198; oral testimony of Gertie Roche. Interview recorded 16 March 1993, at the informant's residence.
78 Burton, for example, offered a rise of 2 pence above the national agreement, as well as a preferential rate for the male pressers. Gold, 'Collective action', pp. 198-9. The strategy may have had a temporary impact, as Burton workers were inconspicuous in the early stages of the strike. They did eventually become involved, however, and years later, one of the strikers, Silvia Patey Johns, reflected that 'Burton's shouldn't have been involved because employees were already being paid more than the increase'. Interview with Silvia Patey Johns recorded 16 May 1993 at the informant's residence
79 Honeyman, *Well suited*, p. 212.
80 The strike committee aimed to directly represent as may firms as possible.
81 The chair, Arthur Asty, and his three supporters, were all members of the John Collier factory committee. Gold, 'Collective action', p. 205; Honeyman, *Well suited*, pp. 212-213.
82 Oral testimony cited in Gold, 'collective action' and Honeyman, *Well suited*, p213, suggest the view of women strikers that while they were not confident public speakers, they nevertheless communicated effectively with other women and generated movement in the strike.
83 *Yorkshire Evening Post*, 18 February 1970; *Daily Telegraph*, 18 February 1970; Gold, 'Collective action', p. 212.
84 *Sunday Times*, 22 February 1970.
85 *Daily Mirror*, 26 February 1970.
86 *Yorkshire Evening Post*, 26 February 1970.
87 Gold, 'Collective action', p. 211; Honeyman, *Well suited*, p. 217.
88 *Yorkshire Evening Post*, 25 February 1970.
89 The mass demonstration held on Woodhouse Moor on 25 February 1970 also rejected the clothing employers' offer of immediate negotiations on their pay claim if they returned to work. *Yorkshire Evening Post*, 25 February 1970.
90 *Yorkshire Evening Post*, 13 March 1970; *Yorkshire Post*, 14 March 1970.
91 *Men's Wear* 2 April 1970.
92 *Yorkshire Post*, 26 March 1970; *Financial Times*, 26 March 1970; *Yorkshire Evening Post*, 26 March 1970.
93 Gold, D. 'Collective action', p. 198, quoting one of the women strikers.
94 *Yorkshire Evening Post*, 1 August 1970.
95 Honeyman, *Well suited*, p. 224.

96 For more detail on the contraction of the industry, see Honeyman, *Well suited*, p. 226-253.
97 *Yorkshire Factory Times* 10 August 1894.
98 The employers refused the claim, arguing that 'men and women are not generally engaged in the same processes in the trade'. *Men's Wear*, 22 March 1913.
99 Honeyman, 'Gender divisions', p. 59.

'The inspector can check a workroom is insanitary by means of his own eyes and nose': rethinking the sweatshop in Victorian and Edwardian Britain

Sheila C. Blackburn

Sweated labour formed one of the most intractable social problems of the nineteenth and early twentieth centuries. Yet, despite the recent appearance of a number of scholarly books and articles on the subject, historians have failed to fully account for sweating. Gareth Stedman Jones and James Schmiechen see it as a peculiarly London problem.[1] Moreover, Schmiechen, together with Duncan Bythell, Shelley Pennington and Belinda Westover, regard sweating as a byword for outwork affecting, overwhelmingly, female homeworkers.[2] This leads Bythell and Schmiechen to assume that, when homeworking declined at the beginning of the twentieth century, sweating disappeared. Perhaps the best study of sweating to date is that by Jenny Morris.[3] But even Morris, who argues that sweating encompassed both outwork and the factory sector, restricts her survey to domestic and small workshop tailoring; and she assumes sweating was the product of de-skilled work which was subcontracted, in the main, to female homeworkers. On the contrary, it is argued here that sweating cannot be analysed within such a static framework – it was a dynamic phenomenon and formed an integral part of a developing capitalism. Nor was it identical with outwork or women's employment. If initially loosely identified with small-scale production, by the opening decade of the twentieth century, sweating was associated with a wide range of occupations unconnected with industrial homeworking. The issue became linked to poverty pay – wherever this occurred.

Earlier writers, it is suggested, have accepted too readily the late-nineteenth century demonization of the homework shop as inefficient and obsolete, in contrast to the modern ruled and regulated factory, given currency by, amongst others, Sidney and Beatrice Webb. This chapter proposes that depictions of sweating went through three main stages. First, the mid-nineteenth century 'discovery' of sweating focused on the cries against the de-skilling of the male-dominated 'honourable' trades. Second, the late-nineteenth century witnessed the scapegoating of middlemen (especially Jews) as the engines of sweating (and 'unmanly' Jewish workers as some of the chief victims). Non-Jewish workers and the well-to-do could both be attracted to this scapegoating of outsiders – and the effect could be to see the main (non-sweated) economy as healthy and functioning efficiently. The third decisive stage in the portrayal of sweating was to erroneously categorise it as a phenomenon centred on women's paid work in the home. This 'traditional' view, focusing on women, emerged in the late-nineteenth century as a combination of the rallying cries of well-intentioned reformers on the one hand, and the desire of large businesses and male trade unionists to suppress outwork on the other. Pressure groups like the Women's Industrial Council (WIC) tactically concentrated on 'vulnerable' women; and growing numbers of employers found it convenient to divide workers into categories such as 'sweated female homeworkers' (who needed protection), and 'casual male workers' (who could safely be left to fend for themselves). At the same time, national efficiency enthusiasts argued that such 'wretched' women were hapless breeders of a casualised residuum. In other words, Victorians and Edwardians sought refuge in the fallacious idea that, if homework were highly regulated or banned, then sweating would die out. As it was, the legal solution to sweating, the Trade Boards Act of 1909, regulated the pay of both males and females, homeworkers as well as factory labour. The chapter concludes that only when sweating is viewed in the wider ambit of a gendered-class analysis can its true nature and extent be revealed. The three main aims of the chapter are: (a) to assess the anti-sweating agitations of the Victorian and Edwardian eras; (b) to locate the causes of sweating; and (c) to establish why, by the late-nineteenth century, sweating became conveniently, but mistakenly, linked with female homeworkers.

I

The mid-century writings of Thomas Hood, Henry Mayhew and Charles Kingsley initially provoked public discussion on the sweating issue. But their disturbing disclosures proposed little by way of remedies for the problem. Hood's seamstress in *The Song of the Shirt* was brushed aside as an isolated instance of distress.[4] His poem also served to focus attention on London and away from other centres of sweating.

Mayhew and Kingsley, on the other hand, by concentrating on the oppressed, male artisan (especially in metropolitan tailoring), were misled into believing that sweating was a separate industrial order revolving around small-scale employment, domestic piecework and subcontracting.⁵ Yet the most extreme instances of sweating, such as shirtmaking, had no necessary connection with these. And where Mayhew had portrayed the middleman as victim as well as villain, Kingsley typecast the so-called 'sweater' as a manipulative and sinister Jew. The upshot was that the public associated sweating with a single figure (frequently Jewish) who could be despised and scapegoated, despite the fact that there were fewer than 20,000 Jews in London.⁶ As the distinguished economist J.A. Hobson was later to observe: '*Alton Locke* gave us a powerful picture of the sub-contracting tailor, who spider-like, lured into his web the unfortunate victim, and sucked his blood for gain.'⁷ Whilst Kingsley condemned London's 'sweating dens', and 'slop shops' as supposedly belonging to rapacious Jewish entrepreneurs, Americans later coined the expression 'sweatshop' as a censure applied to the premises of exploiting masters.⁸

When the outcry against sweating was renewed in Britain in the 1870s and 1880s, it was Kingsley's overblown rendition, not Mayhew's more nuanced approach, that was recalled. The influx of poor Jews into East London heightened the mistaken belief (but one held by a large section of British society) that the Jews were simultaneously both avaricious moneymen and also vicious under-cutters of indigenous wage earners.⁹ Private and government reports alike depicted the Jew as anti-social, a danger to public health, upwardly mobile ('princes of the sweating system') and deficient in scruples.¹⁰ Although Jewish immigrants possibly made a bad situation worse, there was little evidence that they displaced native labour to any significant extent. Sweating had existed in the 1840s prior to the arrival of the most significant wave of immigration, and it prevailed in trades like chainmaking, which were unaffected by any foreign element. Nevertheless, the alarm generated by such respected journals as the *Lancet* and the reports of John Burnett (Labour Correspondent to the Board of Trade) led directly to the hysterical clamour for a select committee urgently to investigate sweating.¹¹

Prior to the Select Committee on the Sweating System (SCSS) (1888–90), sweating had been viewed (and still is by historians such as Stedman Jones) as an East London issue. But after five months, the committee was forced to admit that the problem was a national one and that it touched the manufacture of a large range of goods. However, the 1880s were far from being a watershed for anti-sweating reform. Working-class witnesses were intimidated and unwilling to appear. The popular journalist and eugenicist Arnold White produced witnesses of doubtful provenance who were only prepared to testify against the iniquities of alien labour.¹² Even pioneering investigators such as Beatrice Potter (later Webb), although she dismissed the emotive explanations for sweating dating back to Kingsley and the 1840s, only advocated more stringent domestic workshop regulation.[13]

Nevertheless, Potter's statements set the agenda for the anti-sweating campaigns that followed. In 1894 the Royal Commission on Labour blamed outwork for sweating. In the Minority Report signed by the trade unionists William Abraham, James Mawdsley, and Tom Mann but largely written by the Webbs, there is a fervent plea concerning the benefits which factory legislation had brought to the cotton workers of Lancashire.[14] Fabian pamphlets also attributed sweating to the unregulated sector. One Fabian Tract asserted that: 'The remedy for sweating lies in a quickening of the industrial revolution – in taking such steps as will hasten the transformation of the Sweated Trades into factory industries ...'.[15]

From 1894, moreover, the WIC, together with paternalistic employers like George Cadbury and the organised labour movement, increasingly highlighted not simply the problems of outwork but also the special difficulties of female homeworkers. The WIC sought, in particular, to make homeworking an issue central to public discussion. It published books and pamphlets on the subject, arranged conferences, conducted campaigns, and gathered data on the issue from other countries. The American licensing system for homework especially impressed the WIC. In several states, outwork was prohibited unless the dwelling place had been inspected and licensed. The workers had to apply for this license, and were to produce it when applying for work. Margaret and Ramsay MacDonald, two leading figures in the WIC, made a visit to the USA on behalf of the organisation and were converted.[16] Consequently, from 1899 the WIC sponsored bills to license all those who worked in their own home.

A minority, though, increasingly associated sweating not simply with homeworking (practically a gendered category), but with low waged exploitation (a class explanation). This line of thought led them to advocate, instead of licensing, a legal minimum wage for *all* low paid workers. An initial challenge came in 1896 with the publication of Hobson's article 'A Living Wage'.[17] The following year, the Webbs, despite their earlier enthusiasm for homework regulation, advocated a national minimum wage as the only remedy in their *Industrial Democracy*. A minimum wage, they contended, was a logical progression of the factory acts governing hours of work and sanitary conditions.[18] At the same time, the Liberal politician Charles Dilke, with the aid of the Women's Trade Union League (WTUL), considered that the wages boards of Victoria (Australia), with their industry-based minimum for a few, selected trades, might be a possible solution for Britain.[19] But the MacDonalds took the view that such attempts to contain sweating were utterly misguided. They continued to press for a licensing scheme. Their efforts were rewarded when, in 1906, Cadbury's *Daily News* was persuaded to stage a sensational sweated industries exhibition. Using her connections within the WIC, Margaret Macdonald helped to supply the majority of the workers for the event.[20] Significantly, the exhibition 'rigorously excluded sweated industries other than home industries'. Moreover, of the forty-six homeworkers who participated, no more than three were males.[21] The success of the exhibition led directly to the establishment of a powerful, all-party pressure group, the National Anti-Sweating league (NASL) and to the appointment, in 1907, of a Select Committee on Homework (SCH) to investigate sweating. The SCH reported that sweating prevailed extensively not only amongst homeworkers but factory workers too.[22] This statement was welcomed by the NASL which, by now, had abandoned homework regulation in preference for a legal minimum wage – irrespective of where a trade was practised.

Yet in doing so, the NASL rejected a universal subsistence minimum for a variation of Dilke's more modest wages board scheme. Indeed, the NASL's secretary, J.J. Mallon, believed that a national minimum wage would be inflationary since higher-paid workers would oppose any narrowing of differentials. Additionally, he felt that British industry could not afford a national minimum wage and that its implementation would raise the thorny issue of whether the rates set should be equal for both men and women.[23] Frightened of alienating the League's wealthy patrons, and mindful of the need to assuage those unions who feared the minimum might become the maximum, the NASL leadership convinced Winston Churchill, then President of the Board of Trade, to abandon the concept of a universal minimum, (which he had imbibed from the Webbs), for the more limited experiment of wages boards.[24] This switch from licensing to wages boards split the WIC. Whilst the MacDonalds vehemently continued to support licensing, others did not: the well-known feminist Clementina Black resigned from the presidency of the WIC because it refused to endorse the NASL's wages boards.[25] The MacDonalds' ardent espousal of licensing also caused considerable tension within the ranks of the other organisations to which they belonged – including the Independent Labour Party, the Labour Party and the Women's Labour League.[26]

The NASL justified its change of strategy on the grounds that 'the condition of the home worker is bound up with the condition of the underpaid factory worker'.[27] When legislation to curb sweating in the form of the 1909 Trade Boards Act was finally passed, the Act went beyond women homeworkers to include factory hands, and was gender neutral. As Churchill, the minister in charge of the legislation, patently understood, Parliament could not help sweated female workers without, at the same time, extending its protection to men as well.[28] He candidly acknowledged that, if earnings of less than one pound a week were 'sweated', then one-third of the workforce suffered from the complaint.[29] When the Act was extended in 1913, it included three wholly factory trades: hollow ware, confectionery and laundry work.[30]

II

If, as we have argued, homeworkers were not isolated victims of sweating, then what caused it? Two inter-related elements were necessary preconditions for sweating to develop: an over-supply of labour and a lack of trade union organisation amongst the workforce. These were both linked to unregulated labour markets.

The main reason for the first problem was ease of entry into a trade and lack of *bona fide* apprenticeship requirements. The sweated were not necessarily devoid of dexterity or inbred talent. But many of the processes that the low waged were engaged upon could be acquired in the district or region where sweating occurred. This caused a surplus of labour, a 'reserve army' competing for work, and barely adequate rates for the workers. In nail and chainmaking, for example, children were literally born and reared in the chain shop and learnt their trade at their mother's block.[31] Similarly, boxmaking was started young and ran in families.[32]

Before 1870 and the more rigorous enforcement of the Education Acts, children constituted a significant source of sweated labour. Even after 1870, reliable evidence indicates that the education laws were widely flouted. The inter-departmental committee on the employment of school children in 1901 found at least 200,000 of the latter in paid employment. Although these occupations included homework, they also encompassed drudgery in brickfields, bakery factories, and shops (as errand boys).[33] Added to this was the misuse of the half-time system – even in the well-organised textile districts.[34]

A further factor was the over-supply of adult workers. Many women were undoubtedly sweated due to the sexually segregated labour market. Married women were doubly disadvantaged because their family obligations restricted their employment to an even narrower range of jobs. But it should also be remembered that the sweating of women workers was frequently associated with the low pay or under-employment of males. In the eastern counties of England, women were exploited because they were forced to take in tailoring to augment the meagre earnings of male breadwinners engaged in fishing or agriculture. R.H. Tawney cites the case of the wife of an undertaker compelled to toil at tailoring because 'people aren't dying half fast enough'.[35] The same applied to East London where the irregular wages of dockworkers necessitated sweated tailoring on the part of their wives.[36] Charles Booth confronted the cultural image of masculinity when he demonstrated that one-third of east London families depended on the wages of both husband and wife for survival.[37] In chainmaking the sweated circumstances of women were frequently tied to those of their husbands. The majority of women chainmakers were married to casually employed workers and, in view of the fluctuations in their partners' wages, these women would often discontinue work when the male breadwinner was fully employed, and recommence during periods of low earnings for their spouses.[38] In effect, women were often exploited because they were married to sweated males.

Age, lack of skill, a temporary personal misfortune (such as ill health or alcoholism), could also cast many adult males into the sweated labour market. The social reformer, Constance Smith, highlighted this specifically when she commented: 'In individual cases, the illness of the breadwinner, or the failure of an employing firm is often sufficient to bring a whole family within the grip of the sweating system.'[39] The problem of sweating – if defined as inadequate pay – also embraced some practically all-male activities such as farming, fishing, transport and the Sheffield cutlery trades.[40] As the staunch opponent of minimum wage legislation Sir Frederick Banbury declared on the Second Reading of the Trade Boards Bill:

> A great number of people say that the agricultural labourer who receives only 12 shillings. or 15 shillings. a week is sweated ... So far as I know the only standard fixed by Hon. Members ... is the wage standard – a wage on which the person who receives it can live comfortably ... but that opens the door practically to all trades.[41]

The Labour MP J. R. Clynes retorted that long hours, bad conditions and poor pay: 'exist in connection with ... thousands of the workers of our railway systems'.[42] On this basis, many government contract workers, despite fair wages resolutions, could also be classed as sweated.[43] Even branches of well-organised crafts like engineering were susceptible to sweating.[44] That sweating could not be combated without extending protection to males was clearly demonstrated by the attempted legal solution to sweating, the 1909 Trades Boards Act. This piece of legislation initially embraced approximately a quarter of a million workers; at least ten per cent of whom were men.

By 1921, when the Act had been widely extended, over a million workers, of whom one third were males, had their wages legally regulated by trade boards.[45]

The second vital factor contributing to sweating was the absence of trade union organisation. Collective action was not unknown amongst the sweated and they did not lack agency. Those who assume that poor workers seldom joined unions or were incapable of mounting strikes, that the self-esteem of casual, women workers between 1880 -1914 was tied up with household management, are not entirely correct.[46] Clara Collet, in particular, insisted that homeworkers were not necessarily weak and isolated. Some had extensive networks. Many East London homeworkers had previously been employed in the factory, fraternised with their former work colleagues, and gathered in groups to collect their outdoor work. As a result, they had 'ample opportunity of discussing innovations or reductions' with their factory counterparts.[47]

The sweated chainmakers, too, lived in a self-enclosed community with dense neighbourhood and family ties. The women at Cradley Heath were not simply passive victims borne down by fatalism. They defended themselves and their interests, and defiantly asked of visitors to their 'industrial plague' spot, what they thought of England's most notorious white slaves now that they had seen them.[48] Although they decried their low pay, they professed to taking great pride in their work, and had been organised by the WTUL from as early as 1886.[49] Jewish workers were also involved in bitter strikes over sweating in London, Leeds, Manchester and Glasgow.[50]

But such resistance was seldom permanent. Even the celebrated match girls' dispute of 1888 was only temporarily successful.[51] Sweated workers were never strong enough to negotiate standard rates of pay. Collective action only occurred when prices were forced down to near starvation levels. Once the workers had won an advance of wages, the trade society would typically fall into abeyance. Only when the rates reached a low point again would another strike be declared. Poverty meant that workers could only exert intermittent demands on their employers. The constant pressure required to maintain wage rates was beyond their financial ability. As one union official told the sweating committee, speaking particularly of the chainmakers:

> They cannot afford the 3 pence per week [to the union] simply because their condition is such that 3 pence means a loaf of bread to them; and a loaf of bread short a week means a piece for each child or a meal short ... I have told them it would be better to suffer a bit longer to

make the union much stronger, but they said they could not really do it, they thought they were suffering enough as it was.[52]

Mary Macarthur of the WTUL put the same case, but more succinctly. Sweated workers, she informed the SCH in 1907, were unorganised because they were low paid and poorly paid because they were unorganised.[53] She also made it very plain that starvation wages were not confined to homeworkers. Organisation was equally difficult amongst low-waged factory labour. Indeed, even in the factory, the rate for the same job was frequently not only different in the same district, but even in the same establishment.[54] Black made a similar point to the SCH regarding an East London shirt factory:

When we came to take a register of the wages we found that in the two workrooms in that same firm where the women were actually working upon the very same sort of shirts cut out by the same people from the same bale of material there was a difference in wages of between 45 and 50 per cent.[55]

Social reformers such as Black sometimes alleged that women were more difficult to organise than males because females were only transient wage earners.[56] But sweated females' inability to establish stable unions should not be reduced to a gender issue. As surveys in the past as well as the present demonstrate, males are equally likely to be non-unionised and to be deficient in what Tawney termed 'economic resisting power', when employed in comparable low-paying establishments.[57] Nor should male antagonism be blamed entirely for women's lack of trade union success. Gender relations at work were a good deal more complex than such simplistic depictions allow. Whilst gender rivalry undoubtedly occurred, mutuality across gender lines often existed. Male chainmakers, for example, although they paid lip service to the breadwinner norm, understood only too well, in what was still overwhelmingly a family trade, that union membership for their women folk was vital. This eventually led the men to assist in organising the women and to unite with them to campaign for a legal minimum wage.[58] Studies that foreground gender conflict fail to take into account the implications for trade unions of local labour markets, regional variations, change over time and the fact that attitudes differed not only between but also within unions. As Jonathan Zeitlin reminds us, British employers had the capacity to render impotent even the strongest union objections to the engagement of female labour.[59] Male trade union prejudice, patriarchy and notions of male breadwinning norms do not, on their own, account for women's inability to form durable unions. To fully understand the causes of collective resistance (and lack of it) among sweated workers, we need to investigate, as Marcel van der Linden has proposed, relations between males and females in the household and the community as well as in the work place. It is essential to focus on the 'private' as well as the 'public' sphere.[60]

In addition to the two principal elements of an excess of labour competing for work and the individual haggling over wages, several secondary factors intensified the sweating problem. These included trade swings, seasonality of demand for a product and lack of sound management. Those employers who were guilty of sweating frequently engaged in cut-throat competition. As Smith remarked, 'the typical sweating employer ... rarely takes a long view: his aim is the immediate gain to be snatched out of the competitive struggle'.[61] During a recession, when wages were depressed, these unscrupulous employers would habitually stockpile merchandise and sell it at a greatly enhanced price when business improved. This haphazard and speculative method of management resulted in a deficiency of investment, innovation and training. It also contributed to trade fluctuations, much short-time working and product market instability. But it also included factories as well as the outwork sector. Indeed, Tawney viewed many small Jewish-tailoring workshops as highly efficient.[62] On the other hand, some large clothing factories, like Barran's of Leeds, were notorious for their employment of workers at sweated rates.[63]

The jam, pickle, match and confectionery manufacturers of London's East End were far from being 'responsible' employers. Despite being Quakers, the proprietors of the Bryant and May match factory were, until the late 1888s, renowned for their wretched conditions.[64] Large employers in Dundee – although they numbered in their ranks household names – were the despair of the WTUL in the late-nineteenth century.[65] The owners of trade board establishments by no means conformed to the Webbs' stereotype of sweating masters as the impecunious proprietors of unimportant, retrogressive concerns exploiting predominantly female labour. As Marx had recorded years before the publication of the Webbs' *Industrial Democracy*, factories and workshops were not separate but interconnected: the latter were not 'antiquated' but part and parcel of *modern* industrialisation.[66] Indeed, at the present time, homeworking is playing a major role in the global restructuring of capital – in Japan and Italy it is associated with the most streamlined systems of production and distribution.[67]

III

Why, then, did pressure groups such as the WIC focus their anti-sweating campaigns around the plight of women homeworkers? The most obvious explanation would appear to be that homework was an issue which united a whole range of disparate interested parties: tariff reformers, imperialists, social radicals, economists, feminists, trade unionists, socialists, sociologists, and religious organisations. Although further research is required on the motives of these various bodies, it is possible tentatively to suggest seven overriding considerations.

First, the WIC attempted to arouse popular opinion by portraying sweated female homeworkers as helpless victims. This was a strategy capitalised upon by the various sweated industries exhibitions. The women could be depicted as pale and pinched, widows and mothers of emaciated children, working day and night to keep body and soul together. Drunken and idle husbands, it was darkly hinted, used the opportunity of homeworking to force their wives to toil all hours – or be thrashed.[68] Whilst sweated males could be dismissed as the casual poor (and responsible, therefore, for their own actions), women, as with the passage of the factory acts, could be depicted as not being enlightened agents. Even *The Times* thought that exploited females could be helped without establishing a precedent for men:

> Few can doubt that large and organised industries are best left to settle all questions between themselves and their employers by the agency of combinations of their own. But this principle, however sound in many cases, does not apply to weak and half-starved women, to whom even an attendance at a meeting would mean the loss of at least one scanty substitute for a meal.[69]

Gertrude Tuckwell of the WTUL put the same case rather more bluntly. She declared that:

> the public attitude to the sweated woman worker is not the same as that of the average man or woman to the powerful trade unions and their members. Money is given and sympathy shown for the suffering of the former class, when the statements of the latter class arouses only irritation and contradiction.[70]

A second reason why the WIC found it appropriate to focus on women was that the WIC's campaign for protective legislation for female homeworkers found favour with trade unionists because it neither interfered with free collective bargaining nor impinged on male trade union arrangements. Homeworkers, male trade unionists believed, were isolated and scattered and, therefore, virtually impossible to organise.[71] Above all, trade unions feared the potential of outwork to undermine the wage levels of even highly organised labour. Regulating homework, they hoped, would eventually lead to the abolition of all outwork – whether it was performed in the home or not. Factory workers could then form strong trade unions to campaign for a rise in the workers' standard of living.[72]

Third, homework could be associated with the spread of infectious and dangerous diseases. Representatives of the WIC remarked that shirts, on which female homeworkers were engaged, were undoubtedly used as bedding for the homeworker's family. The WIC, therefore, maintained that the noxious slum of the homeworker acted as a medium for the dissemination of dirt, disease and vermin among the unsuspecting purchasing public.[73] Since clothing could go through many different hands, this was especially perturbing with regard to tailoring. The wealthy, the WIC pointed out, bought clothes which should be fumigated; the uniforms of admirals and vice-admirals were made in filthy hovels; even King Edward's coronation robes – 'perhaps the finest velvet ever woven' – had been produced in unspeakably squalid conditions.[74] Similarly, chocolates, ostensibly made under hygienic factory conditions, were likely to be packed in attractive boxes produced in a room where a consumptive homeworker lived, worked, slept – and where some of her children had died. The same, it was maintained, applied to paper bags designed to hold pastries and wedding cake boxes.[75] Inspection of home workshops, Margaret Macdonald thus insisted, would encourage mothers to at least make the beds, and to use disinfectant more liberally![76]

Fourth, the WIC believed that curbing homework would not pose a threat to the economy, that the bogey of foreign competition need hold no fears for the supporters of homework regulation. As the WIC was keen to point out, several states in America already had a system of licensing for homeworkers in place, whilst Germany (the scene of the first sweated industries exhibition) and France were already embarking on legislation to control the homework sector.[77] However, the WIC insisted that, since the anti-sweating movement was becoming international, legislating for homework need not raise the vexatious question of Protection. One leading WIC member pronounced:

> Protection of home industries is sometimes urged as a possible remedy for sweating. The evidence collected for the Berlin exhibition of

sweated industries shewed however that sweating is quite as rampant in protected Germany as in free-trade England; and there are colonies of home-workers in Chicago and New York where even the very high tariff maintained in America does not make wages or conditions any better than in the worst parts of London. Regulation of sweating would do far more for trade than any import duty on manufactured goods ....[78]

Nevertheless, leading Tariff Reformers like Lord Milner and Alfred Lyttelton believed that curbing homework would strengthen their case.

Fifth, the WIC considered that homeworking undermined the nation's efficiency. It ruined the health of mothers, caused high infant mortality whilst, at the same time, helping to spawn a new generation of underfed and sickly workers. Physically weak, these children were brought up without training to pass into blind-alley occupations. Moreover, children forced to work long hours in the home were in no position to take advantage of educational opportunities. Government expenditure on education, as a result, was wasted.[79]

A sixth factor, one of major importance, concerned 'good' employers. 'Good' employers could be persuaded that stricter regulation of homework would marginalise small-producers. Many large manufacturers were convinced by WIC literature that there was a very real danger of homework undercutting the factory owner. Forced by law to treat their workers fairly, factory owners thought that employers of homeworkers obtained cheap labour, which was subsidised by charity or the poor law.[80] In effect, they believed, like Winston Churchill that 'the good employer is undercut by the bad, and the bad employer is undercut by the worst.' [81] *Justice*, the organ of the Social Democratic Federation, was rather more cynical. It referred to this line of thinking as 'dog eat dog, big capitalist kill small capitalist is the game under this cut-throat system of competition.'[82] No doubt George Cadbury (who was Vice-President of the WIC) would have agreed! The Webbs also shared these sentiments. They welcomed the growth of monopolies believing that, if homework was eliminated, the small and incompetent employer would be crushed out. If this was achieved, business would be propelled into the best-managed and best-equipped factories – where responsible employers and responsible unions would flourish. The prosperous nature of the cotton industry, they indicated, bore out these general observations.[83]

Finally, the MacDonalds hoped that linking sweating to homework would undermine the growing campaign for a legal minimum wage. Since the abandonment of the paternalistic wage-fixing machinery at the beginning of the nineteenth century, economic philosophers had steadfastly held that state interference in the wages contract would be ruinous for the British economy. Hobson, the Webbs, Dilke and the WTUL, amongst others, had increasingly challenged this position from the mid-1890s. But the MacDonalds took the view that if such a solution was ever introduced in Britain, then more work would be driven into the home – so defeating the purpose of the initiative. As Margaret MacDonald remarked in 1907:

> I do not think that any legal regulation could be efficiently put into force amongst the worst paid workers under our present industrial system. Indeed, I believe that it would really increase the number of sweated homeworkers, for the minimum wage could be enforced more easily in the factories and workshops than in the homes, and the unscrupulous employer would put more work out in order to evade the law.[84]

Later, she suggested, the minimum wage would become a maximum one, and employers would increasingly mechanise their concerns – consequently crushing out the homeworker. Alternatively, she predicted, the boards would need an army of inspectors to enforce their decisions and workers would be forced to collude with under-paying masters to protect their employment.[85] As for the Webbs' argument that minimum wage setting was simply an extension of the factory provisions governing hours and conditions of work, she retorted:

> The inspector can check the fact that a workroom is insanitary by means of his own eyes and nose ... he can prove by reference to the clock that an employer is keeping his employers beyond the legal hour for closing. But he has not such independent knowledge of what money has gone into a worker's pocket for wages ....[86]

At this stage, it is probably premature to attempt to assess which one of these seven factors weighed most heavily with the WIC. The WIC was a fairly broad organisation embracing those of a socialist, labourite or liberal persuasion. Morris, however, feels that the WIC was a body of decidedly middle-class women primarily motivated by the ideology that the employment of mothers with young children was socially unacceptable, that such paid work had severe consequences for the future generation.[87] There is no doubt that Margaret MacDonald privileged maternalism and the sanctity of the home above equality for women in the labour market. The WIC executive committee member, Barbara Hutchins, also believed that if poor women were deprived of their meagre but essential earnings from homework, then the case for their state support (through, for example, more generous poor relief, widows' benefits, maternity grants and pensions) would become irresistible.[88] George Cadbury shared these sentiments. (On marriage, women were expected to discontinue their employment at his Bournville factory).[89] But Morris' view is rather unilinear, and fails to take into account the ulterior motives of some WIC supporters. Those, such as Black, while they were prepared to invoke the language of national efficiency and the family wage, did not necessarily believe in these ideologies. Some middle-class social-feminists, like Black, had come to terms with the fact that the key issue for sweated labour was state protection, and it was quite justifiable, therefore, to utilise any argument to achieve this end result. Members of the WIC were often pragmatists rather than theorists.[90]

IV

To fully understand sweating, it is necessary to examine the issue not simply in the context of sweatshops and a gender division of labour. Changes over time, variations in local labour markets, the particular circumstances of the household, and the general distribution of wealth in Victorian and Edwardian society also need to be taken into account. The expression should not be used to denote a remnant of the industrial system that preceded the factory. Furthermore, to decant sweated workers into categories like homeworkers and outworkers is to interpret the problem through a single lens. The spheres of home and factory intersected, and to separate them as if they coexisted independently is to misconceive the complex reality of sweating, and to misunderstand its importance within the development of modern industry.

A gendered-class approach reveals that starving female homeworkers were no more than the most extreme manifestations of sweating. They were merely among the most conspicuous of the 'super-sweated'. Although middle-class female reformers like Margaret MacDonald had brought sweating to the forefront of public debate, her propensity to blame the female victim and her insistence on the 'restorative power of character', was far removed from the NASL's class perspective which held the economic system accountable.[91] But in denouncing the old remedy of licensing for homeworkers, the male-dominated NASL committed itself to only a partial solution – the 1909 Trades Boards Act. The legislation, even if it encompassed males and the factory sector, was limited initially to four trades, covered only a quarter of a million workers and failed to make an impact on income redistribution. Prior to 1918, additional industries could only be granted trade board status by means of a provisional order, a time-consuming process requiring parliamentary approval.[92] Trade board inspection, too, left much to be desired. By giving its approval to the NASL's trade boards, it can be argued that the organised labour movement missed a vital opportunity. Trade boards, like licensing schemes, could not hope on their own to remedy the sweating evil. Viewed as an intricate social problem lying at the heart of poverty and inequality, even though exact statistics are difficult to obtain, it is clear that the extent of sweated labour at the inception of the First World War remained considerable.[93] It continued to persist, as *Justice* poignantly remarked, because:

> Sweating is due to unrestrained and furious competition among propertyless men and women for starvation wages, accepted only because they can keep body and   soul together in no other way. It is the real basis of capitalism and the source of modern riches.[94]

Notes

1. Stedman Jones, G. *Outcast London*, Oxford: Clarendon Press, 1971; Schmiechen, J. *Sweated Industries and Sweated Labor. The London Clothing Trades, 1860-1914*, London: Croom Helm, 1984.
2. Bythell, D. *The Sweated Trades: Outwork in Nineteenth Century Britain*, London: Batsford, 1978; Pennington, S. and Westover, B. *A Hidden Workforce. Homeworkers in England, 1850-1985*, Basingstoke: Macmillan, 1989.
3. Morris, J. *Women Workers and the Sweated Trades*, Aldershot: Gower, 1986.
4. *Punch*, 16 December 1843.
5. Thompson, E.P. and Yeo, E. eds, *The Unknown Mayhew*, London: Merlin Press, 1971, pp. 181-227. For Kingsley, see 'Cheap Clothes and Nasty', *Tracts by Christian Socialists*, 2, 1850 and *Alton Locke*, London: Chapman and Hall, 1850.
6. Feldman, D. *Englishmen and Jews. Social Relations and Political Culture, 1840-1914*, New Haven, CT: Yale University Press, 1994, p. 21.
7. Hobson, J.A. *Problems of Poverty*, London: Methuen, 1891, 76.
8. The *Oxford English Dictionary* (1902) attributes the term 'sweatshop' to American Civil War sewing establishments, but Laura Hapke traces its origins to the 1890s: 'A Shop Is Not A Home: Nineteenth-Century American Sweatshop Discourse', *American Nineteenth Century History*, 2, 2001, pp. 47-66.
9. Probably some two million Jews migrated out of Russia, Austria and Rumania between 1880 and 1914. Although most proceeded to the United States of

America, possibly some 120,000 to 150,000 settled in Britain. The majority of the latter (around sixty per cent) established themselves in East London: Feldman, *Englishmen and Jews*, p. 141.

10 *Lancet*, 3 May 1884, pp. 817-8. See also, *Report to the Board of Trade on the Sweating System at the East End of London*, Parliamentary Papers (PP) 1887, LXXXIX, p. 259.

11 *Hansard* (Lords), 28 February 1888, cols 1,598-609.

12 Dyke, J. 'The Jewish Workman', *Contemporary Review*, 73, 1898, p. 45.

13 Select Committee on the Sweating System (SCSS), *First Report*, PP 1888, XX, QQ. 3,313, 3,339, 3,366. The 1878 Factory and Workshops Act exempted women's workshops and homeworkers from the legal requirements governing cleanliness, effluvia and overcrowding. In women's workshops and domestic workshops (where only family members were employed), work could be undertaken at any time between 6.00 am and 9.00 pm. In the home there were no restrictions on women's working hours and practically none for child labour. Potter ascribed the lax system of regulation in women's workshops to the opposition of the women's rights movement of the 1870s: Potter, B. 'The Lords and the Sweating System', *Nineteenth Century*, 27, 1890, p. 899.

14 Royal Commission on Labour, *Minority Report*, Parliamentary Papers XXXV, 1894, Pt. 1, pp. 136-46.

15 Macrosty, H. 'Sweating its Cause and Remedy', *Fabian Tract*, 50, 1894, p. 10.

16 MacDonald, J.R. *Margaret Ethel MacDonald*, London: Hodder and Stoughton, 1912, pp. 137-46.

17 Hobson, J.A. 'A Living Wage', *Commonwealth*, 1, 1896, pp. 128-9, 165-7.

18 Webb, S & B. *Industrial Democracy*, London: Longmans Green, 1897, p. 774.

19 Dilke, C.'Sweating and Minimum Wage', *The International*, 1, 1907.
The Factory Act of 1896 empowered the governor of Victoria, Australia to appoint special boards to fix legal minimum wages for persons employed in or outside a factory in specified trades. Representation on the boards was divided equally between employers' and workers' delegates. Initially, five boards were established. They held office for four years and were under the direction of a chairman appointed by the elected members. By 1905 the boards ceased to be *ad hoc*, and other Australian states followed Victoria's lead.

20 MacDonald, *Margaret Ethel MacDonald*, p.157.

21 Mudie-Smith, R. ed., *Sweated Industries: Being a Handbook of the Daily News Exhibition*, London: Bradbury, Agnew, 1906, pp. 7, 92-117.

22 Select Committee on Homework (SCH), *Report*, PP VIII, 1908, pp. vii, xi.

23 Mallon, J. 'Industry and a Minimum Wage', in British Institute of Management (BIM), ed., *Industry and a Minimum Wage*, London: BIM, 1950, pp. 5-7.

24 Stewart, M. and Hunter, L. *The Needle is Threaded*, Southampton: Heinemann, Newmann, and Neame, 1964, pp. 140-2.

25 Mappen, E. 'Strategies for Change: Social Feminist Approaches to the Problems of Women's Work', in John, A. ed., *Unequal Opportunities: Women's Employment in England, 1800-1918*, Oxford: Blackwell, 1986, p. 27.

26 McBriar, A. *Fabian Socialism and English Politics, 1884-1918*, Cambridge: Cambridge University Press, 1962, p. 328; Collett, C. *For Labour and For*

Women: The Women's Labour League, 1906-1918, Manchester: Manchester University Press, 1989, pp. 118-19, 182.

27 National Anti-Sweating League (NASL), *Sweating and Wages Boards*, London: NASL, 1908, p. 4.
28 *Hansard* (Commons), 24 March 1909, col. 388.
29 Stewart and Hunter, *The Needle is Threaded*, p. 140.
30 Women's Industrial Council (WIC), *Women's Industrial News (WIN)*, July 1913, p.136.
31 *Reynolds's Newspaper*, 4 September 1910.
32 Bulkley, M. *The Establishment of Minimum Rates in the Boxmaking Industry, Under the Trade Boards Act of 1909*, London: Bell, 1915, p. 66.
33 NASL, *Report of Conference on a Minimum Wage*, London: Co-operative Printing, 1907, p. 43.
34 Adler, N. 'Child Employment and Juvenile Delinquency', in Tuckwell, G. *et al.*, *Women in Industry From Seven Points of View*, London: Duckworth, 1908, p. 126.
35 Tawney, R.H. *The Establishment of Minimum Rates in the Tailoring Industry, Under the Trade Boards Act of 1909*, London: Bell, 1915, p. 191.
36 Ibid., p. 112.
37 Booth, C. *Labour and Life of the People in London*, London: Macmillan, 1889, vol. 1, pp. 37-49.
38 *Report as to the Condition of Nailmakers and Small Chainmakers in South Staffordshire and East Worcestershire*, PP 1888, XCI, p. 502
39 Smith, C. *The Case for Wages Boards*, London: NASL, 1908, p. 40.
40 Black, C. *Sweated Industry and the Minimum Wage*, London: Duckworth, 1907, ch. 4.
41 *Hansard* (Commons), 28 April 1909, col. 406.
42 Ibid., col. 410.
43 The House of Commons adopted Fair Wages Resolutions in 1891, 1909, and 1946. The Fair Wages resolution of 1946 was rescinded in 1983 on the grounds that it was a relic from the days of sweated labour. Fair Wages resolutions specified that government contractors should pay rates commonly recognised as current for a competent workman in his trade, that contracts should not be sub-let. Although the resolutions applied to central government contracts, they were customarily adopted in local government contracts as well. They were rarely effective. Bercusson, B. *Fair Wages Resolutions*, London, Mansell, 1978, chapters 1-6.
44 Cole, G.D.H. 'Living Wages', *New Fabian Research Bureau Pamphlet*, 42, 1938, p. 32.
45 Webb, S & B. *English Local Government: English Poor Law History, Part II: The Last Hundred Years*, London: Longmans, 1929, vol.9, p. 559.
46 Roberts, E. *A Woman's Place*, Oxford: Blackwell, 1984, *passim*.
47 Collet, C. 'Women's Work', in Charles Booth, ed., *Labour and Life of the People in London*, London: Macmillan, 1902, vol. 4, p. 307.
48 Bigg, A. 'Female Labour in the Nail Trade', *Fortnightly Review*, 39, January-June 1886, p. 831.

49 Busby, K. 'The Women's Trade Union Movement in Great Britain', *Bulletin of the Bureau of Labor*, 83, July 1909, p. 56.
50 Buckman, J. *Immigrants and the Class Struggle. The Jewish Immigrant in Leeds*, Manchester: Manchester University Press, 1983.
51 Satre, L. 'After the Match Girls' Strike: Bryant and May in the 1890s', *Victorian Studies*, 26, 1982, p. 2.
52 SCSS, *Third Report*, PP 1889, XIII, Q. 19,342.
53 SCH, *Minutes of Evidence*, PP 1907, VI, QQ. 2,693-5.
54 Ibid., QQ. 2,704-7, 2,712-14.
55 Ibid., Q. 2,856.
56 Black, C. 'Some Current Objections to Factory Legislation for Women', in Webb, B. ed., *The Case for the Factory Acts*, London: Richards, 1901, p. 209.
57 R.H. Tawney, 'Poverty as an Industrial Problem', in Jay Winter, ed., *Tawney, R. H., The American Labour Movement and Other Essays*, Brighton: Harvester, 1979, p. 121. See also, Purcell, K.'Militancy and Acquiescence Amongst Women Workers', in Burman, S. ed., *Fit Work For Women*, London: Croom Helm, 1979, pp. 112-33.
58 Tawney, R.H. *The Establishment of Minimum Rates in the Chainmaking Industry under the Trade Boards Act of 1909*, London: Bell, 1914, pp. 25-6.
59 Zeitlin, J. 'Theories of Women's Work and Occupational Segregation', *Bulletin of the Society for the Study of Labour History*, 54, 1989, p. 6.
60 van der Linden, M. 'Connecting Household and Labour History, *International Review of Social History*, 38, 1993, Supplement 1, p. 63.
61 Smith, *Case for Wages Boards*, p. 7.
62 Tawney, *Minimum Rates in Tailoring*, p. 135.
63 Morris, *Women Workers*, p. 57.
64 Harrison, B.'The Politics of Occupational Ill health in Late-Nineteenth Century Britain: The Case of the Matchmaking Industry', *Sociology of Health and Illness*, 17, 1995, pp. 20-41.
65 Gordon, E. *Women and the Labour Movement in Scotland, 1850-1914*, Oxford: Clarendon Press, 1991, ch. 5.
66 Marx, K. *Capital*, London: Dent, 1962 (1st published 1867), vol. 1, pp. 496-518.
67 Rowbotham, S. *Homeworkers Worldwide*, London: Merlin Press, 1993, p. 33.
68 SCH, *Minutes of Evidence*, 1907, Q. 4,333.
69 *The Times*, 6 September 1910.
70 Tuckwell, G. 'The Regulation of Women's Work', in Tuckwell *et al.*, *Women in Industry*, p. 373.
71 Mudie-Smith, *Sweated Industries*, pp. 65-7.
72 NASL, *Report of Conference*, pp. 45-7, 59-60, 87-8.
73 Mudie-Smith, *Sweated Industries*, pp. 26-7.
74 Black, *Sweated Industry*, p. 14.
75 Black, C. 'Legislative Proposals', in Tuckwell *et al.*, *Women in Industry*, pp. 186-7.
76 SCH, *Minutes of Evidence*, 1907, QQ. 4502-5.
77 WIC, *WIN*, September 1907, pp. 568-70.

78 Hutchins, B. 'Homework and Sweating', *Fabian Tract*, 130, 1907, pp. 7-10.
79 WIC, *WIN*, December 1897, p. 8.
80 WIC, *The Case For and Against a Legal Minimum Wage for Sweated Workers*, London: WIC, 1909, p. 3.
81 *Hansard* (Commons), 28 April 1909, col. 388.
82 *Justice*, 3 September 1910.
83 Webb and Webb, *Industrial Democracy*, pp. 435, 748.
84 *Labour Leader*, 17 May 1907.
85 WIC, *Case For and Against*, p. 11-23.
86 Ibid., p. 12.
87 Morris, *Women Workers*, pp. 148-50.
88 Hutchins, 'Homework and Sweating', p. 2.
89 Dellheim, C. 'The Creation of a Company Culture: Cadburys, 1861-1931', *American Historical Review*, 92, 1987, pp. 41-2.
90 Mappen, 'Strategies for Change', p. 27.
91 MacDonald, *Margaret Ethel MacDonald*, pp. 90-91, 105-6.
92 At their peak, just before the Second World War, there were forty-seven boards covering approximately 1,136,000 employees. In 1945, in order to rid the system of the old stigma associated with sweating, trade boards were re-named wages councils. Wages councils were abolished in 1993, leaving the way clear for Britain to institute a national minimum wage in 1999. See Dorothy Sells *British Wages Boards*, Washington, D.C., The Brookings Institution, 1939, pp. 49.
93 Hobson, J.A. *Work and Wealth: A Human Valuation*, London: Macmillan, 1914, p. 179.
94 *Justice*, 5 May 1906.

Skilled versus qualified labour: the exclusion of women from the construction industry

Linda Clarke and Christine Wall

Introduction

This chapter is about the exclusion and occasional inclusion of women in the building trades in England, a subject of considerable significance given the scale of the United Kingdom construction sector, employing over 1.8 million and accounting for approximately 10% of Gross Domestic Product.[1] Gender equality has actually worsened since the early 1990s, with female participation falling from 11% in 1992 to 10% by 2004, at a time when women represent 46% of the economically active population.[2] Even this proportion is misleading as for craft and trade occupations the proportion is as low as 0.3%, indicating extremely intense gender segregation and, given the higher proportion of women in training in these areas, serious discrimination.[3]

The chapter focuses first on the ways in which 'skilled' status since the eighteenth century has been preserved as a masculine property. Secondly, it describes the barriers to entry for women into the trades, above all through denial of access to craft apprenticeship and the institutional support given to this, including from the trade unions. Thirdly, it explores those periods and areas where women have succeeded in entering the industry, such as into building materials production, into 'semi-skilled' work in periods of war and into training schemes from the 1970s. It concludes by challenging the maintenance of traditional social relations in the industry.

1. Skill as masculine construct

In 1980, Anne Phillips and Barbara Taylor argued that: 'far from being an economic fact, skill is often an ideological category imposed on certain types of work by virtue of the sex and power of the workers who perform it.'[4]

The following decades saw this claim investigated by feminist sociologists and historians to produce a substantial body of work on gender, skills and technology in a range of industries including, textiles, engineering, potteries, clerical work and many others, with the notable exception of the building trades. This chapter returns to the clarity of Phillips and Taylor's original statement in order to examine some key aspects of the construction and maintenance of the 'ideological category' of skill in the building industry: the concept of skill, access to training and the limited representation of women at work.

The common British notion of skill, as the ability, usually physical, to fulfil a particular task or activity in the workplace in order to produce a given output, can be traced from the eighteenth century, from Adam Smith through Ruskin to Braverman. It is a peculiarly Anglo-Saxon notion, used in a similar way to 'know-how' and 'technique', the worker with 'skill' being understood to possess know-how appropriate to the task in hand.[5] 'Possession' is in this sense equated with a property, in the nineteenth century sense of 'property in skill'. Smith was in fact rather disparaging about 'skilled' work, which he associated with 'dexterity' and at the same time with the 'policy of Europe' which 'considers the labour of all mechanics, artificers and manufacturers as skilled labour, and that of all country labourers as common labour'.[6] He added: 'No species of skilled labour seems more easy to learn than that of masons and bricklayers ... the high wages of these workmen therefore are not so much the recompense of their skills.'[7] Smith's criticism of 'skilled' labour is bound up with the fight against the English apprenticeship system which culminated in the repeal of the Statute of Artificers in 1814.[8]

The conception of the skilled worker was enriched through the writings of John Ruskin, in particular in *On the Nature of Gothic*.[9] Ruskin's depiction of the skilled, masculine worker, embodying independence, creativity and autonomy, rapidly became part of the discourse on work for both employers and trade unions.[10] His rhetorical descriptions of physical labour used as part of his argument against the separation of intellectual and manual work came into mass circulation late in the century when reprinted by William Morris. Thus *On the Nature of Gothic* became a manifesto for the Arts and Crafts Movement and a founding text for F. D. Maurice's Working Men's College. Morris re-interpreted Ruskin in a form far less damning of technology and the modern world than those of his mentor and evident in his popular lecture *Useful Work Versus Useless Toil*, published as a Socialist League pamphlet.[11] The nineteenth century craft trade unions wholeheartedly assumed Morris' and Ruskin's portrayals of the noble, male, skilled worker who was made graphically explicit in many of the union banners. For example, the emblem of the Amalgamated Society of Carpenters and Joiners in 1866 depicts the carpenter Joseph of Nazareth at the top, men at work in the middle, between the draped allegorical female figures of Industry and Art, Justice and Truth. The figure of the 'free', 'happy' and autonomous craftsman and Ruskin's idealisation of manual work had a lasting, if somewhat ambiguous, legacy well into the twentieth century, particularly in the construction industry. For instance, in 1962 the General Secretary of the National Federation of Building Trade Operatives (NFBTO), Harry Weaver, echoed the language of *On the Nature of Gothic* in his definition of a craftsman as: '... a worker with the manual skill and dexterity required and exercised for the creation of a finished product from its primary sources of raw materials, combined with knowledge and appreciation of such a creative gift.' [12]

Later in the twentieth century Harry Braverman perpetuated this notion, associating skill with the mastery of a craft described as the: '... combination of knowledge of materials and processes with the practised manual dexterities required to carry out a specific branch of production.'[13] 'Skill' is here again an individual attribute, the physical and mental dexterity of an individual in performing a task in the work process, and still in many respects in accord with the attributes of the traditional apprentice: learning largely on the job, where possible with a journeyman, with little theoretical underpinning and often fairly unsystematically.[14] And the same notion has recently been resurrected by Richard Sennett in his aptly titled book *The Craftsman*, positing obedience and perfection as the standards to live up to and referring to the tacit knowledge passed from the master to his apprentice.[15]

The difficulties of such notions of skill are many, not the least the virtual invisibility of women, which only contributes to the myth that the 'manual skill and dexterity' required for the work itself is inextricably bound up with notions of masculinity. A key problem is that skill refers to the tasks or outputs of the individual worker in the workplace rather than to the division of labour at a collective and social level, between for instance carpenters and bricklayers. The reference point is thus not the realisation of labour potential but *trade* or the *object* of labour, inevitably bound to traditional activities, functional in nature and defined by individual performance.

This Anglo-Saxon concept of skill is equated with what Richard Biernacki[16] terms 'embodied labour' as distinct from the power of labour itself which he terms 'labour power' – a distinction which also has clear gender implications. For our purposes the importance of this concept is that it is divorced from the process of vocational education and training (VET), aimed at enabling labour to integrate knowledge with personal, social and technical competences and to cope with new areas and the changing organisation of work.[17] Yet, as we will show, it is precisely through VET and the development of their qualifications that women have sought to enter the so-called 'skilled', 'manual' occupations of the construction industry.

2. The exclusion of women under capitalist wage relations

The repeal of the Statute of Artificers in 1814[18] meant that henceforth there were:

> ... no longer statutory or legal formularies or instructions binding upon masters or journeymen in the matter of apprentices' but a 'free' agreement between the master, on the one hand, and the apprentices, his parents or representatives on the other.[19]

Without the protection of relatively gender neutral statutory regulation, women were increasingly excluded from apprenticeships in the nineteenth century as the division of building labour changed from the old feudal divisions between master/journeyman/apprentice/ labourers or servants to the early capitalist division between foreman/skilled or craft worker/semi-skilled/apprentice/and labourer. As Snell discovered, between 1841 and 1861 virtually all 'male' trades became more male dominated, including carpenters, bricklayers, plumbers, glaziers, painters, paviours and masons.[20] Conversely, female trades became more heavily female, including glovers, dressmakers and ribbon makers. At the same time the range of occupations open to women declined dramatically, along with the number of female apprentices.[21] Only five out of 75 trades in Middlesex between 1803 and 1822, for example, were mixed, the remainder being totally segregated.[22] This is evident from the Census of 1841, the first to record in detail occupations by gender (*Table 1*): of the 408 females in the category 'plumbers, painters and glaziers' only 27, or 6.6%, representing less than 1% of the work group, were under 20 years old. In contrast, of the 1,143,000 domestic servants, nearly 80% were women and of these 38% were under 20 years old. Nevertheless, the proportion of women recorded in the construction trades, whilst low in 1841, is higher than in subsequent years. Female carpenters and joiners represent 0.3% of those in the trade in 1841, but only 0.1% in 1861, 1871 and 1881, though rising to 0.2% in 1891. Female plumbers, painters and glaziers fell from 0.8% of those in the trade in 1841 to 0.6% in 1861 and to 0.5% by 1881.

In the absence of statutory restrictions, the early trade unions and master associations tended to rely on custom and practice and to fall back on artisan rules and procedures particularly in their attempts to control entry into the different building trades through apprenticeship. The General Union of Carpenters and Joiners set up in 1827, the Friendly Society of Bricklayers in 1829 and the Operative Stonemasons in 1831 all formed 'non-exclusive unions of non-society men' and sought to preserve apprenticeships through imposing age restrictions, a seven year term, limitations on numbers and application only to traditional trades – demands which echoed throughout the nineteenth century.[23] Apprenticeship was invariably confined to men and thus acted as the key means of exclusion and control. The early trade union view was that women should not enjoy the status of artisan and that in effect 'skill' was an essentially masculine quality or 'property'.[24] As Simonton interprets the situation: 'Skill and training were not the root cause of exclusion in the workplace but notions about masculinity and femininity and their relationship to the meanings of work were.'[25] Women represented a 'threat to the rates and conditions given' and 'as a class, the most dangerous enemies of the artisan's Standard of Life'.[26]

By the 1840s women's access to jobs had been delimited and the family wage was openly espoused as a wage paid to a married male worker adequate to raise a family, so emphasising 'patriarchal control of the productive resources'.[27] In the progress of the nineteenth century this sexual division of labour sharpened and reinforced. In 1867, for instance, the Gangs Act outlawed the employment of women or girls in gangs in which men worked. The Ladies Committee for Promoting the Education and Employment of the Female Poor complained in 1894 of the position of women 'grievously and unjustly intruded upon by the other sex ... confined most frequently to a few scanty and unproductive kinds of labour' .[28]

However, one area outside the controls of the traditional 'skilled' apprenticed building trades where women had a significant presence was building materials production, though this was by no means uniform. The proportion of women employed in wood occupations dropped from 22% in 1851 to 11% by 1911, despite a 54% increase in employment (*Table 2*). The proportion of female brick and tilemakers however only dropped from 7% to 5.3% in the same period, though in 1871 the proportion in South Wales was 43% and in Staffordshire 25%; in brick occupations as a whole the proportion rose from 17% to 23% .[29]

Building production lost certain artisanal characteristics by the end of the nineteenth century as the wage system became hourly and time based, the working day was reduced to nine hours, overtime was abolished and building labourers were organised into the Navvies Union and the National Union of Labour and Federated Building Labourers. But the 72 building trade unions, local and national, and the 13 local federations that existed by 1911 remained as exclusive as ever, as apparent from Census figures for 1911, which reveal even fewer women (572) working in the industry than in 1891 (1,850), representing 0.07% of the workforce.

Though the traditional trades had become assimilated to capitalism to become sections of wage labour, with particular abilities and privileges to work with tools related to particular materials, this remained essentially a craft system based on preserving the exclusive privileges governing a particular trade, both through traditional apprenticeship and through maintaining a clear divide between the male craftsman and the labourer.[30] But, though each union sought to preserve its particular trade, this process had become more and more problematic. Much of the responsibility for teaching a trade fell upon the skilled journeymen who often resented training those who would replace them. Not only were trades no longer necessarily confined to special materials, whether carpenters and joiners to wood or plumbers to lead, but with the abolition of statutory apprenticeship the old bond between master and apprentice was broken, so that employers and contractors were free to use apprentices simply as cheap labour. The limits of the tasks encompassed by a particular skilled trade tended to be defined by the 'tools of the trade' and by the 'claiming' of new processes by trade unions, such as cement floors and breeze-block partitions variously by plasterers and bricklayers.[31] And protectionism prevailed as trade unions maintained their own sectional interests and those outside the craft demarcations were not accepted but either excluded (as were women) or classified as labourers, who did not begin to organise separately until the end of the nineteenth century.

3. Political expediency in the wars

This exclusivity was threatened by the severe labour shortages caused by the First World War. Employers were initially reluctant to take women on and the trade unions were highly resistant to the idea. Recruitment was initially aimed at munitions production and the trade unions concerned added the proviso that women were allowed to do only *parts* of a skilled job customarily done by a man; thus semi-skilled men were promoted to skilled jobs and women taken into semi-skilled jobs.[32] This ensured that women remained in subordinate positions, could not earn a fully skilled wage and, like all those recruited into jobs where entry was formally via an apprenticeship, were regarded as 'dilutees'.

Recruitment propaganda, in the form of photographic exhibitions and posters of women war workers, obscured the continuity of women as factory and industrial workers by excluding any images in large workplace groups so that they appear as individual oddities.[33] This approach was echoed by journalists reporting on the 1917 exhibition of photographs of women at work organised by the Ministry of Munitions and reviewed by *Building News* under the title 'Women as Constructors':

> ...women architects, even before the war, we knew, but that women bricklayers, carpenters, woodworking machine operators, and, indeed, workers in almost every branch of the building trades, would have attained in a couple of years to a skill unsurpassed by men...was a development which few would have predicted.[34]

Women were already present, at the outset of the War, in considerable numbers in the building and wood trades and in building materials production (*Table 3*). After relatively short training courses they were in some cases successfully doing jobs previously carried out by a fully apprenticed skilled worker, while employers were paying them merely a third of male wages. It was from the skilled unions that women encountered most opposition, particularly in the munitions industry but also in building trades, for example, the Amalgamated Society of Carpenters and Joiners never allowed women to join.[35] There was, however, a significant increase in the number of women belonging to general trade unions, from 24,000 in 1914 to 216,000 in 1918 which contrasts with the relatively small increase in the Wood Trades from 1,000 women members in 1914 to 5,000 women members in 1918.[36]

Although women's presence during the First World War in the building trades was brief, it was considerable. Ministry of Labour figures record that the numbers of insured female workers in building between 1914 and 1918 increased from 7,000 to 31,400.[37] Table 3 reveals the scale of labour market change in men and women's participation in the building trades and building materials production during the war years. The passing of the Restoration of the Pre-War Practices Act in 1919 saw the majority ejected from their jobs and directed back to traditional employment, mainly in domestic service, shop or clerical work. Thousands of auxiliary members and 'dilutees' were also thrown out of the electrical industries and were entitled to draw unemployment benefit, though they had no prospect of returning. Once this benefit was exhausted, they drifted too out of the Electrical Trades Union.[38] Although many thousands of women disappeared, 21,000 from the building trades and 17,000 from the wood trades, overall, the numbers employed in these sectors increased compared to before the war. Despite the efforts of the government to ensure women's employment was only temporary, wartime recruitment of women resulted in a gain of 3,000 women in building, 18,000 in the wood trades and 3,200 in building materials, in semi- and unskilled jobs, compared to 1914 figures.

A very similar story can be told of women in the Second World War. State policies delayed their recruitment into male jobs until the very last available man had been employed and then young, inexperienced women were favoured as 'dilutees' over older women with experience from the First World War.[39] Building occupations were not reserved in the early years of the war and many thousands of men signed up so that by 1941, although the schedule of reserved occupations had been amended, the industry was short of 50,000 building workers.[40] As war contracts for factories, workers' housing and airfields increased, so did the need for both skilled and unskilled labour.[41] In October 1941 the National Joint Council for the Building Industry, consisting of representatives of employers and employees organisations, agreed the terms on which women would be employed in the industry 'during the period of the war'. These were a set of restrictions on the employment of women, requiring any employer to first consult with the appropriate trade union on whether any men were available and that:

> ...no man shall be discharged in order that his place may be filled by a woman; and, if at any time the Trade Union concerned can supply the Employer with male labour of the appropriate class, the number of women may be correspondingly reduced.[42]

The Ministry of Labour and National Service noted that these conditions on the engagement of women, in practice only possible through the relevant trade union, would result in very few women entering building employment[43]. The agreement also specified that the basic rate of wages for women engaged on craft processes was one shilling and sixpence (1s 6d.) per hour, 20% less than the corresponding male rate. Despite these restrictions, in 1939 there were 15,700 women employed in the industry and by 1945 this had risen to 24,200, giving a participation rate of 3.8% of the total construction workforce.[44]

There was criticism of the discrepancy in earnings between men and women, often working side by side on the same job.[45] In 1943 the National Joint Council Building Agreement was amended so that where a woman did the job of a craftsman 'without special guidance assistance or supervision' she was eligible for the same rate of pay.[46] In practice however women, in both industries, were largely kept in semi-skilled positions and this was reflected in their earnings, almost half those of men (*Table 4*). Very few were sent to government training centres to learn manual trades and acute labour shortages resulted in some employers, Bovis for example, setting up their own training schemes for women.[47]

The industry journal, *The Builder*, omitted to document women's participation during the war years, apart from one short item in 1944 that reported on a conference entitled 'Women in the Building Industry'.[48] Here, one of the speakers described how, even though she had been 'born and bred' in the building industry, it had been extremely difficult to persuade her father to let her train and work as a builder. The conference resolved unanimously that, in the light of the looming housing crisis, the government should provide training for women in the building trades and trade unions should introduce the necessary changes to their rules and practices to enable the employment of women trainees. This call from women already working in the industry was ignored. At the end of the war and facing an acute labour shortage, the Minister of Labour, Ernest Bevin, demanded that all men up to the age of 60 with any experience of building register for reconstruction work and refused to recruit any women into the skilled trades, despite their recent war experience.[49] Once again women were directed into jobs deemed suitable for their gender.[50]

4. Recognition, training and skill in the post-war years

Union leaders appear to have downplayed women's role on the home front during the Second World War. Richard Coppock, Secretary of the National Federation of Building Trade Operatives (NFBTO), President of the Building Industry National Council, Member of the Central Council of the Ministry of Works and Planning, and present on practically every committee and sub-committee during the war years that had anything to do with employment and training in the building industry concluded at the end of the war that: 'Over the last twenty years the number of women in the building and public works contracting industries barely exceeded one per cent of the total personnel.'[51] This figure directly contradicted the Labour Research Department's estimate and the government's own statistics.

By 1950 a series of amalgamations had reduced the number of trade unions for the building industry to nineteen; fifteen craft, three labourers' and one mixed. Their representative body was the NFBTO and throughout the 1950s the NFBTO's own magazine, *The Operative Builder*, published industry statistics which included records of women employees. In 1953 there were 31,680 women working in the building industry in Britain and in 1960 they numbered 69,000, representing 3.1% and 4.9% respectively of the total workforce: considerably higher than Coppock's estimate.[52] However, these industry records end when *The Operative Builder* ceased publishing in 1962 and for most of the twentieth century reliable statistics for employment in the building industry are rare with no systematic gender breakdown. Census records do nevertheless indicate general occupational trends and show that some women did succeed in staying in the industry, particularly as painters and decorators, who numbered 2,863 in 1921, dropped to 2,564 by 1931 and increased after the Second World War to 3,606 in 1951 (*Table 5*). These figures also chart the strength of the craft unions in maintaining gender segregation through the very low participation rates of women in the carpentry and bricklaying trades. By contrast, where the craft unions did not hold sway – in building materials production – women workers made up 14% of the total workforce in 1951.[53]

Only in the electrical industries, determined not to repeat the experience of the First World War, was the union especially organised to take in women. The Electrical Trades Union set up a war emergency section for those never in the industry before and, in 1943, a female section with about 5,000 members, mostly 'dilutees' in semi-skilled positions. In 1954 alone altogether 2,836 women were recruited into the union in a special campaign on the basis that 'craft sectarianism has never protected the skilled man' and in 1961 6%, or 15,000, of the nearly 250,000 membership were women.[54]

G.D.H. Cole, as part of the Nuffield Reconstruction Surveys, undertook an extensive investigation into the supply and training of labour for the construction industry in 1942.[55] Although Cole's proposals were radical, emphasising the importance of a broad general education, the regulation of the institution of apprenticeship, and a formal system of training resulting in a recognised register of skilled workers, they did not include any mention of training for girls or women. His proposals were, anyway, not heeded and the 1943 Training Act defined the terms that continue to distance apprenticeship from mainstream education: 'Apprenticeship training ... will not be provided and paid for by the State and the various questions which arise in controlling apprenticeship are traditionally settled by the industry itself.'[56]

The White Paper endorsed the traditional view that apprenticeship training was 'the recognised method of training in employment and of entry into the ranks of the skilled workers', but conceded that it needed reviewing. This was to be through the establishment of the Building Apprenticeship and Training Council (BATC), consisting of employee and industry representatives together with members of various government departments.[57] This body sought to systematise and standardise apprenticeship training but there was no attempt to transform and broaden out apprenticeship to include provision for girls. After the BATC disbanded in 1956, training was again left in the hands of the industry itself, where 'custom and practice' masked the ingrained prejudices of both trade unionists and employers. There was no central co-ordinating body at all for construction training until the Construction Industry Training Board was established in 1964.[58]

Not surprisingly, Census returns show the total number of women in the building industry declining in the post-war decades to only 1,066 in 1971. Although this period coincides with a period of relative union strength, women's employment was not noticeably on the building trade unions' agenda.[59] The craft trade unions still adhered to a nineteenth century notion of skill acquisition via apprenticeship and refused to recognise anyone attaining the status of skilled worker outside the apprenticeship route, thus barring all those trained in Government Training Centres and, effectively, all women. However, it remained the case that many women continued to be employed in the industry despite not having been through an apprenticeship. Their presence caused friction and uncertainty among male trade unionists over key issues of skill and wages and debates on these issues were aired at the annual conferences of the NFBTO.[60] Many of the women in the industry worked for joinery manufacturers and it is not surprising that it was the Amalgamated Society of Woodworkers (ASW) which, in 1955, was finally instrumental in amending the Building Agreement to include women. The motion demanded equal pay for equal work for women, their right to a place in the building industry as skilled workers and the organisation of women, so that when engaged on a craft process or part of a craft process they became members of a craft union[61]. This was duly agreed, although during the discussion there was resistance from members arguing that women were incapable of carrying out the tasks required of a fully skilled worker but, at the same time, that there was a place for them in the industry providing they came in 'at the same age as the boys come in and serve a five year apprenticeship'.[62] Despite the amending of the Agreement there was no great influx of women into the industry or the craft unions because the means to acquiring skilled status remained via an apprenticeship, accessed at the discretion of the employers and trade unions.

5. Entry into construction through Vocational Education & Training (VET) schemes

It was not until the passing of the Sex Discrimination Act (1975) that a third period of women entering construction began. This piece of legislation, which made it illegal to discriminate against anyone on the grounds of their sex in employment or education, had no immediate and direct effect on the employment of women in the construction industry. It did, however, provide the lever for women to access training in government training centres on TOPS (Training Opportunity Programme) courses.[63] These were six-month, intensive training courses in Skill Centres under industrial conditions at the end of which the trainee emerged with a full set of tools, as an 'improver'.[64] After 18 months continuous employment and/or attaining a City and Guilds Certificate, they were then classed as skilled workers. This route proved revolutionary for women, being the first time that the acquisition of craft skills was possible without the patronage of an employer through the apprenticeship system.

The actual numbers of women who succeeded in training on TOPS courses was small and in the early 1980s a number of local authorities, in response to grassroots campaigning by the feminist movement, funded the setting up of women-only training workshops to provide initial trade training, which included provision for childcare. Close links were maintained with the local authority building departments known as Direct Labour Organisations (DLOs) and many women went on to adult training schemes run by their local councils. For example, by the mid 1980s Hackney DLO was running one of the largest training schemes for building workers in Britain, backed by the construction union UCATT (Union of Construction and Allied Technical Trades). Throughout the time that Hackney ran its new-build training scheme over 50% of the adult trainees were women.

This challenge to the entrenched segregation of the construction industry was, however, short lived. In the late 1980s successive pieces of legislation curbed the autonomous functioning of local authorities, including their power to build new houses. The effect on the DLOs was devastating and many ceased to exist; those that remained curtailed their activities to repair and maintenance operations only and the adult trainee schemes collapsed. The operative workforce of DLOs was reduced from 238,000 in 1970 to 86,000 by 1995, with tradeswomen suffering 'last in first out' redundancy policies in exactly the same way as after the two world wars.[65] In a survey conducted in 1997 there were only 231 tradeswomen found employed in 93 DLOs in England and Wales compared with 266 women – fully skilled, adult trainees and apprentices – employed in just seven London DLOs alone in 1989.[66]

Nevertheless, the legacy of the systems set up in the 1980s survived, albeit in reduced form. The DLOs have continued to address the very low numbers of young women applying for apprenticeships by creating links with the local schools careers services.[67] Many are highly proactive in their recruitment, stressing the importance of positive female images in recruitment literature and advertising, a range of advertising outlets and having women form part of the recruitment team. For example, of the 283 apprentices appointed by Leicester DLO between 1985 and 2002, 84, or 30%, were women, and in 2003, 40 or one in 12 of the 480-strong workforce were women, employed in all the trades including as carpenters, electricians, plasterers, painters and decorators, bricklayers, heating and ventilating engineers, gasfitters and metal workers .[68]

Targeted advertising using positive female images has also been at the centre of the Construction Sector Skills Council's efforts to attract women into the private construction industry, though the proportion remains similar to nineteenth century levels.[69] Higher proportions of women are evident in painting and decorating at 0.8%, but for bricklayers, plasterers, scaffolders, plumbers and civil engineering no more than 0.1% were found to be female in a survey of 2001.[70] Nevertheless, 2% of UCATT's membership is now women, though the union has no female representation at national level and no female regional or national officers.[71] Female first-year trainees also constituted 3% of all construction trainees in 2004, down from 4% in 2000.[72] The vast majority is to be found in full-time Further Education (FE) college courses where they represent 7% of all trainees, rather than as apprentices dependent on obtaining a placement with an individual firm.

This concentration in FE college training rather than as apprentices is not, however, exclusive to women. In what has been termed the 'employers' retreat', the majority, nearly two-thirds, of all construction trainees is now based in FE, whilst a dwindling minority are able to find placements with employers as work-based apprentices.[73] The problem for college-based trainees is, however, that they fail to gain the valued and necessary transitional work experience and as a result acquire qualifications with little currency on the labour market. Work-based training schemes for construction have anyway increasingly been criticised for their often low theoretical content and variable quality, the failure to integrate practical, technical and educational elements and the fragmented and narrow skills produced, which impede social and occupational mobility.[74] Such difficulties in maintaining the traditional apprenticeship system offer at the same time, therefore, an opportunity to introduce a more comprehensive and coherent VET scheme and to restructure entry into the industry for greater inclusivity.

6. Conclusions

In many respects the roles of the traditional craftsman and of apprenticeship as an induction to a collectively agreed and recognised occupation no longer exist. This is evident from the construction collective agreement where the categories of both labourer and apprentice/trainee have disappeared.[75] It has become more and more difficult to rely simply on a work-based apprenticeship process, dependent on generalisation through experience, as skills required have become more abstract and their level no longer expressed though dexterity in the physical work process.[76] With the Modern Apprenticeship too the trade unions are no longer party to the agreement, indicating a severance from the industrial relations system. The great change in the apprenticeship system, one denoting the growing need to articulate with a more complex labour process, has been the recognition of technical education and theoretical knowledge as essential elements in training for an occupation. With greater prefabrication and mechanisation, including the use of power tools and precision instruments, setting out and planning skills are required as well as greater accuracy and precision. In this sense there is a clear break with the nineteenth and twentieth century understandings of skill as an individual and masculine property, symbolised by ownership of a bag of tools. In another sense the labour process itself has become more abstract as the pace of work has come to be determined collectively rather than on an individual basis or as driven by the foreman or gang leader. A craft system founded and paid according to the output of the individual worker cannot apply in this situation. Increasingly, therefore, the construction process is coming to rely on 'qualified' labour, with qualifications acquired through formal VET, as advocated by G.D.H. Cole[77]. As a result, the possibility is opened up for women – long dependent on their qualifications as the only means of entry into the industry – to be included, provided that discrimination in recruitment and selection can be overcome and that good employment and working conditions are in place.

Table 1. Men and women in building trade occupations 1841-1891

Occupation		1841	1861	1871	1881	1891
Builder	Total	9,188	15,757	23,300	30,699	37,815
	Female	81	99	171	135	194
	% female	0.9	0.6	0.7	0.4	0.5
Carpenter, joiner	Total	162,984	177,869	205,824	235,233	221,009
	Female	459	151	200	216	348
	% female	0.3	0.1	0.1	0.1	0.2
Bricklayer	Total	39,806	79,158	99,945	125,140	130,446
	Female	107	35		85	66
	% female	0.3	0.04		0.1	0.05
Mason, paviour	Total	82,650	81,133	95,199	97,540	84,717
	Female	188	31		108	123
	% female	0.2	0.04		0.1	0.1
Slater, tiler	Total	6.348	5,266	6,079	7,483	6,789
	Female	25	4		14	
	% female	0.4	0.08		0.2	
Paper hanger	Total	1,076	2,318	3,442	4,272	
	Female	12	18		95	
	% female	1.1	0.8		2.2	
Plasterer	Total	13,238	18,557	24,575	28,841	
	Female	83	25		41	
	% female	0.6	0.1		0.1	
Plumber	Total				37,400	46,873
	Female				240	226
	% female				0.6	0.5
Paper hanger, plasterer, whitewasher	Total					29,408
	Female					183
	% female					0.6
Painter, glazier	Total				100,130	123,829
	Female				454	710
	% female				0.5	0.6
Plumber, painter, glazier	Total	48,207	74,619	103,912		
	Female	408	447	530		
	% female	0.8	0.5	0.5		
Total female		1,363	810	901	1,388	1,850
% female		0.4	0.2	0.2	0.2	0.3

Notes:
Categories of occupations change in 1881 so that *plumbers* and *painters, glaziers* are counted separately and *plasterers* are counted with *paper hangers*.
All totals include workers in all age groups.
Data taken from the Occupation Tables of the Census for Great Britain 1841, 1861, 1871, 1881 and 1891 published by HMSO.

Table 2: Proportion of women employed in building materials production

Occupation	1851 Total 000s	% female	1881 Total 000sl	% female	1911 Total 000s	% female
Building	429	0.2	765	0.3	947	0.1
Wood	184	21.6	180	10.6	284	10.6
Brick	83	16.8	128	18.7	174	22.5
Brick and tilemaker	30	6.9			52	5.3

Source: Based on Jordan E. (1989) 'The Exclusion of Women from Nineteenth Century Britain' in *Contemporary Studies in Society and History,* Vol. 31, No. 2., April, 273-296.

Table 3: Changes in the numbers of men and women employed in Building, Wood Trades and Building Materials between July 1914 and November 1920

Industries	July 1914 No. employed	November 1918 No. employed	Increase or decrease on July 1914	July 1920 No. employed	Increase or decrease on November 1918
Building Trades	M 920,000 F 7,000	M 438,000 F 31,000	M - 482,000 F +24,000	M 796,000 F 10,000	M + 358,000 F – 21,000
Wood Trades	M 239,000 F 32,000	M 158,000 F 67,000	M - 81,000 F +35,000	M 226,000 F 50,000	M +68,000 F – 17,000
Bricks and Cement	M 100,000 F 5,000	M 40,000 F 8,100	M -60,000 F +3,100	M 76,000 F 8,200	M +36,000 F +100

Source: Table XIII (facing page 107) in Grier, Ashley and Kirkaldy (1921) *British Labour, Replacement and Conciliation 1914-1921*

Note: Wood Trades = sawmilling, joinery, cabinetmaking.

Table 4. Average weekly earnings of men and women employed in selected industries in July 1943

	Men	Youths under 21	Women 18 years and over	All workers
Building, contracting, etc.	108s 4d	46s 10d	61s 5d	100s 4d
Metal, engineering and shipbuilding	138s 3d	50s 9d	69s 10d	108s 3d
Woodworking	102s 3d	37s 8d	56s 9d	79s 4d

Source: Ministry of Labour Gazette 1943, HMSO.

Table 5: Men and women manual workers in select trades in the construction industry in England and Wales 1931-1971[1]

Occupational division		1931	1951	1961 10% sample	1971 10% sample
Carpenters and joiners	Total	246,856	244,929	26,130	29,412
	Women	49	716	106	92
	% female	0.02	0.3	0.4	0.3
Bricklayers	Total	692,898	141,852	15,616	14,330
	Women	775	153	4	16
	% female	0.1	0.1	0.02	0.11
Labourers	Total	172,491	289,506	22,964	25,382
	Women	139	607	24	98
	% female	0.1	0.2	0.1	0.3
Painters and decorators	Total	206,323	253,470	26,337	28,780
	Women	2,564	3,606	738	860
	% female	1.2	1.4	2.8	2.9
Total in above building trades only	*Total*	*1,318,568*	*929,757*	*91,047*	*97,904*
	Women	*3,527*	*5,082*	*872*	*1,066*
	% female	*0.3*	*0.5*	*1.0*	*1.0*

Source: Census returns for 1931, 1951, 1961 and 1971.
1. Data for all years from Occupation Tables. Between 1951 and 1961 there was a complete change in the classification of occupations making comparisons between years difficult. For example in 1951 category XIV (Workers in Building and Construction) included Foreman, Gangers; Clerks of Works; Builder's Labourers; Bricklayers; Bricklayer's Labourers; Other workers (mainly navvies). In 1961 navvies were included under the new occupational category XVIII (Labourers).

Notes

1 Business Enterprise and Regulatory Reform (BERR) Department (2007) *Construction Statistics Annual 2007*. London: BERR.
2 Briscoe G 'Women and minority groups in UK construction: recent trends' *Construction Management and Economics*, Vol. 23, 2006, pp.1001-1005.
3 Byrne, J., Clarke, L. & van der Meer, M. 'Gender and ethnic minority exclusion from skilled occupations in construction: a Western European comparison', *Construction management and economics* 23,1025-1034, 2005
4 Phillips, A. and Taylor, B., 'Sex and Skill: Notes towards a Feminist Economics', *Feminist Review*, no.6, 79-88, 1980.
5 Clarke, L. and Winch, C. 'A European skills framework? – but what are skills? Anglo-Saxon versus German concepts', *Journal of Education and Work*, Vol. 19, No. 3, July, 255-26, 2006.
6 Smith, A. *The Wealth of Nations*, Vols 1, 2, London: Everyman's Library, 1910, p. 90.
7 Ibid., p. 92.
8 Derry, T. K. 'The Repeal of the Apprenticeship Clauses of the Statute of Artificers', *Economic History Review* 1st series 3, 1931.
9 Ruskin, John 'On the Nature of Gothic Architecture: and herein of the true functions of the Workman in Art'. Reprinted from the sixth chapter of the second volume of *Mr. Ruskin's Stones of Venice*, London: G..Allen, 1892.
10 Unrau, John (1981) 'Ruskin, the Workman and the Savageness of Gothic', in *New Approaches to Ruskin*, ed. Robert Hewison, London: Routledge, pp. 33-50.
11 Morris, William *Political writings of William Morris* (ed. A.L. Morton) London: Lawrence and Wishart, 1972.
12 Weaver, H.J.O., 'Innovation and the operatives' in *Innovation in Building. Contributions to the CIB Congress, Cambridge,* Amsterdam and New York: Elsevier, p. 65., 1962.
13 Braverman, H. *Labour and Monopoly Capital*, New York: Monthly Review Press, p. 443, 1974.
14 Clarke, L. 'The Changing Structure and Significance of Apprenticeship with Special Reference to Construction' in Ainley, P. and Rainbird, H. (eds) *Apprenticeship*, London: Kogan Page, 1999.
15 Sennett, R. *The Craftsman*, Allen Lane, 2008.
16 Biernacki, R. *The Fabrication of Labour: Germany and Britain 1640-1914*, Californian Press, 1995.
17 Brockmann, M., Clarke, L. and Winch, C.. 'Competence-Based Vocational Education and Training (VET) in Europe: the cases of England and France', *Vocations and Learning*, 1 (3) (forthcoming), 2008.
18 Op. cit. pp 74-81.
19 Howell, F. 'Trade unions, apprentices and technical education', *Contemporary Review* 30, p. 842, 1877.
20 Snell, K. D. M. *Annals of the Labouring Poor: Social Change and Agrarian England 1660-1900*, Cambridge: Cambridge University Press, 1985, p. 290.

21 Ibid., p. 278.
22 Ibid., p. 285.
23 Postgate, R. W. *The Builders; History*, London: The National Federation of Building Trade Operatives, 1923.
24 Clark, A. *The Struggle for the Breeches: Gender and the Making of the British Working Class*, London: Rivers Oram Press, p. 119, 1995; Hobsbawm, E. 'Man and Woman in Socialist Iconography', *History Workshop Journal* 6, Autumn, p. 132, 1978.
25 Simonton, D. *The Education and Training of Eighteenth Century Girls with Special Reference to the Working Classes*, PhD thesis, University of Essex, p. 35, 1988.
26 Webb, S. and B. *Industrial Democracy*, National Association of Operative Plasterers, London, 1898, p. 497.
27 Kenrick, J. 'Politics and the Construction of Women as Second Class Workers' in F. Wilkinson (ed) *The Dynamics of Labour Market Segmentation*, Academic Press, p. 186, 1981; Pinchbeck, I. *Women Workers in the Industrial Revolution 1750-1950*, 1930; Humphries, J. "...the most free from objection..' The Sexual Division of Labour and Women's Work in Nineteenth Century England' in *The Journal of Economic History*, Vol. 47, No. 4, December 1987, 929-949.
28 Cited in Pinchbeck, ibid., p. 304.
29 Jordan, E. 'The Exclusion of Women from Nineteenth Century Britain' in *Contemporary Studies in Society and History*, Vol. 31, No. 2, April, 1989, 273-296, p. 295.
30 Clarke L. 'From Craft to Qualified Building Labour in Britain: a comparative approach', *Labor History*, Vol. 46, No 4, November 2005, 473-493.
31 Hilton, W. S. *Foes to Tyranny*, London: AUBTW, 1963; Postgate, op. cit.
32 Braybon, G. and Summerfield, P. *Out of the Cage: Women's Experiences of Two Wars*, London: Pandora, 1987.
33 Thom, D. 'Free from Chains? The Image of Women's Labour in London 1900-20' in Feldman, D. and Stedman Jones, G. (eds.) *Metropolis London: Histories and Representations since 1800*, London: Routledge, 1989, p. 94.
34 *Building News and Engineering Journal* (1917) 'Women as constructors', 28th March, p. 268.
35 Braybon, G. *Women Workers in the First World War*, p. 69, 1981.
36 Grier, Ashley and Kirkaldy *British Labour, Replacement and Conciliation 1914-1921*,1921, p. 86.
37 PRO, CAB 21/1527 Production Council, the building industry and the war 1941-3.
38 Lloyd, J. *Light and Liberty: a history of the EEPTU*, London: George Weidenfeld and Nicholson, 1990, p. 275.
39 Braybon and Summerfield, op. cit.
40 Kohan, C.M. *Works and Buildings*, History of the Second World War United Kingdom Civil Series, HMSO, 1952.
41 PRO CAB 21/1527, op.cit.
42 TUC HD 6661, NFBTO, *The Operative Builder, 1953-60*, B9.
43 PRO LAB 8/464 *Memorandum of war time agreement on employment of women*

in the building industry 1941-42.
44 Hall, D. *Cornerstone. A study of Britain's Building Industry*, London: Lawrence & Wishart, 1948, p. 82.
45 Labour Research Department, *Women in War Jobs*, 1942.
46 Hooks, J. *British Policies and Methods in Employing Women in Wartime*, United States Department of Labour, Washington, 1944, p. 29.
47 Cooper, P. *Building Relationships: the history of Bovis 1885-2000*, London: Cassell, 2000.
48 *Builder, The* 'Women in the Building Industry', vol. 166, 2nd June, p. 452.
49 Briar, C. *Working for Women. Gendered work and welfare policies in twentieth century Britain*, London: UCL Press, 1997, p. 84.
50 Boston, S. *Women Workers and the Trade Unions*, London: Lawrence & Wishart, 1980, p. 242.
51 Coppock, R. and Heumann, H. *Design for Labour,* London: Dent, 1942. p. 23.
52 TUC HD 6661, op.cit.
53 See Occupation Tables, 1951 Census.
54 Lloyd, op.cit., p. 326.
55 PRO LAB/8/518, G.D.H. Cole, *The Post-War Demand for Labour in the Building and Civil Engineering Industries* undated document.
56 Cmd 6428 *Training for the Building Industry*, Ministry of Works, 1943.
57 BATC, Building Apprenticeship and Training Council *First Report.* HMSO. 1943.
58 CITB, *Report and Statement of Accounts*, HMSO, 1966.
59 Wood, Leslie W. *A Union to Build: the Story of UCATT*, London: Lawrence & Wishart, 1979, p. 84.
60 MRC MSS. 78/BO/UM/4/1/18-30, *NFBTO Annual Conference Reports 1947-1959*
61 Ibid., 26.
62 Ibid., 45.
63 Payne, J. *Women, Training and the Skills Shortage: the case for public investment*, London: Policy Studies Institute, 1991.
64 Clarke K. *Women and Training: A review,* Equal Opportunities Commission, 1991.
65 DoE (Department of the Environment) (annual) *Housing and Construction Statistics*, London: Stationery Office.
66 Wall C. and Clarke L. (1996) *Staying Power: Women in Direct Building Teams,* London Women and the Manual Trades, 1996; Michielsens, Wall, E.C. and Clarke, L., *A Fair Day's Work. Women in the Direct Labour Organisations*, LWAMT and ADLO, 1997.
67 Beck, V., Clarke, L. and Michielsens, E. *Overcoming marginalisation: structural obstacles and openings to integration in segregated sectors, GB National Report*, Report submitted to European Commission, 2003; Housing Forum, *Housing Skills: approaches to the current challenges*, London: Constructing Excellence. 2004.
68 Clarke L., Michielsens E and Wall C. 'Women in Manual Trades' in A. Gale and L. Davidson (eds) *Managing Diversity in the Construction Sector*, Taylor

and Francis, 2006.
69 CITB, *Construction Skills Foresight Report 2003*, Bircham Newton, 2004.
70 CITB, *Survey of Employment in the Construction Industry 2001*, prepared by A. Humphrey, S. Joy and R. Taylor, National Centre for Social Research, 2002.
71 *Labour Research* (2008) 'Women's union profile is on the rise', March 2008, pp 10-11.
72 CITB *Trainee Numbers Survey*, Bircham Newton, 2004.
73 Keep E. 'The changing meaning of skill and the shifting balance of responsibility for vocational education and training – are employers calling the shots?', paper to Conference on Training, Employability and Employment, Monash University Centre, London, 2002 Construction Skills *Trainee Numbers Survey*, Bircham Newto, 2006.
74 Ryan, P. Gospel H. and Lewis P. 'Educational and contractual attributes of the apprenticeship programmes of large employers in Britain', *Journal of Vocational Education and Training* 58(3): 359-383; Clarke, Linda & Wall, Christine, *A Blueprint for Change: Construction Skills Training in Britain*, Bristol: Policy Press, 1998.
75 Construction Industry Joint Council (CIJC) *Working Rule Agreement for the Construction Industry*, London, 2002.
76 Clarke, Linda and Christopher Winch 'Apprenticeship and Applied Theoretical Knowledge', in *Educational Philosophy and* Theory, Vol. 36, No. 5, Nov. 2004, 509-521.
77 Op. cit., footnote 55.

Black women and work in England, 1880-1920

Caroline Bressey

British labour history, indeed British history in general, has largely ignored black women in analyses of the nation's working class. Those that do take account of black experiences have tended to focus upon male labour, particularly sailors.[1] Conversely, researchers of black history have tended to focus on long-view overarching historical narratives that insist on the need for the black experience to be included within broader narratives of British history.[2] Issues of class, for example the relationship between intellectual elites from the African diaspora who initiated the Pan-African movement from London in the late 1890s and early 1900s and the black working class in Britain are still to be fully examined.

The focus of this chapter is on black women's experience of work in England between 1880 and 1920. It considers how newspaper archives enlighten our understandings of the work undertaken by black women and also how racism impacted upon their everyday experiences. The empirical focus of the chapter is based upon research of women who advertised themselves as domestic workers in newspapers between 1880 and 1920. These entries are brief, often only a couple of sentences. Despite their brevity they are important moments, creating a space in the archives where black women become temporarily visible and present themselves in their own words. However, the reasons why these women appear raise complex questions around race and racism and the chapter ends with a discussion of the racial hostility which black women faced in the 1920s, both on the streets and within an evolving labour movement.

Black women and the history of labour

To date, our knowledge of the social and economic positions of black women during England's long nineteenth century is limited. The information that can be gleaned from national census data is uneven as in England the colour of people's skin was not recorded as a matter of course. The majority of black people still languish in anonymity and a bottom-up approach is required to bring forth the histories of such ordinary folk. Working women who have come to light tend to have been marginalised during their lifetime.[3] They are known because they occupied spaces in asylums, prisons or children's homes, spaces that, for various reasons and in differing ways, recorded the colour of their skin. Yet these records suggest that many of these women were part of 'ethnically mixed' families who lived within integrated working-class communities. However, our ability to understand their day-to-day lives to, for example, measure how much women earned, is very limited, and evidence of the occupational structures they were a part of is thin.[4]

In her research on black survival in white society between 1780 and 1830 Norma Myers has pointed out that black history in Britain has been dominated by elite black males such as Ignatius Sancho and Olaudah Equiano, both of whom had privileged access to the public sphere. Despite an increased interest in black history, particularly from the early 1980s, the focus has generally remained on unique and exceptional characters like Mary Seacole.[5] In her effort to address this imbalance Myers turned to a variety of archives including the Newgate Calendars, baptism records, indictments brought before the Commissioners of the Peace and Gaol Delivery recorded in the Old Bailey Session Papers. She found eleven women accused of theft in her samples of the Old Bailey and Newgate Calendars between 1791 and 1810, including Mary Goring, who stole a silk handkerchief, and Elizabeth Mandeville, who with her white accomplice Ann Grace, was accused of theft.[6] Post 1810, a change in format to the Newgate Calendars excluded physical descriptions, a practice which seems to have been maintained by the criminal system throughout the Victorian era.[7] The legacy of slavery meant that the majority of men and women from the Caribbean had British surnames and an Anglican religion. So, unlike Jewish and Irish communities who can be identified through a combination of place of birth and religion, these fields are of limited help in recovering black histories.

As the above examples reflect, the presence of black working women in Victorian England did not pass completely unrecorded. They appear as barmaids in illustrations that depict urban dandies. In a painting of colonial produce at the Great Exhibition, Joseph Nash (1852) included a black nurse with her two young white charges. Of course, not all black women were poor or marginalised. In 1879 the circus performer Miss La La, also known as the 'African Princess', toured London and Manchester. Miss La La, who was born in Stettin (then in Germany and now in Poland), was a popular attraction and painted by Degas in Paris earlier in the year. Some women also supplemented their income with occasional work, such as sitting as an artist's model. In May 1899 an artist placed a request in the *Liverpool*

Mercury for a 'coloured lady' to work in such as position and some women became part of well known images. Born in Jamaica Fanny Eaton lived with her family in the King's Cross area of London in the 1850s and 1860s. Working as a charwoman, she earned extra income as a model and was painted by a number of artists including Joanna Wells, D.G. Rossetti and J.E. Millais. When the 1881 census was taken Fanny was widowed and living in Chelsea with her seven children. By the time of the 1901 census she had moved to Oakfield in the Isle of Wight and was working as a domestic cook.[8] Images, be they paintings or photographs, have proved an important tool for researching the black presence in Victorian Britain, offering a way into archives that could not be reached through the written word.

Two novels by Dinah Craik (1850), *Olive* and *The Half-Caste* (the latter concerning the daughter of a white Englishman and an Indian Princess) discuss the place of race in middle class families more directly than those suggested by the literally and metaphorically marginalised Jamaican creole woman who resides in the attic of *Jane Eyre*. These literary examples and the presence of privileged women such as Sarah Davies (an African orphan who became a god-daughter of Queen Victoria) and members of the black bourgeoisie suggest discussions of race and class, not just race and labour, require more research within a British context.[9]

For many historians the absence of knowledge about black women in the historical record has been assumed to reflect extreme marginalization, but Norma Myers found no figures to support previous assumptions that black women were forced into prostitution during the nineteenth century. Ian Duffield's examination of records in the archives of New South Wales and Tasmania located six black women who were transported to Australia between 1832 and 1838. All were domestic servants and included a skilled needlewoman, a plain cook, a laundress, a housemaid and a laundry maid. In his research on Black Edwardians, Jeffrey Green recovered insights into the lives of female servants and entertainers, some of whom suffered abuse from their employers.[10] The work I present here supports similar findings for the later decades of the century. The examples also allow questions around black women's strategies for economic and psychological survival to be raised, if not answered.

Colouring Labour

Recent changes in research technologies have altered access to historical data on the black presence in England. Digitalisation and the ability to remotely search the national census along with newspapers such as *The Times* are proving to be significant methodological tools.[11] They allow researchers who can access them to undertake 'needle-in-a-haystack' searches that previously would have taken an entire career to complete, if at all. The ability to search newspapers and census returns via keywords allows similar searches to be undertaken in a matter of weeks or months. The use of these research tools has formed the basis of the research in this chapter but, of course, it is not a perfect method. Scanning these vast archives does not always capture the intricacies of identity. It is very difficult to search around very broad terms such as 'black' which will refer to the colours of horses, surnames and 'bad days' in politics or on economic markets. Moreover, the method only locates those who had the colour of their skin recorded in the archives for some reason.

This paradox raises two major issues. Firstly, it speaks to fundamental questions of race and racism in Britain. If it was not the normal practice to record the colour of a person's skin why have some people, and not others, been coloured in particular archives? Secondly, this uncertainty raises interesting but difficult issues of 'authenticity'. That is, how do we know someone who is given some identification of blackness is a person with African ancestry? In the nineteenth century a man from India might be described as a 'negro', a creole woman could have white or black skin.

In the 1881 census six women with identities connected to imaginaries of blackness were documented by census numerators. There were others, but I have chosen to highlight these women as they reflect the complex issues of racial identity in English archives. The oldest of this group was Eliza Louthean, who was born in Jamaica in about 1830. Married, she lived at Homewood in Wimbledon, south London. Catherine L Lloyd, a twenty-four-year-old Jamaican woman was living in Portsea, Hampshire. She too was married, to a Royal Navy Captain. The fact that these women were born in Jamaica is no assurance of blackness, both women could have been white or of Indian or Chinese descent. Mary Ashley, born in London in about 1853 was married to the Birmingham born Charles Ashley and living at 2 Chapel Street, Rickergate, Cumberland at the time of the census. Mary and her husband were both working as a 'professional negro singer'. But it is impossible to be certain from the entry if Mary and Charles were a black couple who made their living as professional singers, or if they made a living by performing a 'blacked-up' minstrel routine? They were not the only couple to be given such a job description. Annie Albery was born in Brighton in 1861 and was still living there at the time of the 1881 census, although she was then married to Londoner Henry Albery. They also worked in the entertainment business. Annie was a 'nigger minstrel musician' and her husband a 'negro' minstrel. Henry's occupation suggests a white man who blacked-up to perform, but there is nothing to confirm that the difference in Annie's employment record identification indicates an ethnic difference between her and her husband.

Among the many women working as domestic servants and living not far from the Alberys, twenty-seven-year-old Margaret Prince worked at Cannon Place, Brighton as a domestic servant. Born in St Vincent, Margaret's ethnicity is confirmed by her full description as a 'domestic servant negress'. Mary was twenty at the time of the 1881 census and working for the Harpur family in Wavertree, near Liverpool. Her place of birth is given as Africa (she is noted to be a naturalised British subject), but as well as noting her servant status the recorder also registered that she was an 'emancipated slave'. Maria Laurence also worked as a domestic servant. A Jamaican woman of thirty-five Maria worked as a housemaid in Elvaston Place in London. She too is recorded as being a naturalised British subject. Of all these women we can only say with any confidence that Mary, a domestic servant with no given surname, and Margaret Prince were black.

The difference between these entries and the personal advertisements placed in the 'wanted' columns of England's newspapers is that colour was specified both by black women looking for work and by employers seeking to fill specifically racialised jobs. A host of racialised and sometimes racist search terms have to be inputted to reveal them; 'coloured chambermaid', 'negress servant', 'coloured kitchen maid', 'coloured cook', 'West Indian cook', 'African nurse', 'coloured servant', and 'West Indian governess' are among the many combinations I have tried. Not all bore results. Those that have reveal a bias towards domestic service and the entertainment industry. Further research into women's employment in other industries such as cotton weaving, which employed 31-year-old Mary Gregson in Blackburn in 1901, is required.

Looking for work

The majority of women who feature in this chapter were, like so many working-class women, employed as domestic servants. The nature of the industry and the London base of *The Times* newspaper means there is a bias towards London, where domestic service was the largest sector providing employment for women.[12] However, these women were not the poorest domestic workers. Placing an advert in *The Times* cost money and these women, whether from their own pockets or with the support of employers, were able to pay the required fee.[13]

The adverts prove that black women have been associated with the nursing and caring professions for far longer than the histories of their roles in the NHS suggest. In May 1886 a thirty-year-old 'coloured woman' with very good references advertised her desire to find a new position as a nurse. The following year a 'West Indian coloured nurse' advertised her services. She was only willing to work with one baby and only for 'a gentleman's family'. In April 1891 another 'West Indian Coloured Nurse' began looking for a new position, as well as being able to bring up an infant she was also a skilled needlewoman. On 5 September 1899 an advert for a West Indian 'black nurse' appeared in London's *Daily News*. This middle-aged woman was looking for a new position in a gentleman's family that would start by the end of September. John Gillis has argued that women did not find that their wages in domestic service increased with experience and most avoided the label of 'old maid' by leaving service by their early thirties.[14] It is hard to glean whether the advert placed in the *Daily News* reflects a woman's inability to leave the ranks of domestics because of the colour of her skin, or a desire to remain independent within a relatively stable employment sector.

It is likely that a substantial number of black domestic servants would have been born in Britain but longings to return home – subtly revealed in these advertisements – reflect the broader travels of the women from the African diaspora. In 1887 a 'coloured' woman, then working at Oakhill Road in Putney, south-west London, advertised for an engagement that would enable her to return to the West Indies. She would work as a maid or nurse. The following decade, in October 1899, 'a young negress, from Jamaica, anxious to return home' advertised for a position as a nursemaid 'to any lady' who would pay for her passage home. Women's employers would sometimes place similar adverts on their employee's behalf. One such recommendation was placed by Mrs Caulfield of Sunninghill in April 1881. She wished to recommend a 'nurse (West Indian)' with a 'view to sending her out to her native country'.

Explicit desires to travel did not always have connotations of a yearning to return home. On Tuesday 20 September 1881 an advert placed by a 'young coloured woman' who spoke English and Spanish appeared. She hoped to work for a woman who was travelling to New York in early October. In May 1885, a 'middle-aged coloured woman' advertised for a position as a nurse with a baby, but she was very specifically looking to work for a family who were travelling to Australia. Two months later a 'coloured woman' who worked as a nurse at 35 Linden Gardens in Bayswater, west London, placed an advert. She was looking to continue working as a nurse and hoped to find a position caring for an elderly lady or one child. She did not object to travel as part of the job. In May 1907 another nurse, a 'West Indian. Coloured' who could take care of a young baby placed an advert. Aged forty, she was also prepared to travel if required.

Very occasionally black women would be specifically requested for posts which included travel. In October 1892 an advert was placed in *The Era* for a 'good-looking coloured lady to travel'. *The Era* was a London based weekly paper that reported on the world of entertainment. It carried numerous classified adverts, including personal ones for actors and performers and those seeking to employ them. This particular position was permanent with 'good wages' and housing. Further details would be sent on receipt of a photograph, but no more about the position or the potential employer was revealed. Even less could be gleaned from an advert in the *Liverpool Mercury* in April 1900. Inserted between adverts for coca rooms and pastry girls a request for a 'coloured lady' appeared. She was wanted for 'light business'. What this might have entailed was not mentioned.

Black women from outside the realms of the British empire also travelled to England to find work. In November 1900 an American 'negress' applying for assistance to help her get back to the United States of America stood before Mr Horace Smith in Westminster. She had left New York for Paris, planning to pay for her passage and more, by selling her services to rich American and British visitors at the Paris Exhibition. But the tourists she had expected to serve had not come, and those who had attended did not wish to employ her. She had left Paris to try her luck in England, but found the streets of London equally hostile. She had thought, it was reported, that everybody made money in England, but now she had spent all her savings and was at a loss as to what to do in a country that was making her 'full of rheumatism and cold'. She had worked as a hairdresser in the United States, and was willing to work as a cook, a waitress, anything 'respectable', but she had found that 'folks did not care for black people' in England. Horace Smith hoped that she would be helped, not in finding employment, but in being returned to the United States.[15]

Two years later *The Times* announced the opening of a new club in London. The Columbia was to be located at the Avondale Hotel in Piccadilly, its aim to act as a meeting place for British subjects and US citizens 'for the convenience of American visitors, and the furtherance of mutual good feeling between the citizens of the two countries'. In order to provide authentic cuisine, 'a skilled chef from the United States and an "Aunt Sally" negress cook from the South' were to be employed in the club's kitchen.[16] The implication that a black woman could not be a chef adds another component to the processes of de-skilling women faced in the labour market, although some did demand a minimum level of income for their services. In March 1910 a Clapham based West Indian cook advertised her desire to find a new position, but only in a household that kept a kitchenmaid and would pay her at least £33.

The 'exotic' on display

The pages of adverts also confirm that the world of entertainment provided employment for black women as actors, singers and also behind the scenes. In November 1900 a 'coloured young lady' placed an advert requesting a job as an assistant in a bazaar or playhouse, but most of the adverts reflect a demand for black women for particularly racialised and sexualised roles. In April 1885 an advert appeared in the *Liverpool Mercury* for a woman who would entertain guests at a hotel and pleasure gardens. An attractive 'young coloured woman' who could sing and play the piano was preferred. In July 1887 The Old Ship in Worksop advertised for a 'coloured lady' to perform as a pianist and singer.

Five years later two positions for 'coloured' women appeared in the same column of *The Era* in August 1892. The first offered suitable 'coloured lady vocalists' comfortable and permanent situations. Those interested were asked to attend rehearsals at the Assembly Rooms at Crewkerne in Somerset. The second advert came from the Lyric Theatre in west London which required a 'coloured lady singer' as a lead performer. In September 1885 an advert was placed for a barmaid in Stockton which specifically asked for a 'coloured lady' – no experience required. In Birmingham in June 1895 a position as a barmaid at the Manchester Hotel came up. Again no experience was necessary but only a 'coloured lady' would be successful, and all applicants were asked to enclose a photograph with their references.

While these adverts could be seen as inclusive, others clearly located black women within the realm of the exotic, and hint at broader motives than revealed in these enquiries. In 1890 the Coliseum Music Hall in Sheffield advertised for 'novelties' to perform on dates in April and beyond. Particularly desired were a 'Giant, dwarf or coloured lady'.[17] An advert, again placed in *The Era* for a position in Sheffield, requested sober applicants for a 'bar novelty'. Male barmaids, giants, giantesses and 'coloured' women were highlighted as most 'desirable'. In May 1891, the Volunteer Inn in Salford placed an advert for 'all kinds of bar novelties and attractions' as well as for a 'coloured lady or Zulu man'.[18]

There were also acting roles to be had on stage. An illusionist based in Newcastle-upon-Tyne in February 1886 urgently needed a 'good looking young lady', a 'coloured lady and a negro boy' for his act. The ladies applying were once again asked to include a photograph with their application.

Black women were also sought to take racialised roles. The stage version of Harriet Beecher Stowe's 'anti-slavery novel' *Uncle Tom's Cabin* remained popular in late Victorian England and there was even an Uncle Tom's Cabin Company. In December 1884 the company advertised for a 'coloured lady and gentleman vocalists or dancers' for an immediate start and a long engagement at the Theatre Royal Cheltenham, and again in October 1885 when the company was based at the Theatre Royal Canterbury.[19] In October 1892 another 'young lady (coloured)' was wanted for the role of Topsy in Uncle Tom's Cabin then on at the Theatre Royal, Doncaster with a run in Grimsby to follow. The influence of perceived and real African-American culture was reflected in a request for a 'coloured lady' soprano to perform Jubilee singing in Colne, a town in east Lancashire. She did not have to be attractive but she had to be 'good'.[20]

Women wanting to work on the stage were not only limited to England. For a woman interested in travelling to Belgium there was an opportunity in Ghent for 'a coloured woman to sing and make herself useful in plays and concerts' in 1892. A woman at the beginning of her career would be considered, and the position came with board and lodging and a salary for three months. For women hoping to travel further from London, the prospect of performing 'at the most brilliant variety establishment and pleasure gardens' in St Petersburg might have seemed attractive. Along with dancers, women gymnasts and 'novelties' of every description, 'American coloured lady vocalists and dancers' were requested to apply with photographs, lithographs and their terms to an international agency in Russia.[21]

How women felt about taking these parts, or the opportunity they had to take non-racialised positions, particularly on the stage, is hard to determine. There are hints that non-racialised roles were not often available. The singer Amy Height, a well respected 'soprano and semi-comic vocalist', was described by the Cardiff *Western Mail* as 'the only coloured lady on the music-hall stage' in 1891.[22] The adverts above suggest that this was something of an exaggeration, but it does probably reflect the limited roles and opportunities available to black women as performers in their own right.

Race, labour and racism

On Tuesday 8 April 1919, Jamaican born Grace Ann Matilda Stevenson was found dead in her bedroom on Kings Avenue, Ealing, in west London. Grace, aged thirty eight, had only been working for Ivy McLachlan for about three weeks before she died, but McLachlan served as the major witness at the inquest describing Grace's final days to the court. Grace was a live-in servant, and the weekend before her death she had complained of not feeling well and her mood had been snappy although on Monday morning she had got up and cooked breakfast as usual. McLachlan had gone out to visit her mother, leaving Grace in but giving her keys so she could go out in the afternoon. Returning after 10 pm that night McLachlan noticed that Grace had not completed all her duties. The blinds had not been closed, nor had the slops been emptied. McLachlan went upstairs to see if Grace was in bed, but got no answer when she knocked on her employee's door. Despite seeing something white underneath the door, which she took to be a light, McLachlan went to bed.

At 7.15 on Tuesday morning, not hearing Grace up and about, McLachlan knocked on her door again. Once again there was no answer, she tried once more a bit later in the morning, but there was still no answer. Shortly after her second attempt, two women came to the house, one of whom remarked on the smell of gas. When the women left, McLachlan went to visit Grace's friends to see if they had seen her on Monday. They had not, so on her way home McLaclan went to the police station and got an officer to come back with her to King's Avenue. The policeman forced Grace's door. Inside the pair found the room filled with gas. The window, door and chimney had all been padded and Grace lay on the bed fully dressed. She had been dead for seven hours.

Grace's friend Martha Cockram was also a witness at the inquest. She had last seen Grace on the Sunday before she died. The two had had tea together and Grace had left Martha's place at about 9.30 pm. Martha confirmed that her friend was depressed. She was upset that she was unable to return to Jamaica and she had not heard from her sweetheart. She was also upset that people would make racist jibes about and to her when she was walking down the street. The pair had agreed to meet again on Tuesday, and although she knew Grace was depressed, Martha had never heard her talk of suicide and was surprised when she heard she had taken her own life.

Grace had left her suicide letter on the dressing table. It does not survive among the inquest papers, but part of it was reproduced in *The Times* below the headline 'Black woman's suicide / taunted about her colour':

> I am black, but I didn't make myself, but people look at me and think I have no feeling, I cannot bear it any longer. I am a lonely, broken-hearted girl, and I have no one in England. I tried to go but cannot do so; I have not enough money. … I cannot face the work any longer; it is too hard. I have no strength left in me. God knows.

The verdict was suicide by gas poisoning.

While Grace's letter does not imply that racism was the only reason for her deep depression it certainly played a significant part and, despite having some friends, she felt lonely and isolated. Racist attacks on black and Asian people in Britain, which had been on the increase since 1917, may well have played a role in her feelings of isolation and an atmosphere which led to her receiving racial abuse on the streets of London. In 1917 reports of direct racism impacting upon black individuals and their families appeared in local and national newspapers. It was, according to *Empire News*, the war that had forced 'the colour problem into prominence', but most articles focused upon the presence of black men. It was not only their presence in the labour market that was seen as a threat (for the *Empire News* this was seen as a necessary part of the war effort), but the perceived increase in 'mixed' relationships and marriages. The need for a Salvation Army officer to encourage parents to warn their daughters of the 'danger of association with coloured strangers' and the *Empire News*' declaration that white men who married black women were not '*white* ... far from it' reflect the hostile atmosphere that was developing around black men and women.[23] In July 1917, East London's *Stratford Express* reported on a Canning Town landlord who had attempted to force out a black man and his family. His mother-in-law argued that it was because her daughter was married to a black man that the family had been targeted. The paper also reported an attack on Mrs Lynch, a 'half-caste', which had resulted in a Mrs Beard being summoned before a magistrate for assault.[24]

Josephine Esther Bruce was born at 15 Dieppe Street in Fulham, west London, in November 1912. Her father was born in Georgetown, British Guiana (now Guyana) and worked on ships before he settled in London. 'Aunt Ester', as she was known to her biographer, Stephen Bourne, recalled her childhood in Fulham as one belonging to a close-knit, friendly and supportive community. However, she also recalled that at her school in North End Road, Fulham, teachers were openly racist:

> We had a teacher called Mrs Carson. She was a funny old dear. One day she said to the class: 'I am going to teach you how to talk to people.' She taught us how to be polite to each other and then she said: 'Now, when you meet coloured people, you do not talk to them ... Don't forget, you do not talk to coloured people.'[25]

Esther Bruce's teacher was sacked, but Neil Evans has argued that by 1919 a combination of white demobbed soldiers looking for work and the expansion of the British Empire to its greatest geographical area further focused tensions around issues of race and empire at home.[26] The so-called race riots that resulted from these tensions, again often discussed in the media through the sexual relations between white women and black men, were violent and murderous. Three days of rioting in London in 1919 was followed by an outburst of violence in South Wales and Liverpool in June. These 'pogroms', as they were described by the *Negro Worker* in 1932, resulted in hundreds of African and West Indian seamen, who had defended the British empire during the First World War, being beaten by mobs in the streets of London, Liverpool, Barry, Newport and Cardiff. The *Negro Worker* blamed the majority of the attacks on 'ship owners and the trade union reformists' who they believed organized the majority of 'rioters'.[27] These rioters were responsible for gunfire, the burning of black and Asian homes and the murder of twenty-three-year-old Charles Wootton. A West Indian, Wootton was chased by a white mob to Queen's Dock in Liverpool. He fell or was pushed into the water and as he swam to get away was stoned from the banks. He was hit and drowned. Despite a police presence no one was arrested for his murder.[28] This, Marika Sherwood argues, was Britain's first official lynching.[29]

An awareness of racism in England is reflected in some of the adverts placed by employers. Isaac Green placed one such example in *The Era* in 1880. He was looking for 'a good attraction' for his Sheffield bar. In his advert he made it clear that he would not object to employing 'a coloured woman'. Similarly in *The Times* in November 1919 a woman who lived at Holly Bush, which she described as a small house in Hampstead, north London, advertised for help. She was looking for a domestic servant who would work in the house but also help look after her 'unspoiled' 18 month year old son. The position came with its own bedroom and the support of daily help. The woman would have to be good natured, but the fact that it was clearly stated that a 'coloured woman or foreigner' would be made welcome, seems to reflect an understanding that life for these women was becoming increasingly difficult.

There are many questions around black family lives raised by these violent crises and everyday forms of racism that existed before, during and after. For Grace, racism impacted upon her ability to live her day-to-day life. Her situation reflects a lonely experience, with an employer who, perhaps because she had not known her for very long, or because she was not that concerned, did not attempt to understand Grace's problems until she neglected the duties for which she was employed. How were black women (of whom many would have had white friends and relatives, lovers and 'mixed' children) affected by these troubles? How did it impact upon their ideas of identity, class solidarity or their ability to work?

In March 1914 a good 'plain cook' then based in Brixton advertised for a new position. Accustomed to working for 'good families' she was looking for a position that would come with the help of a kitchen maid. Of interest here is the fact that she described herself as a trustworthy and superior '*light coloured* West Indian'.[30] Did the increasing hostility towards black people encourage this kind of personal identification? Like all the women who placed adverts that have been highlighted here she brought attention to the colour of her skin in a public advert. Why did these women do this? Was it because they were hoping to attract employers drawn to particularly 'exotic' employees, or was it a way of making themselves stand out from the crowd? Were there certain positive attributes associated with black female nurses, perhaps a legacy of Mary Seacole? Or was it because these women wanted and could afford to save themselves the humiliation of turning up for another interview when a door would open and then be slammed? How the need to live within such a racially structured society impacted upon individual members of the black community is yet to be fully explored, but the experience of Grace Stevenson suggests there were serious difficulties associated with fighting racial prejudice in everyday life.

Concluding questions

These brief accounts of black women's work highlight some of the questions of race, racism and labour that need to be better explored within histories of work in Britain. New research technologies mean that assumptions that they were not present can no longer be maintained. However, these tools often deliver scant personal information about these women and give us little sense of their position within working-class communities. This chapter has focused on England, but this is not to say that examples are not to be found in Scotland, Wales or Ireland during this period. For example, an advert was placed by Mrs Love who wished to recommend a 'nurse (black)' to a family going to Demerara (now within Guyana). Mrs Love's advert appeared in the *Glasgow Herald* on 21 August 1888, although it appears she lived in Strevithie Mains in St Andrews. Did her 'black nurse' live with her in St Andrews or was she placing the advert on behalf of a friend?

These questions advocate the need for more research on the black population in Britain to be undertaken in spaces not usually associated with a black presence which remains located in urban imaginaries. This essay also excludes the experience of 'Asian' women and there is a need for further research both on the experiences of Asian women at work and the employment networks that might have been developed between black and Asian women.³¹ For the Victorian period the concept of a 'black community' is questionable – there is as yet no evidence to establish its presence. It is difficult to gauge how important such ideas were to the black working class in London. It is also difficult to guess whether they had an identity as a black community, or if they felt any sense of connection with members of the black diaspora and, if so, whether this was one that cut across national and class boundaries. Indeed, it is hard to know whether the women here would have recognised the placing of their lives in a historical geography of black women.

Norma Myers has argued that in England the oppression of black and white means that class solidarity through 'racially mixed' communities was the most likely support network used by black workers. But what were these support networks and how did they manifest themselves? How and why did these relationships seemingly break down in the 1910s and 1920s?³² There is a need for issues of race and racism, in their broadest context including anti-Irish and anti-Semitic forms, to be included in feminist and labour histories. Without these discussions our understandings of class, gender and work will remain incomplete.

Acknowledgements

I would like to thank the Working Lives Research Institute for organising the conference in 2006 where I first gave a version of this chapter, and all those who made comments on it. Since then aspects of it have become part of an essay on Black women and men's work for a special issue of *Immigrants and Minorities*, volume 28, issues 2/3, 2010. I would like to thank Daniel Grey and Mary Davis for our discussions. The research for this chapter was supported by a fellowship from the Economic and Social Research Council.

Notes

1 For examples: Frost, D ed., *Ethnic Labour and British Imperial Trade: A history of ethnic seafarers in the UK*, London: Routledge, 1995.
2 For examples Fryer, P. *Staying Power: The History of Black People in Britain*. London: Pluto Press, 1984; Adi, H. *West Africans in Britain 1900 -1960: Nationalism, Pan-Africanism and Communism*, London: Lawrence and Wishart, 1998; Sherwood, M..Lynching in Britain. *History Today* 49, March 1999.
3 For examples see Green, J. *Black Edwardians: Black People in Britain 1901 – 1914*, London: Frank Cass, 1998, especially pp 42 – 67 on 'The working class'.
4 Lebsock, S. Free Black Women and the Questions of Matriarchy, in Newton, J, Ryan, J. M and Walkowitz, J. eds., *Sex and class in women's history*.

London: Routledge and Kegan Paul, 1983. For references to black women and institutional histories see Bressey, C. 'Forgotten Histories: Three Stories of Black Girls from Barnardo's Victorian Archive', *Women's History Review*, vol. 11, (3) 2002; Bressey, C. 'Invisible Presence: The Whitening of the Black Community in the Historical Imagination of British Archives', *Archivaria* 61, Spring, 2006.

5   For a more diverse reflection upon the black community in Britain see Marsh, J. ed., *Black Victorians: Black People in British Art 1800 – 1900*, Hampshire, Lund Humphries, 2005.

6   Myers, N. *Reconstructing the Black Past: Blacks in Britain 1780-1830*. London: Frank Cass, 1996. For further research on eighteenth century London see Chater, K. 'Black People in England, 1660 – 1807' in Farrell, S., Unwin, M and Walvin, J *The British Slave Trade: Abolition, Parliament and People*, Edinburgh: Edinburgh University Press, 2007.

7   For example archives from Pentonville Prison illustrate that on black (males) prisoners' records there was no mention of their colour from registers recovered between 1876 & 1883. These men were first identified in photographic albums. London Metropolitan Archives PCOM 2/99-PCOM 2/103 & PCOM 2/76-/78.

8   For further biographical information on these sitters see Marsh, J. ed., *Black Victorians: Black People in British Art 1800-1900*, Hampshire, Lund Humphries, 2005.

9   Craik, D. *Olive* (first published 1850) Oxford: Oxford University Press, 1996; Bressey, C. 'Of Africa's brightest ornaments: A short biography of Sarah Forbes Bonetta', *Social and Cultural Geography*, 6, April 2005.

10 Myers, N. 'The Black Presence Through Criminal Records 1780-1830'. *Immigrants and Minorities* 7(3) 1987; Ian Duffield. Skilled Workers or Marginalised Poor? The African Population of the United Kingdom 1812–1852, *Immigrants and Minorities* vol 12, no 3, 1993; For examples see Green, J. *Black Edwardians: Black People in Britain 1901-1914*, London: Frank Cass, 1998.

11 Unless otherwise stated all advertisements come from *The Times*.

12 Gillis, J. 'Servants, sexual relations and the risks of illegitimacy in London, 1801-1900' in J Newton, J. M Ryan, and J Walkowitz, eds., *Sex and class in women's history*. London: Routledge and Kegan Paul, 1983.

13 I am grateful to Nicholas Mays, Deputy Archivist at News International, for the following information. As the Manager of the Classified Advertisement Department noted in a circular letter to prospective advertisers in February 1915, *The Times* was the foremost organ of the *'servant-employing classes'* and *'the most certain way of satisfactorily finding a well-trained servant'*. The regularity of situations required advertising indicates that the cost of advertising was not beyond the means of domestic staff, though the far greater level of 'situations required' advertising reveals the difference between the wealth of the employers and their servants. The *Times'* archive includes about twenty original documents for classified advertisements for situations vacant or required which were inserted in the newspaper between 1833 and

1835. These reveal that the price for 3, 4 and 5 line advertisements was 1s 6d, while 6 and 8 line advertisements cost 5s, the 9 line advertisements cost 6s and the single 11 line advertisement cost 6s 6d. The next evidence is from the copy of the paper published on March 17, 1914 where it states that these advertisements cost one penny a word. The earliest scale of charges Mays has found was printed in the paper in an issue dated December 3, 1919 (page 1), where the scale of charges is 2s for a minimum of two lines with 1s per line payable thereafter.

14 Gillis, J. op. cit.
15 *The Times*, November 14 1900.
16 *The Times*, May 29, 1902.
17 *The Era*, April 1890.
18 *The Era*, May 2 1891.
19 *The Era*, December 1884 and Theatre Royal Canterbury October 1885.
20 *The Era*, March 1887.
21 *The Era*, April 1883.
22 *The Era*, August 1885 and the *Western Mail*, August 1891.
23 See Daily *Dispatch* (Manchester), 8 August, 1917; *Empire News*, August 12 1917, original emphasis.
24 *Stratford Express*, July 14, 1917.
25 Quoted in Bourne, S. and Bruce, Esther *Aunt Esther's Story*, London: Hammersmith and Fulham Ethnic Communities Oral History Project, 1996, p. 4.
26 Evans, N. 'Across the Universe: Racial Violence and the Post-War Crisis in Imperial Britain 1919-192?', in *Ethnic Labour and British Imperial Trade: A history of ethnic seafarers in the UK*, London: Routledge, 1995.
27 *Negro Worker*, March 1932.
28 Evans, N op cit.
29 Sherwood, M. 'Lynching in Britain', *History Today* 49, March, 1999.
30 *The Times*, my emphasis.
31 For discussion of the experience of Asian women see Visram, R *Asians in Britain: 400 Years of History*. London: Pluto Press, 2002.
32 For some suggestions see Kirk, N. *Comrades and Cousins: Globalization, workers and labour movements in Britain, the USA and Australia from the 1880s-1914*, London: The Merlin Press, 2003; Marc Brodie, *The Politics of the Poor: The East End of London 1885-1914*, Oxford: Clarendon Press, 2004.

United we stand: class issues in the early British women's Trade Union Movement

Gerry Holloway

Women's participation in the British Trade Union Movement has a long but problematic history. The barriers to women's participation are persistent and are still with us today.[1] The main reason offered is the gendered nature of work where men have been regarded as the primary breadwinners and women's work has been regarded as primarily private and domestic and therefore beyond the remit of union intervention whether the work was paid or unpaid – though there were a few failed attempts to organise domestic workers in the 19th and early 20th centuries. Further, where women have worked in the public sphere they have still been regarded as having primarily a domestic role and their paid work as a necessary evil or undertaken for pin money. This assumption allowed male trade unionists to privilege their own demands at the expense of those of women for decades. Exacerbating this has been the masculinised nature of trade union organization and the focus on male cultural practices such as after work pub meetings that have served to exclude women. Even when large numbers of women have been trade union members, their voices are silenced.

There is a growing literature on the gendered barriers to women's participation in trade unions and some championing of women only organization,[2] but few papers explore the ways that gender and class have operated together as a barrier to women's participation in trade unions. In this chapter I want to examine how the women's trade union movement developed before the First World War. I particularly want to explore the ways that both class and gender shaped the development of the movement and suggest that some of the problems of the organizing women in trade unions were sown in its very early years because of the over-focus of gender issues over class issues in the minds of the organizers of the movement.

Women were involved with the trade union movement throughout the nineteenth century. Indeed, Drake notes examples of women belonging to informal unions in the latter years of the eighteenth century.[3] However, these early examples of women's trade union activity were sporadic and short-lived. The one exception was the textile industry where women joined the unions in large numbers, but there is little evidence to show that women took a lead in either shaping the unions or being able to influence policy-making. Women in the cotton unions were amongst the best paid in the country but, according to Schwarzkopf, this had less to do with their influence in the union than male weavers' fear of being undercut by women workers on low wages.[4]

The first systematic attempt to organise a woman-only umbrella organisation that could represent women clustered in small skills-based unions was the Women's Protective and Provident League [WPPL], which was established in 1874. This organisation came about at a time when the 'Woman Question' was a focus of many people involved in social reform. Women's employment was seen as a burning issue in the later decades of the nineteenth century for both working-class and middle-class women. The notion that all women were oppressed also led some women social reform activists to feel that they had a common bond with working-class women that transcended class affiliations and was expressed in terms of sisterhood. This led reformers to want to set up an organisation that would help working-class women fight for their rights.

The catalyst that led to the establishment of the WPPL was a letter that appeared in *Labour News*. In June 1874, Emma Paterson, an assistant secretary to the Workingmen's Club and Institute Union, wrote this seminal letter which was entitled 'The Position of Working Women and How to Improve It'. It began by examining the shocking case of a woman worker who had starved to death despite being in full-time work. Paterson, who had already worked as a teacher and a bookbinder before becoming a speaker for the suffrage movement, argued that blaming employers who paid starvation wages was counterproductive because they were just responding to market forces. Women needed to organise in trade unions so that they could protect their interests through their own efforts rather than protest against laws that restricted the sort of work they could undertake. Furthermore, until they organized, women would always be at the mercy of their employers and working men would continue to regard them as a depressant on men's wages. However, she warned, male trade unionists who excluded women from their trades because they lowered wages were short-sighted because it was better for men and women to work together to improve working conditions for all workers rather than to promote one group of workers at the expense of the other. That is, male trade unionists ignored class unity at their peril. Further, she concluded that a separate organisation for women would be preferable as it would teach women how to take responsibility for their own actions, be good citizens and not be at the mercy of employers or dependent on male trade unionists.

This letter was well received in social reform circles and a conference was organised to which were invited people involved in the Working Man's Club and Institute Union and the Society for the Promotion of the Employment of Women [SPEW]. At the conference it was mooted that an organisation be established that would educate women in the benefits of union solidarity and offer women a social space in which they could meet, participate in co-operative workshops for unemployed women and find out about training and emigration possibilities.[5] Although Paterson had wanted the organisation to be a national general union, in practice the London-based WPPL never became one; rather it developed as an umbrella organization to promote trade unionism among women working in a range of London-based skilled activities, such as bookbinding, tailoring and upholstery work. A general union was established in Bristol, but a national women's general union was not achieved until 1906 when Mary Macarthur established the National Federation of Women Workers [NFWW].[6]

The aims of the organisation were take from Paterson's experience of working with the Men's Club and with women's rights activists in both Britain and the United States. With Paterson as its secretary, these influences shaped the way that the women's trade union movement would develop. The WPPL, as it's name suggests, was a mixture of a friendly society and trade union, although its founders were always careful to exclude the words 'trade union' as it might have deterred wealthy supporters. This engendered immediate suspicion among some male trade unionists, who were quick to dismiss the League as another middle-class philanthropic endeavour, a charge that was denied fervently by Paterson and her co-workers.[7] Amongst its supporters were several members of the Langham Place-based Society for the Promotion of the Employment Women, including Jessie Boucherett, Emily Faithfull and Caroline Ashurst Biggs. Others influential women's advocates included Frances Power Cobbe, Josephine Butler and Millicent Fawcett. The influence that these equal rights feminists had on the movement was double-edged By equal rights in this context I mean feminists who thought women should work on the same terms as men and should not be subjected to legislation that restricted their work to undertake any types of work. It was useful to have influential people involved with the movement but they pushed the movement in directions that weren't necessarily what working-class women wanted. Crucially, from the outset working-class women were absent from decision-making. Paterson, who was to become the voice of the WPPL, was uncompromising in her stance on equal rights. Equal Pay, no gender-based employment legislation and an end to sexual harassment in the workplace were her three main platforms. In a paper to the Social Science Association in 1874 she made a strong case for equal pay:

> It is said that men are PAID HIGHER WAGES than women because they have FAMILIES TO SUPPORT, but no one ever proposes to pay single men lower wages than married men. WOMEN ARE OFTEN the sole protectors for themselves and their CHILDREN, OR THEIR AGED OR INFIRM PARENTS; yet their earnings are insufficient not only for a support of a family, but also, in many cases, for the barest subsistence of one person.[8] [Emphasis in the original]

This radical position did not reassure male trade unionists, who regarded women as competitors and who were already engaged in a struggle to be recognised as the breadwinners of the family.[9] The tension that emanated from the two opposing factions – male trade unionists and middle-class feminists – who both placed gender before class, was of little help to working-class women who had to constantly struggle against employers *and* working-class men who resented them because they believed women undercut their pay. The identification of Paterson with the arguments of the predominantly middle-class equal rights feminists led to her status as a working woman being ignored or discounted and she was labelled a 'middle-class meddler' by many male trade unionists eager not to address women's real grievances if they clashed with their own interests. To some extent this class epithet had some substance. Equal rights feminists assumed that they knew what was best for women and made policy without proper consultation with the women it affected. Further, the executive committee of the WPPL consisted of mainly middle-class ladies rather than workers, as did the secretaries of the individual unions. For example, Edith Simcox (1844-1901) was the secretary of the Shirt and Collar and Underlinen Makers Society. She wrote for the journal *Nineteenth Century* and associated with the Langham Place Group and the intellectual group around George Eliot.[10]

However, others came from more humble backgrounds. For example, Jeannette Gaurie Wilkinson was the daughter of respectable working-class parents and from the age of seventeen earned her own living as an upholsteress. She sought to improve herself by attending evening classes at the Birkbeck Institute in Chancery Lane so that she could work as a teacher. From 1875 she was also the secretary of the Upholsteresses' Union, representing them nine times at the Trades Union Congress until her death in 1886.[11] Wilkinson was probably the model trade unionist in Paterson's eyes. A woman who had been able to overcome some of the handicaps of her class to become a widely respected member of the growing women's movement of the 1880s, interested both in the unionisation of women and their inclusion in the body politic. Even more importantly, she took an equal rights stance on employment legislation. However, women like Wilkinson were scarce in the newly fledged WPPL, possibly because, as we shall see, the issue of protective or restrictive employment legislation was highly contentious in the 1870s and 1880s.

Paterson was aware that the dominance of middle-class women in the women's trade union movement was a problem and believed that middle-class women putting their organisational skills and leisure time at the disposal of working-class women as they did for women in refuges and penitentiaries could overcome this. Like many feminist activists, she evoked the idea of an essential womanliness which could unite women across the social divide. This idea ignored the power dynamics that operated between women of different classes. The obvious inequality in the relationships between lady social reformers and the women they sought to help was ignored in this proposition. Further, as Fuerer argues, they confounded the problem of what to do about exploitative work practices by regarding the problem as social rather economic.[12]

However, not all women trade unionists believed that the women who organised penitentiaries were the right type of women to encourage working women to be independent and organise autonomously. Even Paterson became impatient towards the end her of her life with middle-class 'do-gooders' who believed it was possible to cure all social evils by 'a half crown and a bunch of grapes'.[13] Philanthropy was to become an anathema to some women trade unionists as it stifled women's anger and ability to resist the role of helpless victim unable to help themselves, a role that such charitable exercises inevitably thrust upon them. Isabella Ford, a protegée of Paterson's[14] writing nearly thirty years later, was even more scathing of what she regarded as the unhelpful intervention of school and Sunday school teachers, who tried to impose their own values on working girls.

In the early 1890s Ford, like Paterson, believed that legislation without unionisation was ineffectual and that women needed a 'well-organised rebellion'[15] to change the appalling lives most working women led. The notion of 'well-organised rebellion' reflected Ford's feminist definition of female responsibility that extended beyond the home. Although Paterson agreed that women had a place in the public world, she did not share Ford's socialist leanings and, consequently, she failed to appreciate that class antagonism was inherent to the capitalist system and underplayed the differences between women of different classes. She believed that there should be an entente cordiale between worker, employer and consumer and the role of the union was to keep the balance right.[16]

The liberal ideology that underpinned this notion showed the weakness of the WPPL from the outset as it failed to grapple with the problem of exploitative employers, both male and female, as well as hostile male trade unionists. This attitude also meant that the WPPL did not provide strike funds and, indeed, actively discouraged strikes. Ford and other socialist women felt that this position was never going to appeal to the large number of working women beyond the respectable craft unions.[17]

From its earliest days, even within the WPPL there was dissent between the leadership and the membership, but at least the leadership did try to represent the membership's wishes, even if they differed from their own. The Protective Legislation debate was raging furiously in the 1870s. In 1875, Paterson and others gave evidence to the Royal Commission on the Factory and Workshops Acts. This Commission was enquiring into limiting the length of the working day for women. The WPPL policy was against this move but it did not carry its members with it. Paterson was asked if the members objected to a limitation and she replied:

> I do not say that they all object; our league committee thinks that it is objectionable, but I do not think that the workers generally at present do, although I believe that they are now beginning to see the great value of combination for these purposes, and that very soon they will be in such a position as not to require legal interference, and not to wish for it.[18]

Tensions were obviously present at this first attempt of the League to act as a representative of working women. The members did not appreciate the fine points of equal rights feminist thinking. However, the League ploughed ahead assuming that it was merely a question of educating the membership rather than listening to and reflecting their views.[19] In the future movement they did not always solicit working-class women's opinions at all but imposed policy from above. Unfortunately for the Executive, it was never possible to mobilise working women in the large numbers needed to obviate the need for legislation to protect them. One possible reason for the difficulty in mobilising women was that they welcomed the legislation as the best in the short term and in the day-to-day struggle to survive had little inclination to fight for the abstract benefits of power through unionisation. Another issue that may have discouraged women from joining the WPPL unions was the benefits offered to them. Although the WPPL conceded that as women earned less than men they could not be expected to pay the same membership rates, they made no other concessions to gender difference. Consequently, no contributions were refunded to women who gave up work on marriage and there was no provision for women to re-enter the union after their childrearing years.[20] This policy, of course, corresponded with the WPPL's equal rights stance. However, as previously mentioned, the membership of the unions did not necessarily share these beliefs and possibly, like the woman bookbinder appearing before the Royal Commission of Labour in 1892, felt that, as there were no special benefits, no strike fund and opposition to protective legislation, there was 'no use in joining, you get nothing out of it'.[21]

Patterson died quite suddenly of diabetes in 1886 and left a huge gap at the head of the WPPL. Her work had prepared the ground for the formation of the women's trade union movement. However, she also helped sow some of the seeds of tension and these were carried forward into the next phase of the movement, the Women's Trade Union League [WTUL]. Despite her efforts to ensure that the membership could express their views at meetings with government bodies and the TUC, the organisation of the WPPL was by no means democratic. The Executive was a close, self-appointed middle-class dominated clique and there was no decision-making machinery to decide policy. This lack of democracy allowed critics to dismiss the movement as a 'middle-class enterprise' and probably discouraged more working women than it attracted to becoming activists. Moreover, like her future successor Mary Macarthur, Paterson did not find delegation easy. She ran the organisation almost single-handedly, including writing and editing the *Woman's Union Journal*, the organ of the movement, and running the savings bank and social club. This element of 'rule from above' made it difficult to ascertain what the rank-and-file wanted, especially when the membership expanded into thousands rather than hundreds. Dilke and Macarthur tended to carry on this practice during their leadership of the WTUL.

Paterson predeceased the rise of New Unionism and some of her ideas developed primarily from a liberal rather than socialist ideology. In line with her liberal outlook, Paterson's brand of feminism concentrated on the issue of gender and underplayed the importance of class in the movement. For Paterson, sisterhood and self-help were the keywords to helping working-class women improve their lot. She believed that middle-class women could help working-class women to organise, so that they had the power to choose how long they would work and in what trades. In this analysis, the state was tyrannical. Indeed, when the Women's Trade Union League under Lady Dilke changed its policy towards protective legislation, Heather-Bigg, Boucherett and Blackburn founded the Women's Employment Defence League to carry on the opposition to state intervention.[22] Mid Victorian feminists justifiably saw the law as inequitable to women. They had no say in its making and were often its victims as their campaigns to repeal the Contagious Diseases Acts and marriage laws indicate. However, later feminists were to turn increasingly to the 'tyrant' state to remedy their ills. Victorian feminists also used a notion of sisterhood to denote a feeling of solidarity with working-class women but this notion of sisterhood did not mean that they regarded all women as equal. Feminists appear to have regarded their poorer sisters as younger, more vulnerable sisters in need of big sister's guidance and advice. Not many working-class women would have been happy with such a role and some even regarded themselves as much better equipped to deal with life than middle-class ladies.[23] Unlike Ford, Paterson and others in the WPPL did not develop a class analysis that took into account the possibility that the different values of the masses of working-class women were as valid as those of the middle classes. This was not a bias confined to equal-rights feminists; many middle-class activists found it difficult to appreciate the different cultural values of the working classes and this gap between theory and experience was crucial to the movement.

Before the 1880s, unions focused on skilled work. This was, of course, impractical for the vast majority of women, whose work was considered unskilled and casual. Furthermore, working women tended to regard their working life as a necessary interlude between school and marriage and therefore were less interested in the long-term benefits of trade unionism. Both Jeannette Wilkinson and Emma Paterson were exceptional working women. They both grew up in families that had valued the importance of education for girls. Neither woman had children to care for. Consequently, their project to mould working women into their own vision of the female worker and citizen, and to work with them to improve the lot of all workers, was fraught with difficulties. Despite their experiences as workers, it was still difficult for them to closely identify with the masses of under-educated, overworked, impoverished women who, both before and after marriage, had to bear the burden of industrial and domestic work. The WPPL was a small organisation but at least it was a beginning. Its work was carried on by a new generation of social reformers many of whom had their roots in socialist politics. It was Lady Dilke, Isabella Ford, Clementina Black and the younger women such as Mary Macarthur, who were to develop and transform some of Paterson's ideas and increase the numbers of women trade unionists.

If we consider organisational structures and practices, we can see that the Women Trade Union League did not break completely with the WPPL, and indeed the same networks that supported the WPPL continued to some extent to support the Women's Trade Union League and other organisations within the wider Industrial Women's Movement. Losing Paterson was a setback for the WPPL and for a while it was adrift. The secretaryship fell to socialist women, firstly, temporarily to Edith Simcox and then to Clementina Black.[24] These appointments indicate that the WPPL was trying to break with the liberal, 'equal rights' politics of Emma Paterson.[25] Black's involvement with the women's movement sprang largely from her interest in Fabian socialism.[26] However, Black's appointment was short-lived. For Black, unionisation was not enough to change working women's lives. Her involvement with the Fabians and her career as a writer taught her that investigation and inquiry were the key elements in gaining theoretical knowledge of the conditions of workers, and without this knowledge change was impossible. Black's socialist ideas were an anathema to the old guard of the WPPL committee.[27] Black's involvement with the flamboyant socialist Annie Besant during the Matchgirls' Strike in 1888 heightened tensions within the WPPL. There is a terse note in the minutes of the organisation, which indicates that the committee did not approve of Black's involvement with the strikers, and the WPPL committee voted to take no active part in the campaign beyond boycotting the firm's matches.[28] Despite this setback in challenging the old guard, the WPPL changed its name to the Women's Trade Union League in 1889. Along with the change in name, there was a change in policy. Lady Dilke, the League's president, sought to capitalise on her extensive political network and proposed a scheme for the affiliation of provincial unions to the WTUL. Under this scheme, the WTUL offered affiliation for a small annual fee to any trade union admitting women to its membership. Mixed unions took up this offer and the WTUL expanded steadily. By 1895, twelve unions had affiliated to the WTUL and this meant that 8,000 women were members.[29] However, this was still a mere drop in the ocean when it came to the total number of women members of all trade unions which, excluding teachers and professional workers, rose from around 37,000 in 1886 to around 118,000 in 1896.[30] By the end of the century, the aims of the WTUL were very clear. Firstly, it existed to support the organization of women's trade unions or strengthen existing ones around the country. Secondly, it acted as a representative of women trade unionists at parliamentary committees and other legislative bodies. It also undertook to support members in complaints of breaches of factory and public health legislation. Finally, it offered members a social space by helping them to establish working women's clubs such as the Paterson Working Women's Club that met at the League offices in London.[31]

The growth in organization in the provinces meant an increased demand for women speakers and organizers. The WTUL adopted a scheme of annual tours by which organizers could visit districts periodically to offer help and encouragement. The organizer would call a meeting at a local club or meeting room, and later, when working-class women were more commonly employed as organizers, at the factory gate.

The organizer's task was to enumerate the benefits of unionism and help in the early stages of establishing a union.[32] In 1892, the WTUL adopted the practice of employing working women as organizers. The first paid organizer was Annie Marland. These women were not elected representatives of unions but were appointed by the Committee of the WTUL and later, the National Federation of Women Workers. This practice did nothing to enhance ideas of democracy and empowerment amongst union members. The choice of the Committee would not necessarily reflect the wishes of the membership and led to the appointment of educated women rather than industrial women later on.[33] Rubinstein suggests that Lady Dilke decided to employ Marland following a speech she made at the Women's Liberal Federation in 1891 defending unions against the charge of trying to limit women's employment.[34] However, it is possible that Marland was employed as an experiment – one that was to prove successful and led to the employment of more working-class organizers for a time.

Firstly, the committee probably realized that there was resistance from working women in accepting advice from educated women who had no 'hands on' industrial experience. Secondly, the type of help given by some middle-class ladies was considered dubious. Ben Tillett attacked 'Lady Bountifuls' who took up disputes with employers and negotiated with them on behalf of their less 'able' working sisters, leaving the workers to feel grateful and dependent on the largesse of such women. Tillett, like many supportive Labour men, challenged equality advocates, regarding them as at best rather misguided philanthropists. He argued that the 'Lady Bountifuls' methods did not teach working women organisational skills and therefore they remained in the same vulnerable position they occupied before the dispute.[35] Following on from the older WPPL practice of trying to encourage able working women to join unions, the Committee of the WTUL was bound to be sensitive to such criticism. Under the leadership of Lady Dilke, it was increasingly willing to accept a certain amount of change, although the overarching hierarchy of a middle-class executive deciding policy remained in place. Liddington and Norris make a further interesting point on this use of working-class women as organizers in the trade union movement. They argue that it proved a great help to the suffrage movement, as these women were often speakers for both causes.[36] Looking at the working-class women who worked as organisers during the 1890s and early 1900s does bear this argument out. Annie Marland does not appear to have been involved in any suffrage work, but Helen Silcock, Julia Varley, Sarah Reddish, Sarah Dickenson and, later, Ada Nield Chew were all active trade unionists and suffragists. They were certainly the type of women that Emma Paterson had hoped would lead the movement. However, in the years leading up to the First World War, the WTUL moved back to employing educated ladies as their organisers.

Around the same time that the WPPL became the WTUL, Clementina Black left the organisation to establish with other socialists the Women's Trade Union Association (WTUA). This organisation was part of the New Unionism movement of the late 1890s and early 1900s. The unions it organised tended to be in the unskilled, largely casual trades such as rope making and food manufacturing. Consequently it struggled and folded after five years.[37] However, during its short existence it tried to include working women on the Committee and also employed Clara James, a working woman, as an organiser. It was succeeded by the Women's Industrial Council (WIC), an investigative organisation which also employed, where possible, working-class women such as James, Margaret Bondfield and Amie Hicks to investigate women's trades.[38] But given the nature of the work – investigators had to have quite a high degree of literacy – and the need to rely on volunteers rather than paid workers, the WTUA and later the WIC were also organised by middle-class reformers and, like the WTUL, often brought middle-class values into debates and campaigns, and policy was made without proper consultation with the women concerned.[39]

During the early years of the twentieth century, the WTUL grew steadily. By 1902 there were between 40,000 and 50,000 members.[40] The WTUL worked closely with the women factory inspectors whose prosecutions were published in the *Women's Trade Union Review*. Further, sympathetic MPs, such as Sir Charles Dilke, asked questions in the House of Commons on behalf of the WTUL and campaigned for various reforms. In 1903 Mary Macarthur, on Margaret Bondfield's recommendation, became the new general secretary. Under Macarthur's evangelising secretaryship the WTUL flourished and within two years the membership had increased to 70,000.[41] Macarthur was a worker, albeit a white collar one, and this contributed to her popularity with working women. She had been a bookkeeper in her father's shop, and was involved in trade unionism from an early age.[42] Therefore, unlike other leaders in the WTUL, she had practical experience of being a worker and member of a union at branch level. This led to her being less interested in the investigative and theoretical work than propaganda and organisation. Despite the large number of women now affiliated to the WTUL, it was still a small proportion of the potential number of women who could join a union. In 1906, around 167,000 women were unionised, mostly textile workers and in mixed unions. As Drake points out many of the non-unionised women were domestic servants (nearly 1.4 million in 1911) or dressmakers in very small shops and therefore almost impossible to organise. One problem was that women had been approaching the WTUL asking to join unions only to discover that their trade did not admit women or there was no union at all for their trade.[43] Macarthur argued that a general union for women, as originally suggested by Paterson, would aid the organisation of these women. So the WTUL formed the National Federation of Women Workers (NFWW) in 1906. The new union differed from other women's unions because the subscriptions were low, there was a strike fund indicating that strikes were no longer the anathema they had once been and the membership was open to all women workers regardless of skills. Macarthur was the prime mover behind this change, believing that unskilled women needed to identify and unite with a large organisation that would have a more powerful voice than the small, localised unions that withered and died shortly after the organiser left the area.[44] Further, the employment patterns of women working in, for example, the semi-skilled trades in South and East London meant that women moved from factory to factory as work was available, which made it difficult to organise them on traditional lines. Moreover, it was still necessary to circumvent male prejudice against women joining existing unions. Macarthur was successful in organising not only the unskilled factory workers, but also other groups that had been difficult to organise: white-collar workers such as telephone operators and postal sorters at a time when the numbers of women clerical workers was rising rapidly. Inevitably, the NFWW was closely linked to the WTUL. Up to 1908 Macarthur was the secretary of both. Three members of the WTUL were elected to serve as advisory members on the NFWW's executive. Nevertheless, the NFWW was a union in its own right and was affiliated to the TUC and the General Federation of Trade Unions. Despite the close relationship with the WTUL, the NFWW differed most markedly in the way it organised. Organisation often first occurred when workers were on strike and the NFWW supported strikers much more actively than the WTUL. Drake argues that this was a deliberate policy of Macarthur's, which asserted that a strike was the perfect opportunity to demonstrate to both women and employers the benefits of unionisation. By the end of the first year of its existence, the NFWW had over 2,000 members and 17 branches in England and Scotland and by 1914 it had 20,000 members. The NFWW concentrated on women's low pay rather than striving for equal pay.

Macarthur was an advocate of minimum wage policy and used her position in the WTUL to campaign in the Anti-Sweating League for the Trades Board Act, which was passed in 1909, although not all activists supported this policy. This Act established regulatory boards and minimum rates of pay in specific trades. At first, these were chain making, lace making, box making and readymade clothing but more trades were later included. All areas that were notoriously underpaid. However, as Thom has pointed out, the minimum wage soon became the maximum and the Act in some ways undermined the notion that unionisation was the way to strengthen women's bargaining power.[45] However, it could be argued that the Act strengthened women's ability to bargain, especially if they used it and strike action to increase their wages. For example, in 1911 chain makers in the Cradley Heath area of Birmingham struck for the immediate implementation of a pay rise, although the Act gave the employers six months to implement the rise. Supported by the NFWW, WTUL and the Anti-Sweating League, women in small, scattered workshops were able to maintain a sustained strike to achieve their aims and, importantly, to encourage workers in other trades to follow suit.[46]

Boston argues that the early days of the women's trade union movement were a 'strange mixture of feminism, trade-unionism and middle-class attitudes' influenced partly by the ideas and character of Emma Paterson and partly by the ideas of the trade union movement at that time.[47] This characteristic continued into the reigns of Lady Dilke and Mary Macarthur, whose personalities shaped the both organisation and policy. However, as I have argued, this concentration of power at the top of the union hierarchy left the membership too dependent on charismatic or dominant leaders.[48] One problem for the movement was the tension between the leadership wanting to instil middle-class ideas of self-reliance on working-class women while still wanting to have the power to devise and shape policy. For women who had only recently tasted limited power themselves, enabling others was a testing task. Thom has argued that the ideology of the leadership of women's trade unionism offered limited constructions of working-class women.[49] This meant that leaders failed to consult working women and often suggested policy that was not always in working women's best interest. Evidence of this can be seen in the debates around protective legislation, whether married women should work and what sort of work would be suitable.[50] Further, underlying class assumptions about working women's abilities to take on positions of responsibility meant that opportunities were missed for encouraging able working women to take leading roles in the movement, so the emergence of working-class women as leaders was limited. The type of feminism found in the movement also changed over time. By the early 1900s Paterson's strong equal rights stance was replaced by Macarthur's more socialist one. As a member of the Labour Party, Macarthur supported Labour's position on the importance of the breadwinning male and the homemaking female. Despite being a working wife and mother herself, she believed that the wife's place was in the home and that women's domestic role was paramount, despite her ardent support for women workers.

Attempts to unionise working-class women before the First World War were problematic partly because of male resistance to women joining existing unions, partly because working women were usually in short term jobs rather than long term trades or careers and partly because the leadership failed to give them an adequate voice in making union policy. Behind the stereotype of the working-class woman as the passive victim of capitalist exploitation lie alternative stories. As Louise Raw has shown in this book, the women involved in the Bryant and May dispute were tough and resourceful and were not, as the legend tells us, led by Annie Besant. Individual working women do loom out of the shadows of their more articulate, educated sisters and worked long hours traipsing round the country organising working women in unions. But although there was some will to employ working women to do this work, there was never a process in place that would enable the movement to develop a large cohort of paid working women organisers. Nor were the women paid in this role given any say in the policy-making process of the movement.

Today it is recognised that women play an important part in the trade union movement and women's needs are beginning to be recognised as part of the agenda. However, feminist industrial relations literature still shows that women are under represented in union decision-making processes.[51] Women only training courses for activists are recommended as one way forward. It is interesting to note that over eighty years after the WTUL was merged with the National Union of General and Municipal Workers in 1921, separatism is once again being mooted as a way of encouraging women to become trade union activists. The movement is recognising that alongside a trade union identity there is also a need for a gender identity. However, it is to be hoped that in the women only union courses that are taking place today, there will be room for discussion on how the identities of class and gender intersect and that there is a real move to enable the women on the shop floor to participate in the decision-making processes of the union rather than their more highly educated middle-class sisters making the decisions for them.[52] We need to look to the past for sites of identification and models to learn from. Further, we need to uncover the histories of how women of different classes worked together, successfully or otherwise.

Notes

1   For histories of women's involvement in trade unions see for example, Pinchbeck, *Women in Trade Unions*, London: Virago, 1984; Lewenhak, S. *Women and Trade Unions: An Outline History of Women in the British Trade Union Movement*, London: Ernest Benn Ltd, 1977 and Boston, S. *Women Workers and the Trade Unions*, London: Davies-Poynter 1980.
2   Kirton, G. *The Making of Women Trade Unionists*, Aldershot: Ashgate, 2006.
3   Drake, p. 3.
4   Schwarzkopf, J. *Unpicking Gender: The Social Construction of Gender in the Lancashire Cotton Weaving Industry, 1880-1914*, Aldershot: Ashgate, 2004, p. 22.
5   Paterson, E. 'The Position of Working Women and How to Improve It', *Labour News*, June 1874. This is also reproduced in Goldman, Harold, *Emma Paterson*, London: Lawrence & Wishart, 1974.
6   Drake, p. 12.
7   See Fuerer, R. 'The Meaning of Sisterhood": The British Women's Movement and Protective Labour Legislation, 1870-1900' in *Victorian Studies*, 31, 2, Winter 1988, p. 240 for a discussion of how the WPPL reflected feminist-philanthropic biases.
8   Paterson, E. 'The Industrial Position of Women engaged in Handicrafts and other Industrial Pursuits', *Englishwoman's Review*, January XXI (NS), 1875, p. 3.
9   For a discussion of the male breadwinner/working wife question see Holloway, G. '"Let the Women be Alive"! The Construction of the Married Working Woman in the Industrial Women's Movement, 1890-1914', in Yeo, E.J. [ed.] *Radical Femininity: Self-representation in the Public Sphere*, Manchester: Manchester University Press, 1998.
10 Mackenzie, K. A. *Edith Simcox and George Eliot*, Oxford: Oxford University Press, 1961, is primarily concerned with her emotional dependence on George Eliot rather than her own work in trade unionism and feminism. For further information on Edith Simcox see Fulmer, C. M. and Barfield, M. E. [eds] *A*

Monument to the Memory of George Eliot: Edith J Simcox's Autobiography of a Shirtmaker, Garland, 1998.
11   *Englishwoman's Review*, May 1886, p. 227.
12   Fuerer, p. 234.
13   *Women's Union Journal*, December 1886, quoted in Bellamy and Schmiechen (1977) p. 169.
14   Ford's mother was a friend of Emma Paterson and Paterson first encouraged Ford to help the Leeds Tailoresses in 1885. See *Women's Union Journal*, July 1885 and Hannam, J. *Isabella Ford*, Oxford: Blackwell, 1989, p. 31.
15   Ford I. O., *Women's Wages and the Conditions under which they are earned*, London: Humanitarian League, 1893, p. 10.
16   WPPL *Annual Report* 1875.
17   However, see Levine, P., *Feminist Lives in Victorian Britain*, Oxford: Basil Blackwell, 1990, chapter 8, for another reading of middle-class activity in the WPPL.
18   Evidence to the Royal Commission on Factory and Workshops Acts, 1876, XXX, q.435.
19   This evidence suggests that Levine rather overplays the concord between individualist feminists and working-class women over protective legislation. Levine, chap. 8.
20   Olcott, p. 35.
21   Royal Commission of Labour, *Minutes of Evidence and Appendices*, c.6708-VI, 1892, q. 8012 quoted in Olcott p. 39. Also see Bornat, J. 'Lost Leaders: Women, Trade Unionism and the case of the General Union of Textile Workers, 1875-1914', in John, A.V. *Unequal Opportunities: Women's Employment in Britain, 1800-1918*, London: Routledge and Kegan Paul, 1986, pp.207-233 for a study focused in Yorkshire.
22   See Malcolmson, P. *English Laundresses: A Social History*, Urbana, University of Illinois Press,1986 p.51 and Levine (op cit)1990, p.163.
23   For example, see Stanley, L. ed.] *The Diaries of Hannah Culwick: Victorian Maidservant*, London: Virago, 1984.
24   Mackenzie, 1961.
25   For an account of this struggle see *Women's Union Journal* October 1886; Tsukuki, C. *The Life of Eleanor Marx* Oxford: Oxford University Press, 1967 p.61. For an argument that centres the protective legislation debate as crucial to this struggle, see Fuerer [1988].
26   Cameron, M. 'Clementina Black: A Character Sketch', *Young Woman* vol.1 June 1892 pp. 315-6 and Willard, F. E. 'Questions of the Day: An Interview with Clementina Black' *Women's Signal* vol. IV, No.87 29 August 1895.
27   See Caine, C. *Victorian Feminists* Oxford, Oxford University Press, 1992, pp. 224-5 for a discussion of Millicent Fawcett and Josephine Butler's distaste of trade unions although they both supported the WPPL.
28   *Women's Union Journal* July 1888 and WPPL *Annual Report* 1889, p. 5. Also Edith Simcox represented the Matchworkers Union at the International Trades Union Congress in London in November 1888. Nethercott, A. H. *The First Five Lives of Annie Besant*, London: Hart Davies, 1961, pp. 269-75.
29   WTUL, *Twentieth Annual Report*, 1895.

30 Drake, p. 30 and Table I.
31 WTUL, *Twenty-Sixth Annual Report*, 1899.
32 Bulley, A. and Whiteley, M., *Woman's Work*, London: Methuen, 1894, pp. 81-2.
33 For a discussion of this see Thom's article in John, 1986, pp. 261-289.
34 See Rubinstein, p. 125.
35 *Women's Trade Union Review*, Oct 1896.
36 Liddington, J. & Norris, J. *One Hand Tied Behind Us: The Rise of the Women's Suffrage Movement* London: Virago, 1978, p. 98.
37 For the history of the Women's Trade Union Association and the investigative organisation, the Women's Industrial Council, that it later became see Mappen, E. *Helping Women at Work: The Women's Industrial Council, 1889-1914*, London: Hutchinson, 1985.
38 Examples of the investigative work that WIC undertook include Black, C. *Sweated Industry and the Mininum Wage*, London: Duckworth and Co, 1907 and Black, C. *Married Women's Work*, London: G. Bell & Son,1915 and the WIC's organ the *Women's Industrial News* is full of reports of the numerous other investigations undertaken by the WIC.
39 This is an example of middle class activists struggling over the question of minimum wage legislation in the sweated labour campaign. Black and Mary Macarthur were in favour but Margaret MacDonald opposed this policy favouring licensing of home work. The women on sweated pay were not consulted. For a full discussion of this issue see Mappen, E.F. 'Strategists for Change: Social Feminist Approaches to the Problems of Women's Work' in John, 1986.
40 *Reformers Yearbook*, 1902, p. 62.
41 Martin, D. E. 'Mary Macarthur (1880-1921) Trade Union Organiser' in *Dictionary of Labour Biography* Vol. II, 1974, p.256. Drake, B. *Women in Trades Unions*, London: Virago, 1984 claims that by 1906 there were 118,000 women trade union members, over 80 per cent of them working in textiles, p. 30.
42 Martin, p. 255.
43 Thom in John, p. 268.
44 Boston, p. 61
45 Thom in John, pp. 273-275
46 Boston, pp. 65-7
47 Boston, p. 31
48 Drake, p. 46; Thom in John, pp. 277-8.
49 Thom in John, passim.
50 Holloway in Yeo.
51 Kirton, p. xiv.
52 Kirton, p. 158.

The women on strike outside the factory, July 1888
Courtesy of the People's History Museum, Manchester

The strike committee, with Annie Besant at the lectern next to Herbert Burrowes
Courtesy of the People's History Museum, Manchester

Striking a light: Bryant & May revisited

Louise Raw

Introduction

The principal streets and thoroughfares of East London, especially the Mile End Road have been swarmed with the girls who were generally accompanied by men of the lowest orders. Some of the girls marched up and down the streets soliciting coppers, and were quite willing to pour their tale of hardships into every sympathetic ear.

On Tuesday morning, opposite the Earl Grey, a vanload of pink roses drew up and it was presently surrounded by some 200 of the girls. The roses were flung into the street by the two men... it afterwards appeared that the roses had been sent down by a supporter... to be worn by the strikers as badges.[1]

So, on July 14th 1888, the *East London Advertiser* described the spectacle of Bryant & May's matchworkers on strike. Their dispute received considerable media and public attention in its day; in terms of popular appeal, it had everything: the fairytale quality of a struggle between the powerful and the poor; and a mostly young and female workforce with the photogenically waif-like appeal of Hans Christian Anderson's 'Little Matchgirl', a Victorian classic. Before the strike the matchworkers had been dismissed as part of the 'lowest strata of society'[2]: during it they were the subjects of Parliamentary questions. They earned the dubious accolade of being threatened by the serial killer 'Jack the Ripper', or someone claiming to be him[3], and attracted the more wholesome attention of socialist luminaries like Bernard Shaw, William Morris, Eleanor Marx, and, of course, Annie Besant, the Fabian journalist and, according to all previous sources, the woman who organised and led the matchwomen.

No wonder, then, that the matchworkers captured the public imagination, and have not relinquished their hold on it yet: plays and musicals were being written about them well into the 1960s (to the chagrin of Bryant & May, who remained litigiously sensitive on the subject of 19th century industrial relations for decades), and are still performed today.[4]

In the field of labour history, the dispute has been sufficiently written about to provide an exception to the rule that the lives and experiences of most working-class women remain 'hidden from history'[5]: it is almost a cliché of the genre. Almost a century later Sarah Boston, preparing to write a general history of women and trade unions, found that the general reaction to her subject was, 'Oh…the Matchgirls' strike and all that?'[6] and that even those with an otherwise good knowledge of labour history could rarely name any other examples of industrial action by women.[7]

For many labour historians this is exactly the problem: what the matchwomen have gained in fame, they have lost in credibility. History is, as Carr reminds us, more than a neutral record of the past: only certain events are selected from the great morass of human experience to be elevated to the status of 'historical fact'.[8] The matchwomen's strike, to many scholars, achieved this under false pretences, riding into the history books on the coat-tails of New Unionism proper, when the women themselves were externally-organised and 'too different' a group of workers to have influenced the Beckton gasworkers or '89 dock strikers.[9]

Accordingly, although historians seem unable to resist the appeal of the matchwomen's story and most histories of the period include it, it has never been seriously examined. No single study has previously been devoted to it, despite the multitude of volumes on the leaders of the dock strike, and indeed Besant. Despite a wealth of primary evidence, countless newspaper reports, a large company archive, and a surviving strike fund register listing 700 strikers, secondary accounts are usually brief, often confused or conflicting, and emphasise outside agency. Pelling tells us only that 'a few dozen' women struck successfully '…with the help of Mrs Besant and other socialists', when it was in fact 1,400.[10] Morton and Tate state that 700 women came out on strike, and that 'Mrs Besant and another socialist, Herbert Burrows…organised them' after 'Mrs. Besant published a startling exposure of their conditions in the link in *July*'[11] (rather than June). Soldon agrees that 'Mrs Besant deserves the lion's share of the credit' for the dispute, and says that the women 'went on strike after hearing *(her)*'.[12] In fact, there is no evidence that she ever addressed them as a group of workers before the strike. 'In *'Labour's Turning Point'*, Eric Hobsbawm writes that the strike was won '…largely with the help of the Socialists'.[13] Had their strike indeed been as marginal as many suggest, this would perhaps be no tragedy, with so many lives still awaiting rescue from the 'enormous condescension of posterity'.[14]

In fact, the orthodox version of events is seriously flawed, and should not have stood unchallenged for so long. History has not hidden the matchwomen, but it has done them a great disservice.

This chapter will present a reconstruction of the events of the strike drawn from primary evidence, using a timeline constructed for the purpose by plotting all available accounts onto a calendar of the relevant days and weeks, to arrive at the most likely sequence. Besant's voice will not be ignored, but nor will it be allowed to completely shape the narrative, as has so often been the case. The findings submitted in this chapter give surprising but sufficiently overwhelming evidence about the true causes, and leaders, of the strike to challenge not just the received wisdom on this one dispute, but what we understand about the beginnings of Britain's general trade union movement.

'None of the girls would ever say a good word about their employer'[15] – the Matchwomen and Bryant & May

From late June 1888, the matchworks in Fairfield Road had been in an uproar. On June 23 the *Link*, Annie Besant and Herbert Burrows' weekly political paper, published Besant's exposé of the exceptionally low wages and dangerous working conditions at Fairfield. As Besant was quick to point out, these contrasted uncomfortably with the firm's immense profitability and the 'monster dividends' paid to its shareholders.[16] Heightening the discomfort were the firms' status and public image, and also the well-known political leanings of the company's directors.

Bryant & May was a household name, its products ubiquitous in Victorian Britain. Still in family hands in 1888, it had risen to great heights from its beginnings in the 1830s.

William Bryant was the son of a starch and polish-maker from Devon, and he and May, a tea dealer, had set up a general merchants' business in 1839. Originally, they imported the matches they sold from Sweden, but took out their own patent in 1855 when the growing British demand for safety matches outstripped the Swedish supply.

Six years later the men leased the 'Fairfield Works' at Bow, which consisted of three former factories, including a crinoline manufacturers. By 1876 a visitor to the factory noted that, including homeworkers and workers at other locations in East London, Bryant & May employed around 5,000 people in total. They were East London's largest employer of casual female labour, the docks being the male equivalent.[17]

The considerably more ruthless Bryant family eventually forced May out.[18] By 1887, founder's son and company director Wilberforce Bryant had attained a personal fortune sufficient to purchase a vast country estate, where prominent members of the Liberal party, assiduously courted by the company, were entertained.[19]

Bryant & May had become a limited company in 1884. By then it was an active cartel, buying out its rivals (though not always changing their names) and powerful enough to fix wage rates as it chose, forcing them down to such an extent that some of those Besant interviewed in 1888 were earning less than ten years beforehand.[20] Their commercial success and powerful parliamentary friends may have led the firm to feel, by the time of the strike, virtually unassailable. However, a chain of events was in motion which would lead, if not to their downfall, to considerable public embarrassment, and their workforce's unexpected victory.

'White Slavery in London'

London had, of course, always had an eastern quarter, but not until the 1880s did it acquire an 'East End'.[21] Who coined the term isn't known, but its negative connotations were clearly understood:

> A shabby man from Paddington, St. Marylebone or Battersea might pass muster as one of the respectable poor. But the same man coming from Bethnal Green, Shadwell or Wapping was an "East Ender", the box of...bug powder must be reached for, and the spoons locked up.[22]

The area became stigmatised as the home of the disreputable poor, and also as a centre of casual and 'sweated' labour.[23] 'Sweating' was by no means a new feature of the late Victorian period, but would prove to have made its transition into new industries, as well as continuing to thrive in the old.[24]

In February 1886 economic depression was at a peak, and a harsh winter had caused exceptional distress in outdoor trades. A meeting on 'Free Trade' lead to a supposed riot as the fury and despair of the crowd spilled over into Pall Mall, The *Times* considered the situation more dangerous than in the 'revolutionary year' of 1848, reporting that the West End had been 'for a couple of hours in the hands of the mob'.[25] The gates of Downing Street were shut and troops confined to barracks.

Potentially adding to both the fear and guilt of the more affluent was increasing evidence that casual and sweated labourers were not the shiftless 'roughs' of popular stereotype, but men and women who were working themselves sometimes literally to death in East London docks, homes and factories, so close to the affluence and luxury of the West End.[26]

In 1887 both the Board of Trade and the Lancet carried out their own investigations into sweating, and in early 1888 MPs representing East

London constituencies urged the government to take action, leading to the establishment of a House of Lords' Select Committee. Investigations would show a large proportion of sweated workers to be female and, with the exception of construction and dock labour, the Committee would concentrate exclusively on women's work. In the course of the enquiry the Reverend Adamson, vicar of Old Ford where many match-women lived, gave evidence on their behalf, and spoke of the exceptionally low wages paid by Bryant and May. (The company responded furiously, suggesting that '…the Revd. Adamson ought to be locked up for three months for making assertions simply based on hearsay.)[27] This exchange was reported in the media, and Adamson's claims discussed at a Fabian meeting; and this is how the matchwomen first came to the attention of Annie Besant.

Resolving to investigate, she interviewed a handful of women outside Fairfield and found reports of their exploitation to have been entirely accurate. Her resulting piece 'White Slavery in London'[28] was a fearless condemnation of their employers, and Besant made sure that the directors were aware of it, telegraphing them notice of its imminent publication. The copy of the *Link* featuring the article is still in the company archives.[29]

Bryant & May moved swiftly to confident rebuttal, threatening Besant with legal action and attempting to force the matchwomen into signing a statement refuting her allegations. However, either all or most refused to do it – a courageous move when, as casual, unorganised workers, they could be summarily dismissed at any time with no redress. Particular pressure was put upon one woman, about whom it is only known that she was 'a pale little person in black',[30] and popular with her workmates. It seems that Bryant & May suspected her of giving evidence to Besant and, when she again refused to sign the prepared statement, she was sacked, allegedly for disobeying a foreman's instructions on a work matter. I believe that she worked in the Victoria building, right in the middle of the huge site, with about three or four hundred other women who, seeing what had happened to her and why, all walked out immediately in solidarity with her.[31]

'One Girl Began'[32]: the Strike

This walk-out seems to have taken place on July 2, a Monday morning.[33] The women immediately assembled a picket line at the gates and waited until the other workers came out on their break. They quickly persuaded most of them to join the protest, and elected a small deputation of six women to put their terms to the company directors. They were now demanding not just the re-instatement of their sacked colleague but improved pay and conditions, and an end to the fines and deductions which were regularly made from their wages.[34] Bryant & May refused to consider their demands – with what words it is not recorded, but a company which had demanded the imprisonment of a gentleman of the cloth was unlikely to have been conciliatory when faced with its own defiant workers. Certainly the strikers would be threatened with dismissal at other points in the dispute. However, far from being intimidated, the women were '…in a great state of excitement and refused to resume work'.[35]

There were soon 1,400 strikers picketing the factory, parading the streets of East London and collecting funds from passers-by. This attracted sufficient attention to draw reporters from the national press to the scene. The *Star*, which would follow the strike closely, was there at the beginning, and its reporter gave his first impressions of the matchwomen: though sympathetic, he was clearly taken aback by the sight of working-class women *en masse*.

> …just like the girls that one reads about in a story of outcast London, clad in old, worn out, faded jackets, or in ragged shawls and bedraggled skirts, with their heads covered with old brown or black straw or felt hats battered into every conceivable shape, they made indeed a strange gathering.[36]

As with the *Advertiser*'s disapproval of the strikers association with men of the 'lowest orders', such accounts are frequently redolent with class and gender judgements: however, as we will see, these same reporters arrived at a truer estimation of the women's achievements than have most modern historians.

By the end of the week, on Friday July 6, the 'whole factory was lying idle'.[37] Mass meetings were being held every day and the women were on the picket line in the early hours of each morning. The strike was attracting the alarmed attention of the establishment as well as the media:

> …eleven hundred employees paraded the streets in the neighbourhood of Bow on Thursday and Friday. A large number of police have had to be stationed in the neighbourhood.[38]

Word had spread to Lewis Lyons, militant secretary of the tailors' union, who came down to the factory and addressed the crowd but was arrested for obstruction.[39] A large crowd of matchwomen surged around the arresting officers, refusing to abandon Lyons and marching with him to the police station 'singing popular songs and cheering him'.[40]

Only now does Annie Besant enter the story, through her own account of her meeting with the strikers. Working upstairs in her offices, she was informed that a delegation of matchwomen had arrived and was asking for her. Confessing herself non-plussed by their appearance, her first concern was that the women were blocking the pavement below, causing 'serious inconvenience',[41] and she sent them down a note to this effect. Then, following '…a little puzzled delay', she agreed to see a small deputation.[42]

Three women, whom Besant describes only as 'respectable'[43], were ushered in, and she asked them why they were there. They told her that they were on strike. That Besant had to be told would be problematic for her reputation as the strike's orchestrator even had this meeting taken place on the first day of the strike, but the timeline, backed by Besant's account, shows that it occurred four days later, on July 6th. Besant cannot, therefore, have been closely monitoring, let alone directing, events – she had somehow missed all the noisy activity of the strike so far, despite receiving a letter from the matchwomen days before, warning her about the bullying at the factory:

Dear Lady they have been trying to get the poor girls to say it is all lies that has been printed and trying to make us sign papers that it is all lies; nobody knows what it is we have put up with and we will not sign them. We thank you very much for the kindness you have shown to us. My dear Lady we hope you will not get into any trouble on our behalf as what you have spoken is quite true.[44]

Besant did not reply or further investigate the situation at the factory. Once aware of the strike, her next move was also surprising. According to the *Star* she went that evening to speak, as planned, at a Fabian meeting on 'art under socialism', giving 'an eloquent speech, and … plea for music as the supreme form in which the art of the future would develop itself'.[45] What she did not apparently do is to mention the strike. This would surely have been the time to celebrate her success, had she deliberately started it, and discuss arrangements for fund raising and the conduct of the dispute in general. Had she done so, the *Star*, something of a champion of the matchwomen, would have almost certainly mentioned it.

In fact, when Besant first publicly commented on the dispute in the *Link*, she expressed regret at the action the women had taken, saying they should have allowed a few of their number to be dismissed rather than take supportive action. She stressed that 'The Girls Will Go Back To Work' and pressed for a legal solution – 'Why Not Prosecute Bryant and May?'.[46] She also called for a consumer boycott of Bryant & May's products – and this kind of middle-class stand-off between socialists and the firm had, I believe, been her original and sole intention when first publishing the exposé: she had never intended to involve the matchwomen themselves, and certainly not anticipated their taking of matters into their own hands.

Besant and the Fabians, far from originating events, now had to struggle to catch up with them. Organising and fund-raising meetings had to be hastily convened; again showing a lack of the foresight expected had experienced political activists planned the strike. Meanwhile, the matchwomen got on with the publicising of their cause. The media had now tagged the dispute 'The Match Girls' Strike',[47] and reported that 'thousands of people' attended the next meeting at the Mile End Waste, 'for the affair has created enormous sensation in the neighbourhood'.[48]

The strikers were 'in good spirits',[49] several of them addressing the crowd, detailing conditions in the factory and their reasons for striking, and 'warmly welcoming' outside speakers: but not until the next day was Besant among them. [50] Even then her speech fell short of the stirring oration which might be expected of a strike's leader. Again urging a boycott of Bryant & May, Besant went on to categorically disassociate herself from the women's actions:

> With regard to the charge that we instigated the strike – although it is a matter of no importance – we beg to say that this statement is absolutely false, nor were we, as asserted, near the factory on the day it commenced.[51]

On Friday July 13 the strike was the subject of a leader in the *Star*, which reported that shareholders were pressuring Bryant & May. No wonder: many were establishment figures who were being made to look hypocritical:

> Messrs Bryant & May are well known Liberals and have…paraded their Liberalism before the world…more than one shareholder is a well-known member of parliament who in other matters profess to champion the cause of the poor and the oppressed. How could they meet their constituents with large dividends in their pockets… when their employees in the east of London existed on next to starvation wages?[52]

The London Trades Council (LTC), an organisation which had previously 'shunned unskilled workers'[53], now joined the fray, and a committee of matchwomen was formed to liaise with them. The Council's Secretary seemed confident of a gentlemanly resolution:

Mr George Shipton…had written to Messrs. Bryant & May stating that…the London Trades Council, as experienced and unprejudiced workmen, should offer their services to try to bring about an amicable solution. He had received a most courteous reply….[54]

However, on meeting with the firm, the LTC admitted that they would '…make no concession'[55], reporting the employers' demand that the strikers return to work immediately or be replaced, apart from 'the ringleaders', who they would not take back.[56]

The Council proposed a levy of all affiliated trade unionists, an 'almost unprecedented event in the history of labour',[57] indicating the strike's impact. (In 1890 the LTC would change its rules and admit female delegates for the first time.)

Strike funds already collected, from sources including the *Star*'s readership, were first distributed on July 14 and an *Eastern Post* report gives a rare insight into the way in which Besant addressed the strikers:

The women, boys and girls were urged to…remain quiet, to give no cause for legal interference…Mrs. Besant…explained to these poor girls that there were friends ready and willing to assist them provided they always behaved themselves….[58]

The women had by now been without money for days, and must have been experiencing hardship; but their cheerful solidarity remained constant:

…the girls were determined to stand together at all costs. 'I can pawn this for you', 'I'll lend you that', in every direction girls might be seen plotting how they could help one another on until Bryant & May gave them back their pennies.[59]

Pressure on the company grew. Investigators from Toynbee Hall examined Besant's original allegations. She was vindicated, and further grievances and illegally-imposed fines uncovered.[60]

Confronted with these findings, Bryant & May could no longer deny the existence of unjustified deductions.

The directors admit the existence of the charges of sixpence for brushes, sixpence for stamps…(They) have admitted…that the deductions of 3d. a week from wages, alleged by the girls and denied by them, is in fact correct.[61]

The company was discredited and moving towards a position of compromise far removed from their initial hostile defiance.

The company's directors finally met with a deputation of matchwomen and LTC members on July 16. After prolonged discussion all parties agreed to terms to be put to a full meeting of strikers, including the abolition of all fines and establishment of '...a breakfast room for the girls so that the latter will not be obliged to get their meals in the room where they work' (an important concession, as toxic particles settling on food was a contributing factor in 'phossy jaw') and the formation of a union.[62]

The *Eastern Post* reported the meeting that followed:

> ...Mrs Besant...said the firm had suggested that if they were to concede the points demanded by the workers, possibly when the busy time came round the girls would again strike. Now, said Mrs. Besant, I feel sure, I may say, you will do nothing of the kind, will you? [63]

By July 18 the *Post* reported that 'One of the most important strikes that has agitated East London for a considerable time past has happily been brought to a close. The employees of Messrs. Bryant and May have been successful,'[64] The *Star* too enthused over the workers' 'magnificent' victory, 'won without preparation – without organisation – without funds...a turning point in the history of our industrial development.'[65]

The union they formed, the Union of Women Matchmakers, was the 'largest union in England and Wales...composed entirely of women and girls'.[66] Despite Besant's admonishments, its members remained militant: after she had moved onto other things,[67] a disapproving observer noted that '...relations between the girls and the firm remain as bad as possible; none of the girls would ever say a good word about their employer, and small strikes on the most trivial matter are a constant occurrence'.[68]

In fact, the matchwomen's militancy pre-dated the '88 strike. Independent strikes at Bryant & May are recorded by media accounts in 1881, 1885 and 1886. The *National Reformer* reported that the strike in the autumn of 1885, to which Tom Mann also made reference in 'What a Compulsory Eight Hour Working Day Means to the Workers', was over "low wages and 'Phossy Jaw'"[69]

Beatrice Potter (later Webb) reported for Charles Booth's survey that the matchwomen had '...always shown a remarkable power of combination. ... There have constantly been small strikes in the match factories of the East End.'[70]

Eliza Martin and the 'Ringleaders'

Our re-examination of events has provided considerable evidence of a self-organised strike; following the lead of media accounts allows us to go further still. We have already seen the LTC's report of Bryant & May's anger at what they termed 'ringleaders', contrasting with the firm's public willingness to blame Besant for the strike. The *Star* noted the presence at a last strike meetings of a young woman described with no equivocation as 'One of the leaders of the strike…'[71] Her name was Eliza, and she was apparently on the strike committee and involved directly in the administration of the strike fund, also addressing the meetings.

I was able to find evidence in the company's archives supporting both of these accounts. During the strike, the directors had evidently asked their foremen to draw up a list of likely troublemakers. Five women were named: Alice Francis, Kate Slater, Mary Driscol (sic- actually Driscoll), Jane Wakeling and Eliza Martin.[72] After a long search for descendants, I interviewed the grandchildren of Eliza Martin in 2005. Jim Best and his sister Anne Chapman had not known their grandmother, who had died when relatively young, possibly not from natural causes.[73] However, they had learned about Eliza from her children, their uncles, aunts and father. Family tradition had always asserted that Eliza was instrumental in the strike. Jim recalled seeing an article in a local newspaper in the 1980s commemorating it:

> I remember my Dad showing me the article…and saying, That's your Nan, son. Eliza had told Dad that she and her mates started the strike… We're quite proud of that.[74]

Mary Driscoll's granddaughter Joan Harris was also interviewed, and had known her grandmother well, being partly brought up by her.[75] She recalled her talking about conditions in the factory and 'phossy jaw'. It was due to the assistance of Jim Best's family that I was able to ascertain that all of the five 'troublemakers' were voted onto the strike committee, which became the union's organising committee and was elected by the striking women.[76] This further strengthens the hypothesis of self-organisation. If this were not enough, Besant's own words should finally lay the matter to rest. In the same issue of the Link in which '*White Slavery…*' appeared, she discussed trade unionism and women, asking 'How could a union be formed among the girls of Bryant & May, mentioned in another column? Suppose a union was formed, and the girls went on strike: the foreman would simply announce that so many hands were required at so much an hour, and their doors would be besieged within hours.' Trade unionism might, she wrote, 'teach (women) comradeship and stir up social feeling, and improve their business faculty, and brighten their lives in many ways; but raise their wages – no.'[77] This should come as no great surprise – even supposing Besant possessed the organisational genius to bring out a 1,400-strong workforce, all utterly dependant on their meagre wages and with whom she had no real connection, no source asks *why* Besant should have wanted to lead a strike in the first place. If she was some kind of early syndicalist hoping to bring about a general strike, the match industry was not an obvious place to start, and neither was joining the Fabian Society, which prided itself, as founding member Bernard Shaw said, on 'addressing itself to its own class' rather than involving itself in worker militancy.

Two years after the strike, Besant wrote a pamphlet about trade unionism, making no mention of the matchwomen *per se* but condemning 'women workers and unskilled labourers, the two unorganised mobs which have hung round the disciplined army of unionists and have lost them many a fight…'[78]

New Unionism

Primary evidence may allow us to dispense with the myth of Besant's leadership, and finally to give credit to the matchwomen for the organisation of a successful and well-known strike: but this does not in itself mean that their victory was influential enough to deserve a place in the history of New Unionism as more than a minor signifier of events to come. Notable historians have insisted that it was not, with Paul Thompson concluding:

> The strike of matchgirls in July 1888, organised by socialist Annie Besant…was relatively isolated and consequently has been given exaggerated publicity. The real start of the 'new unionism' in London was not until the gasworkers' agitation.[79]

Thompson does not explain what he means by 'relatively isolated', nor provide supporting evidence, but presumably refers in part to the year between the two strikes. The perceived 'isolation' may also refer to the matchwomen as a group of workers: E.H. Hunt also judged them 'too unlike the workers who had the best chance of becoming successful new unionists' to have influenced them, and their strike 'too early'.[80] Certainly the matchwomen's gender set them apart from other New Unionists: Hunt does not explain whether it is this to which he refers, and again gives no evidence to support his contention. The Great Dock Strike, which began 13 months after the matchwomen's victory and within walking distance of the

Bryant & May factory, is usually credited with beginning a 'truly massive advance in trade unionism',[81] in which membership numbers increased from ¾ of a million in 1888 to more than 2 million by 1900.[82] Historians generally agree that it was the dock strike which set off a whole series of agitations and strikes, the formation of new unions and the expansion of existing ones which became known as New Unionism.[83] In fact, the evidence for re-evaluating the matchwomen's strike does not end with its resolution.

As news of the matchwomen's victory spread, the dockers were among groups of workers who contacted the Union of Women Matchmakers to ask for advice on establishing their own organisations: as Besant, in her role as union secretary, noted, 'Then came a cry for…help from tin-box makers…aid to shop assistants…work for the dockers and exposure of their wrongs…'[84]

I have analysed reports of recorded strike action after the matchwomen's victory, and there is a definite upsurge, with the *Times* recording more than double the numbers of strikes per quarter in the first half of 1889, after the match strike, than in the first half of 1888, before it.[85] These included a forerunner of the East End dock strike, which occurred not one year, but only three months after the matchworkers'. In October 1888, Ben Tillett led a strike at Tilbury Dock: it was ultimately unsuccessful, but the inspiration of the matchworkers was indicated in the speaker chosen to address the strikers: Tillett reported that at his request union secretary 'Mrs. Besant came along and spoke to 5,000 dockers'.[86]

An event largely ignored by secondary sources illustrates the widespread fame of the matchwomen's victory, and its direct and immediate impact on unskilled female workers as far away as Ireland. I am indebted to Paddy Logue of the Derry Trades Council for the story of the Derry shirtmakers, who, on hearing of the matchwomen's victory, contacted the local branch of the Boilermakers' Union on their own initiative, asking to be allowed into membership.[87] The Boilermakers contacted the Derry Trades Council for advice, who in turn corresponded with their London counterpart. As a result, Eleanor Marx went to Ireland to advise them, making a celebrated entrance to Derry greeted by large crowds and welcoming processions; and the Derry Trades Council became only the second to admit women and unskilled workers.[88]

The next few months marked the beginning of a resurgence of working-class consciousness, with East London as its centre, and the 8-hour day and minimum wage its 'rallying call'.[89] There was a growing sense that, as a participant in the dock strike had it, 'If the working classes hold together, they can do what they likes'.⁹⁰ Re-examination of primary evidence on the dock strike shows that once it had begun, its leaders frequently invoked the matchwomen's example. John Burns, during one of his famous orations to a mass demonstration, reminded the men, to cries of 'Hear hear', that 'the match girls had formed a union and had got what they wanted, and so had the gas stokers at Beckton, and surely the Dock Labourers could do the same'.⁹¹ It is noticeable that Burns said simply 'the matchgirls' without any further explanation, showing that he expected his audience- tens of thousands of people – to be immediately familiar with the women and their victory.

On a further occasion during the strike Burns would urge the dockers to '...stand shoulder to shoulder. Remember the matchgirls, who won their fight and formed a union'.⁹²

Original sources show the matchwomen also to have been literally present during the dock strike. The *East London Observer* reported on solidarity action with the dockers: '... A week of strikes- coal men, printers' labourers, match girls... are all out'.⁹³

The *East London News* also noted that '...coal men, Matchgirls, parcels postmen...Clothing and railway works have... followed the infectious example of coming out on strike.'⁹⁴ The *Star* described the scene at the final victorious procession marking the docker's victory:

> ...up came the dockers, an interminable array with multitudinous banners...Then came a large contingent of women ...match-makers, among others. Looked at from above they advanced like a moving rainbow, for they all wore the huge feathers of many colours which the East End lass loves to sport when she is out for the day....⁹⁵

Looking back on the dock strike in later years two dockers leaders would make it clear that the matchwomen's victory had been an inspiration. Ben Tillett said simply that the women's strike was '...the beginning of the social convulsion which produced new unionism'.⁹⁶ Mann agreed: '...the girls' won. This had a stimulating effect upon other sections of workers, some of whom were also showing signs of intelligent dissatisfaction...'⁹⁷ The employers brutal re-offensive against New Unionism crushed many of the hundreds of new unions which had been established within a few years: but still the way had been prepared for the modern Brit trade union movement, for general unionism and the organisation of women and semi- and unskilled workers.

Study of the familial and geographic connections of the matchwomen's strike committee has also yielded numerous connections to dockers.[98] Mary Driscoll was a dockers' daughter and married a docker, and Eliza Martin's brother-in-law and nephews were dockers. As Jim Best put it, far from being too dissimilar from the dockers to have influenced them, East London matchwomen and dockers were friends, relatives and neighbours: virtually 'the same people'.[99]

Conclusions

That the Victorians could have had misconceptions about the matchwomen's strike is perhaps understandable: these were women stepping outside of their prescribed roles, who should have been either helpless 'little match girls' or slatternly factory women. Even so, men like Tillett and Mann seem to have had no trouble with seeing them as more than one-dimensional, or industrially militant, and nor did some of the middle-class journalists and commentators covering their strike. Even Bryant & May privately accepted their capability for defiance.

That the erroneous version should have endured for nearly a hundred and twenty years, when so much evidence contradicts it and in spite of developments in working-class and women's history, is more problematic. For some historians it is apparently still preferable to accept that the women were somehow 'made' to go on strike by Besant, who, although obviously female too, can be accommodated within traditions which, as Joan Kelly wrote, feature women 'largely as exceptions; those who were said to be as ruthless as, or wrote like, or had the brains of men'.[100] Throughout her life those who disliked Besant, including Emmeline Pankhurst and Beatrice Webb, often used her supposedly 'unfeminine' appearance or behaviour to castigate her[101]. She too suffered through dominant ideology and achieved a great deal in her life in spite of it – but this does not make her a strike leader. She herself made it clear enough that she was not one, and her well-recorded views and politics should have confirmed this. Indeed, there is a wealth of primary evidence which signals the truth, but historians seem unable to make the obvious connections: it is generally known that the strike began with an unexpected sacking, followed by an immediate walk-out in sympathy – how could Besant have orchestrated that, and if she had, would she have been as puzzled by the matchwomen's deputation to her days later, as her own well-known account makes abundantly clear? Even a recent socialist history of New Unionism which looks in some detail at the strike with thorough use of primary sources, does not question Besant's leadership.[102]

It must be considered, then, that the strike has fallen victim to the incomplete conceptualisation of the workings of gender as well as class oppression in much of British Labour History, which allows the perpetuation of what Sarah Boston has called 'the myths about women workers and organisation which…do not stand up to historical scrutiny'.[103] It is a great pity that this was not understood soon enough for the matchwomen to be interviewed about it in their later years. However, their grandchildren's testimony tells us that, no matter what the 'academic' view, local traditions were more accurate – the strike was still talked about in the East End when they were growing up, and as a victory for the workers. As one said – and perhaps this is a question we should ask ourselves – 'Why should it be hard to accept that the women went on strike themselves? *They* worked in the factory – *they* knew it wasn't right how they were treated, better than anybody else did. They did it for their families too. They didn't need to wait around to be told right from wrong.'

In the course of my research I interviewed one of the dockers' grandsons too, and he showed me a letter which Ernest Bevin wrote to his grandfather in 1940 paying tribute to the strikers:

> Fifty years ago…you were among those who were involved in… a great industrial upheaval – virtually a revolution against poverty, tyranny and intolerable conditions. You little thought during those weeks…that you were laying the foundation of a great Industrial Movement.[104]

If this was true of the dock strikers then, I would argue, it is time we accept it to have been equally true of the Bryant & May matchwomen.

Notes

1 *East London Advertiser*, 14 July 1888, p. 6.
2 Liberal MP John Scurr quoted in the *Morning Star*, 10 July 1988, in Trade Union Congress Archives, Ref: MISC HD 53699.
3 Evans, S. P. *Jack the Ripper: Letters from Hell*, Stroud: Sutton, 2001.
4 E.g. Bill Owen and Tony Russell's musical '*The Matchgirls*', first produced at the Globe Theatre, London, in 1966.
5 Rowbotham, S. *Hidden From History*, London: Pluto, 1977.
6 Boston, S. *Women Workers and the Trade Unions*, Introduction, London: Davis-Poynter, 1987, p. 1.
7 Ibid.
8 Carr, E. H. *What is History?* New York: Vintage, 1990. pp. 7-30.
9 Hunt, E. H. *British Labour History 1815- 1914*, London: Weidenfeld and Nicolson, 1985, p. 305.

10   Pelling, H. *A History of British Trade Unionism*, Harmondsworth: Penguin, 1963, p. 97.
11   Morton, A. L. and Tate, G. *The British Labour Movement*, London: Lawrence and Wishart, 1956.
12   Soldon, N. *Women in British Trade Unions* :Gill and Macmillan, 1978, p. 30.
13   Hobsbawm, E. *Labour's Turning Point 1800-1900*, : Harvester Press, 1974, p. 78.
14   Thompson, E. P. The *Making of the English Working Class*, London: Victor Gollancz, 1963.
15   Interview with Miss Nash, superintendent of the Clifdon House Institute (the dining rooms and social club established for the Bryant & May workers after the strike), 1896, in Charles Booth's notebook, Booth Archive, L.S.E. *B178*, p. 62.
16   Besant, A. 'White Slavery in London', The *Link*, 23 June 1888.
17   Crory, W.Glenny, *East London Industries*, London: Longmans, 1876, p. 43.
18   Rigby, L. *Stoke Poges: A Buckinghamshire Village Through 1,000 Years*, Chichester: Phillimore, 2000.
19   Ibid.
20   Besant, A. op. cit., *The Link*, 23 June 1888.
21   Fishman, W. *East End 1888*, London: Duckworth, 1988, p. 1.
22   *The Nineteenth Century* XXIV (1888) p.262 cited in Fishman, W. 1988, op. cit. p. 1.
23   'Sweating' would be defined by the House of Lords Select Committee as work with one or more of the following characteristics: below-subsistence wages; excessively long working hours; 'an insanitary state of the houses in which the work is carried on.' 5th report of the House of Lords Select Committee on the Sweating System pp. 1980, xvii (Cd 169) pxlii, cited in Morris, J. *Women Workers and the Sweated Trades*, Aldershot: Gower, 1986, p. 8.
24   Morris, J. op. cit., 1986, pp. 1-2.
25   *The Times*, 10 Feb 1888, cited in ibid. p. 292.
26   Morris, J. op. cit., p. 6.
27   Bryant, A. C. cited in Taylor, A. *Annie Besant*, Oxford: Oxford University Press, 1992, p. 206. Besant, A. *The Link* 23 June 1888.
28   Ibid.
29   Bryant & May Archives, Hackney Archives Department: Bundles P/B/BRY/1/2/538-564
30   *The Star* 4 July 1888, p. 4.
31   For further discussion see Raw, L. '*The Place of the Bryant & May Matchworkers' Strike in British Labour History*' Doctoral Thesis for London Metropolitan University, 2008.
32   Quote from an unnamed matchwoman, '*Toilers in London*', cited in Hobsbawm, E.J. *Labour's Turning Point 1800-1900*, London: Lawrence and Wishart, 1974, p. 78.
33   Accounts are conflicting and confusing, but I have arrived at this as the most likely start date of the strike using various sources, including the following comments from an interview with Wilberforce Bryant in the *Star* on July 3rd

1888:
Q: What is the cause of the strike?
A: Why, a girl was dismissed yesterday; it had nothing to do with Mrs. Besant. She refused to follow the instructions of the foreman, and as she was irregular anyway, she was dismissed.
For further discussion see L. Raw, op. cit, 2008.
34 The *Star*, 6 July 1888.
35 Ibid.
36 Ibid.
37 *The Star*, 7 July 1888
38 *East London Advertiser*, July 7 1888 p. 5.
39 *The Star*, 6 July 1888, p. 3.
40 Ibid.
41 Besant in *The Link*, 7 July 1888.
42 Ibid.
43 Ibid.
44 Anonymous letter to Annie Besant, cited in Besant, A. *Annie Besant: an autobiography*, London: T. Fisher Unwin, 1893, p. 117.
45 *The Star*, 7 July 1888.
46 Annie Besant in *The Link*, 7 July 1888.
47 *The Star*, 9 July 1888, p. 3.
48 Ibid.
49 Ibid.
50 Ibid. P. 2.
51 Ibid.
52 *The Echo*, 20 July 1888, in Beer, R. *Match Strike 1888: The Struggle Against Sweated Labour in London's East End*, 1979, p. 42.
53 Poynter, J. 'The London Trades Council and the New Unionism', Dissertation for University of North London (2001), p. 45.
54 *The East London Advertiser*, 21 July 1888, p. 6.
55 *The Star*, 13 July 1888, p. 3.
56 Ibid.
57 *Pall Mall Gazette*, 9 July 1888, cited in Beer, R. op.cit., 1979, p. 41.
58 *Eastern Post*, 21 July 1888 p. 9.
59 Anon, probably Harkness, M. (1889) British Weekly Commissioners, *Toilers in London*: cited in Charlton, J. *It Just Went Like Tinder, The Mass Movement and New Unionism in Britain 1889, A Socialist History*, London: Redwords,1999, p. 21.
60 *The Star*, 17 July 1888, in Beer, R. op. cit. 1979, p. 42.
61 Ibid.
62 *East London Observer*, 21 July 1888, 'The Match Girls' Strike' p. 6.
63 *Eastern Post*, 21 July 1888, op. cit.
64 Ibid.
65 *The Star*, 18 July 1888.
66 Chinn, C. *They Worked All Their Lives: Women of the Urban Poor in England, 1880-1939*, Lancaster: Carnegie, 1988, p. 82

67 Besant soon abandoned socialism for Theosophy, eventually becoming the *de facto* leader of the movement.
68 Charles' Booth's interview with Miss Nash, 1896, op. cit.
69 *National Reformer* 1885, cutting in Bryant & May company archives, Hackney Archives Department: Bundles P/B/BRY/1/2/538-564;Tom Mann (1986) pp. 25-26.
70 Charles Booth, *Life and Labour of the People*, Volume 1, S.l. Williams and Norgate, 1889, pp. 474-5
71 Ibid.
72 Bryant & May Archives, Hackney Archives Department: Bundles P/B/BRY/1/2/538-564.
73 See L. Raw, op. cit., 2008.
74 Interview James Best/ L. Raw 7 February 2005 in L. Raw, op. cit. 2008.
75 See L. Raw, op. cit. 2008, for interview testimony of Joan Harris, June 8 and 9 September 2004, October 2005.
76 It transpired that, because of his family connection to the strike, Mr. Best's brother had kept the original newspaper article, written by the historian and custodian of a local museum: (The *East London Advertiser*, 15 December 1989, 'Make a match', p. 18). I was able to cross-reference this with the 'troublemakers' list.
77 The *Link*, 23 June1888.
78 Besant, A., *The Trade Union Movement*, Self-published pamphlet, 1890, p. 28.
79 Thompson, P., *Socialists, Liberals and Labour: The Struggle for London 1885-1914*, London: Routledge & Kegan Paul,1967, p. 45.
80 Hunt, E.H. *British Labour History*, London : Weidenfeld and Nicolson,1982, p.135
81 Harrison, J.F.C. *Late Victorian Britain, 1875-1901,* London: Fontana, 1990, pp. 142-3
82 Ibid.
83 E. g. Thompson, P., op. cit., 1967, p. 53.
84 Besant, A., *Annie Besant: an autobiography*, 1893, p. 117.
85 For full analysis, using *Palmer's Index to the Times* for the first quarter of 1888 to the third quarter of 1889, see Louise Raw, op. cit., 2008.
86 Tillett, B., *A Brief History of the Dockers' Union*, London: Dock, Wharf, Riverside and General Workers' Union, 1910, p 14.
87 Interview with Paddy Logue of the Derry Trades Council, August 11th 2002, in L. Raw, op. cit.
88 Ibid.
89 Morton A.L. & Tate, G. op. cit., 1956, p. 185.
90 Quoted in *The Daily News*, 19 August 1889. Cited in A. Stafford, op. cit., 1961, p. 107.
91 *The Pictorial News*, 24 August 1889
92 Mann , T. *Memoirs*, S.l.: Labour Publishing Co., 1923.
93 *The East London Observer*, 31 August 1889.
94 Charlton, J. op. cit., 1999, p. 99.

95 *The Star* 5 May 1889.
96 Tillett, B. *Memories and Reflections,* S.l.: John Long Ltd., 1931, p. 122
97 Mann, T. op. cit., 1923, cited in Briggs, A. *Victorian Things,* Harmondsworth: Penguin 1988, p. 203.
98 Raw, L., op. cit., 2008.
99 Interview James Best/ L. Raw 7 February 2005, in L. Raw, op. cit., 2008.
100 Kelly, J. *Women, History and Theory,* 1984, p. 2.
101 See L. Raw, op. cit., 2008.
102 Charlton, J., op. cit., 1999.
103 Boston, S., op. cit., 1987, p. 1.
104 Letter to surviving dock striker John Ravey (1861-1947), provided by his son John Rooney, 29 July 2002, cited in L. Raw, op. cit., 2008.

The fragility of the union: the work of the National Federation of Women Workers in the regions of Britain, 1906-1914

Cathy Hunt

This chapter aims to build a picture of the work of the National Federation of Women Workers in the regions of Britain during the years before the First World War. Although over 140,000 women workers were members of textile (predominately cotton) trade unions by 1906[1], others, if organised at all, belonged to small, individual associations often with insufficient resources and leadership to ensure long term survival. The Federation, an all female trade union founded in 1906 under the guidance of the Women's Trade Union League (WTUL), sought to organise women into a strong and co-ordinated organisation committed to recruiting women workers from all trades, particularly in those where all-male unions excluded them.[2] Although the names of those associated with the national organisation of the Federation, primarily Mary Macarthur, its first President, are reasonably familiar to students of early twentieth century British labour history, far less is known about the work of the Federation's national and local organisers who sought to bring women into the union, or about the women members that they recruited. By July 1912 the Federation claimed to have 15,000 members and stated that as many as 74 branches had been established in Britain.[3] Membership numbers, however, were never static and whilst in some areas local organisation thrived, attracting hundreds of women workers, in other places it would falter, despite promising starts and the considerable efforts of both local and national leadership to re-inject life into the failing branches. This study, by investigating local Federation activity based around strikes and campaigns, questions whether there were any common features that might ensure lasting success for a Federation branch and why it was that some branches, including ones that had experienced resounding victories in disputes with employers, resulting in initially high membership numbers, were not always able to remain strong. In so doing, some of the hidden or neglected details of the working lives of women during this period are highlighted and the consequences of women workers' exploitation exposed rather than remaining as hidden as the workplaces and homes in which so many of them were employed.

In 1986 Deborah Thom wrote that 'for too long women have been the stage army of history, particularly labour history. We need less of seeing them as others saw them, more of seeing them as they saw themselves.'[4] I was reminded of the poignancy of these words a few years ago when asked, after giving a paper on the work of the Federation in one particular region, how it benefited its members. What was the *point* of women joining the union, the questioner asked? What did they get out of it? On reflection, my response sounded as if I was acting as a spokeswoman for the Federation. I mentioned the benefits of organisation, the importance of combining to seek higher wages and the importance of the fight for better working conditions for women, but I realised, even as I was speaking, that I was talking about the *potential* benefits of the union, those that women workers were told about by organisers and speakers rather than those that they had necessarily experienced themselves.[5] I gave no sense of what it might have meant to women to wear the Federation badge, to stand up to management in a spirit of solidarity, to unite on marches and demonstrations and pose for victory photographs after disputes were favourably settled. I certainly gave no insight into the enormity of the efforts put into establishing and maintaining local branches, of life beyond the struggle or of what it was like in the union branch a week, a month or a year after the strike was over. I began to seek more precise answers to questions such as what did being in the union mean in terms of members' relationships with employers, and if women could afford to continue to pay their union subscriptions, did they consider it worthwhile to do so?

It is of course increasingly difficult to find out about the lives of women trade unionists in the early twentieth century. In the 1970s, Thom interviewed women who worked at the Woolwich Arsenal during the First World War about their trade union involvement.[6] Joanna Bornat employed oral history in order to understand more about men and women's attitudes towards their membership of the General Union of Textile Workers between 1900 and 1916 in West Yorkshire.[7] At the start of the twenty first century, what historians need, as Jill Liddington acknowledges in her discussion of her research on the suffrage campaign in Yorkshire, is to employ a combination of detective work and a determination to examine all possible sources.[8] When examining women's trade unionism, this methodological approach needs to be steadfastly adhered to in order to counter the strong tendency that has existed within traditional labour history to overlook women's organisational past. Many large, mixed sex unions had high female membership but because the positions of power within them were held by men, they have been written about almost exclusively in terms of their male leadership.[9] Despite significant advances in the writing of women's history since the 1970s, many general 'mainstream' histories of British trade unionism continue to marginalize the contributions of women within a labour movement widely regarded as belonging to working men.[10] One of the reasons why the Federation has been neglected within traditional labour history may be attributable to a lack of official records;[11] small organisations have always been less likely to retain documentary evidence of their history than large, financially secure (and often male dominated) ones and Anna Davin has noted a tendency amongst historians to focus on those powerful organisations whose records are accessible. She points out that because men have been more likely than women to have well paid, regular work, it is more likely that they would become members of those organisations that retained records.[12] But there is arguably more to the neglect than this. In many traditional accounts, women's trade unionism is seen as small and presumed to be unable to play a significant part in the development of the labour movement. This has arguably contributed to the sidelining of a small, all female trade union such as the Federation.

Despite the marginalisation of the Federation within mainstream labour history, other studies have provided both information and insight into its history,[13] beginning with Barbara Drake's detailed study of women's trade unionism, written after its enormous expansion during the First World War.[14] In the 1970s and early 1980s, Sheila Lewenhak and Sarah Boston published studies tracing women's involvement in British trade unions, including the Federation.[15] Boston provides examples of strikes in which the Federation became involved but neither account has the space to move far from assessments of the national leadership and, specifically, the work of Mary Macarthur. Thom's examination of the organisational practices of the Federation and the Workers' Union before and during the First World War emphasises the importance of investigating *why* women became members of trade unions despite the difficulties that faced them as workers and as trade union organisers.[16] A regional assessment of the Federation and its members is included within Eleanor Gordon's work on the Scottish labour movement, in which she examines the challenges faced by those attempting to organise women in Scotland before the First World War and highlights women workers' strength and unity, challenging traditional, contemporary views that the main obstacles to recruiting women into trade unions were their general apathy and the temporary nature of their place in the workforce.[17]

In the tradition of feminist historians who have uncovered new material and re-examined 'mainstream' sources in order to answer questions about women's historical position in society, this study draws on a wide a range of sources.[18] My research on the Federation began in Coventry, examining newspaper reports[19] and the records of the city's Trades Council.[20] As a result of revisiting some oral accounts from the 1960s,[21] I made contact with the daughter of a Coventry Federation member and branch organiser who provided further invaluable comment on the activities of her mother, Edith Mayell (nee Stringer) who became the Federation's Midlands secretary in the years before the First World War.[22] The research has expanded to include other local case studies and in addition to make use of the Federation's annual reports, which include branch reports from around Britain, the Federation journal, *Woman Worker*,[23] and the Gertrude Tuckwell Collection.[24]

The Federation's annual reports give a strong indication of the intensity of effort that went into its 'strenuous campaigns in England, Scotland and Wales…to break fresh ground and give the Federation a footing in districts previously untouched'.[25] Before the First World War, the Federation and the WTUL directed organisers to help in regional disputes, to organise women into those unions that did accept women or to assist in Federation branch formation. Many accounts refer to the indefatigable energy of Macarthur's tours of Britain to educate women about unionisation, to respond to pleas for help during disputes and to establish new branches. 'How militant our youngest branches are!' exclaims the *Woman Worker* in 1907, 'We have hardly begun to tackle the grievances at Oxford when an imperative call reaches us from Hull [where] dissatisfaction is again rife at the local tin-box works'[26]. The same report confirms that 'the situation at a branch still further north is even more critical. There the wages of some of our members have recently been subjected to most scandalous deductions'.[27] On that occasion, the Federation responded by sending organisers to 'endeavour to secure a satisfactory settlement'.[28] Their schedules were every bit as exhausting as Macarthur's; the volume of work taken on by the Federation's own officials and those 'lent' by the WTUL is evident in the pages of the Annual Reports as well as *Woman Worker*. Strikes were recognised by Macarthur as an effective recruiting tool as well as a means to prove to women that if they had already been in a union, there was a good chance that the dispute could have been avoided in the first place. Organisers rushed to attend disputes at a moment's notice; in 1913 Isabel Sloan left a TUC conference on receiving a wire from the women at the Britannia Cotton Mills in Colwick Junction.[29] Earlier in the year, she had responded to calls from other parts of the country, each time having to be ready to speak at hastily assembled meetings and decide on the best local course of action, endeavouring to bring in regionally based organisers where possible. Depending on recruitment success, some regions were given full time organisers; for example, by 1911, Kate MacLean and Agnes Brown had been appointed to work in Scotland and a secretary had been appointed in Cradley Heath after the chain makers' dispute of 1910.[30] Sometimes officials would rent office space within a district to help with a strike or to co-ordinate a recruitment campaign and both their continued presence and their full time dedication to the cause had a positive effect on membership, particularly within areas which had previously experienced difficulty in organising women. For example, in 1913 Sheffield was noted as having soil 'uncongenial' to women's trade unionism, but Federation membership was reported to have been given a boost by the fact that one its officials had decided to make the city her headquarters.[31]

The help of high profile and popular figures within the labour movement was also appreciated by the Federation, and in 1913 Susan Lawrence, by then a Labour councillor in Poplar, was described as the 'fairy godmother' of the London County Council School Cleaners' branch, despite holding no official position within it.[32] Other branches relied on national officials who travelled long distances, making numerous return visits to ensure the survival of branches. Gordon suggests that it is a tribute to 'the success and tenacity of the WTUL' that it was able to extend its operations into Scotland, attempting campaigns in big cities, small towns and rural districts alike.[33] The Federation was equally enthusiastic and ambitious in its undertakings across the rest of Britain, although for some the strain of the work could not be endured indefinitely. Jessie Main, the Federation's General Secretary, resigned in 1910 owing to 'a complete breakdown'.[34] Ada Nield Chew, who toured the country on behalf of the WTUL and the Federation, gave up her post in 1908, possibly because she had 'become tired of the incessant grind of constant travelling', which she often did in the company of her small daughter, who later recalled that at one stage her mother and Macarthur 'divided the country between them' in order to reach as many women as possible.[35]

The difficulties faced by organisers can also be judged by examining the wide range of establishments and trades within which they attempted to organise. From those mentioned in Federation Annual Reports before the war, four broad categories can be identified. The biggest was that of textiles; whilst women in the largest, particularly cotton, mills were more likely to be members of the textile unions, there were still thousands of unorganised women working in factories, in small workshops and at home, engaged in the production of, for example, lace, thread or dye, and of garments including dresses, hats and gloves. The second largest group related to food production, such as confectionery, biscuits, jam and pickles and also the making of containers used to sell and store food, such as boxes and tins. The third group included women in manufacturing, from metal work such as cycles and safety razors to general engineering, including ammunition. Fourthly, the Reports show that the Federation tried to organise women who engaged in domestic work, for example as school or hospital cleaners and in laundries. Within all four groups there were women whose low pay, isolation and poor working conditions made organisation extremely difficult. Whilst the Federation became publicly associated with campaigning against the worst excesses of sweated labour, its main efforts at the local level went into supporting 'hidden' women in industry. For example, the plight of women who worked in small dressmaking firms, were, despite low pay, long hours and an unhealthy working environment, less likely to arouse society's indignation than that of the chain makers, whose oppression was symbolised by the chains that they made. If women had to work, dressmaking was widely regarded as a suitable occupation for them. In 1914, Mr Cramp, the owner of a blouse-making firm in Coventry, failed to understand the Federation's application for an extra ½ d. per blouse for its female workforce. Despite the skilled nature of the work, his view was that this sort of work was done happily for nothing by 'ladies at home', including his own daughters, and so there could be no justification for the payment of higher wages within his establishment.[36]

Federation organisers needed to be ready to respond to hundreds of localised disputes similar to the one at Cramp's and it was crucial that they understood both the nature of the grievances and working practices of the wide range of trades and industries that they set out to organise within. The evidence from Federation Annual Reports between 1911 and 1914 – years that witnessed increased industrial unrest across Britain – reflects Gordon's assessment of the situation in Scotland that there were more strikes during these years for better pay than there were in protest over wage cuts, suggesting that women were emboldened by the atmosphere of heightened industrial tension.[37] But it was also common for an incident, such as the sacking or victimisation of a woman worker, or the intimidating behaviour of a foreman, to provoke an immediate walkout, followed by the drawing up of a list of demands. The vulnerability of women workers can be illustrated by examining how employers could pay women with one hand and take back money with the other, in the shape of fines and

Members of the Coventry branch of the National Federation of Women Workers in 1914, marking the end of a three week strike at Messrs James Cramp and Sons, Blouse Manufacturers of Coventry. 130 workers, who struck for increased wages, were all enrolled into the union. The dispute ended with the firm granting wage increases to the extent of one half of the workers' demands.

Photo courtesy of Mrs Enid Trent

deductions. Fines could be imposed for anything from 'bad' or 'spoilt' work to behaviour deemed inappropriate on the factory floor; a girl working in a mill in Mansfield was fined a shilling for laughing during working hours whilst another was fined six pence for using the wrong staircase.[38] Louisa Leng, who worked for a clothing manufacturer in Oxford and became secretary of the local Federation branch, supplied Mary Macarthur with details of working conditions within the firm. She explained that although the women were not subject to fines, other ways were found to dock pay. Leng, who also tried to organise women textile workers in nearby Banbury, told Macarthur that anyone who was late was locked out for the half day; if needles were broken they had to be paid for and the sewing machinists had to pay for all cotton that they used:

> Piece machinists have to pay one shilling out of their wage for cotton, we have to pay 3d a reel for glaced [sic] and 2 ¾ for soft. Some of us might have two reels, some three and some four or five – it all depends on how much work you do.[39]

The correspondence between the Oxford and Banbury branches and Federation headquarters gives an indication of the minutiae of detail that national organisers sought when preparing to interview employers during strike periods or disputes. Leng forwarded grievances written by women in different departments of the Oxford factory, outlining inconsistencies within pay; whilst the youngest gown hands might earn between six and ten shillings, the knicker hands 'very rarely had the good fortune to ever earn ten shillings'. Leng and her sister could sometimes earn thirteen shillings but could also see their wages fall as low as nine shillings, 'and we are considered to be good hands'.[40] The need for precise understanding of local situations gives some indication of why organisers frequently spent weeks investigating and supporting local women, staying close by in order to ensure a strong and dedicated presence in the area.

It is not surprising, then, that the Federation made grateful use of local help whenever it was available and national organisers were keen to encourage, advise and protect activists. Its leadership knew that branches, however strong they appeared when first established, risked falling by the wayside unless there were either national organisers or reliable local activists to ensure that lively branch activities kept the attention of members. Branches with activists who sought to maintain membership after the initial recruitment campaign was over, seem to have had a better chance of success than those which continued to rely solely on national impetus. Effective use was therefore made of 'honorary members' many of whom, although not in factory employment, were nonetheless working-class women who had either retired or ceased working after marriage. Getting the right person to do the job could make or break a branch and Federation sources reveal the impact that local organisers had on establishing and strengthening branches. From its inception in 1907, the personnel of the Coventry branch was noted for its enthusiasm and success in attracting new members. Branch President Mrs Williams organised educational events and worked to raise the profile of the Federation within the local labour movement. When she moved to Woolwich in 1912, she was reported to have injected new life into the branch there.[41] The Federation seems to have used honorary members to meet with management rather than exposing working women activists to risks of victimisation from their employers. In Coventry considerable efforts were made to prevent Edith Stringer, as a young factory worker, from being black-listed by local employers. However, Stringer recalled her frustration when she felt that the inexperience or naivety of the honorary members resulted in failed negotiations. According to her, one honorary member, Mrs Griffiths, was persuaded to give management the names of all the women involved in a dispute at the Courtaulds factory. This resulted in the sacking of the women and considerably weakened the Federation's ability to make further inroads into the firm.[42]

In the spirit of trade union co-operation that Macarthur advocated, local efforts were encouraged to persuade the dominant male trade unions to recognise the merits and benefits of the Federation, not just for women workers but for the protection of men's wages and industrial status. In 1907, Derby's honorary secretary is recorded as a Mr Pritchard and in other areas, such as Oxford, where help was forthcoming from Ruskin College, men associated with local socialist politics offered advice and practical support.[43] In Banbury, Mr Walker of the Independent Labour Party played a significant part in building 'a splendid little branch' in 1911.[44] The Federation's pragmatism could have considerable benefits, including gaining the support of local union men during disputes. In some districts women organisers invited men from the skilled trade unions to Federation meetings to talk about the history of their organisation: tactics aimed not just at teaching new women members about labour history but also at proving to the men's unions that the Federation was itself a valuable addition to the labour movement. In 1907, the Coventry branch stated that 'if men trade unionists knew about the movement, they might help us a great deal'[45] and it invited Mr Binks of the Amalgamated Society of Engineers 'who told us interesting things about a trade union that is fifty six years old and impressed upon us the need for unity of action'.[46] Awareness of the need to persuade the men of the importance of women's organisation may have paid dividends – in 1914 the Coventry Trades Council lent moral and financial support to women strikers at a textile firm, reasoning perhaps, with a certain amount of self interest, that a happy female workforce in traditional work might well stem the rising, and to male workers unwelcome, tide of women seeking employment in the city's cycle trade.

Strikes were wonderful recruitment opportunities for women's trade unionism. The Federation's national leadership was not always in agreement over its sanctioning of strike action but organisers were acutely aware of the immediate impact it had on membership. It was not unusual for all those involved in a dispute to fill in application forms for the Federation, creating branches of several hundred members. Boston comments that during the years before the First World War 'one gets the feeling of a sudden welling-up of confidence among women workers. They marched in their Sunday best, picketed, organised and raised funds with gusto'.[47] Certainly trade union membership among women rose from 166,803 in 1906 to 357,956 in 1914 and although the majority of these were women in the large textile unions, Federation reports capture a sense of both excitement and progress in reaching women workers who were traditionally isolated, either at home, in small all-women establishments, or women departments in male dominated factories.[48] The 1914 Annual Report referred to recent 'signs of awakening' among women and includes reports of lively disputes. In Millwall in 1914 there was an all out strike at a food preparation firm, the result of young girls in tin box production having to use drawing presses for the first time. Men and women came out together and whilst over 800 women joined the Federation, the men were enrolled in the Dock, Wharf, Riverside and General Workers' Union. There was a strong procession from Millwall to Trafalgar Square, accompanied by a band and piper and led by the Federation banner. The procession was joined at Aldgate by members from the East End; more women, themselves out on strike in Camberwell, joined at Blackfriars, and Mary Macarthur and Susan Lawrence were among those who gave speeches in Trafalgar Square.[49]

Not surprisingly, collective action that highlighted the generally ignored plight of women workers attracted popular vocal support and there are lots of examples of the enthusiasm that surrounded specific disputes, giving an illusion of union strength and solidarity. The address given by Miss Flowers of the Federation at a mass meeting in support of striking women at Hart and Levy's textile firm in Nuneaton in 1914, 'was the signal for an uproarious volley of cheering, the girls standing up and waving their handkerchiefs in wild enthusiasm'. Flowers was greeted as the hero of the hour, despite the fact that until then there had been no organisation within the factory.[50] Despite the seriousness of disputes that left women workers without pay, or on union strike pay of up to seven shillings, holiday atmospheres often accompanied walkouts and strikes. Thom notes that women strikers often adopted 'suffrage tactics of propaganda and demonstration' in order to give maximum impact to their actions.[51] W. Hamish Fraser draws attention to what he calls the 'new joviality' that women brought to this period of industrial unrest.[52] At the same time, the reasons for such behaviour need to be examined to ensure that there is no danger of trivialising women workers' grievances. For many women strikes represented the first time in their lives that they had collectively challenged authority. The involvement of a trade union in their dispute undoubtedly encouraged many to believe that the struggle was not in vain and strength really could be found in unity and organisation.

However, whilst euphoria generally followed the conceding of strike demands, Federation reports do not suggest that a growing sense of the importance of being unionised was emerging across the country. Rather, they contain regular accounts of branches where membership had lapsed and where, despite local campaigns involving indoor and outdoor meetings and social events, the Federation struggled to persuade women to retain their membership. In 1912 a very heavy percentage of lapsed members is reported. Bournville, for example, previously described as a strong and lively factory based branch had, by 1912 lost 'some very keen members who had gone abroad', a fact which emphasises the importance of local activists to branch life.[53] In 1913 falling membership at Clerkenwell was reported; since a successful strike at the firm of Murray's Confectionery, working conditions had improved.[54] Similarly, in Wellingborough in Northamptonshire, membership had not been maintained since a strike over conditions in a steam laundry had ended in victory for the workers in 1913.[55] Although the dispute had been effectively co-ordinated between the local branch and Federation headquarters, the laundry was small, making it difficult to keep up the show of strength once the strike was over, particularly as laundry work often employed casual labour, which made permanent organisation even harder to achieve than in other small industrial establishments.

Similarly, in other places, the reasons for being in the union did not seem so obvious once disputes were won and it appears that without constant encouragement and pep talks from organisers, membership tended to lapse. The Bridport branch was dissolved in the autumn of 1912 because 'everything had gone smoothly at the firm of Messrs Grundy since the dispute at the beginning of the year and our members thought therefore there was no need to keep up their membership'.[56] The period after a dispute was of crucial importance; it was imperative that branches found ways of persuading women to stay in the union and clearly some struggled to do so. Not all were proactive in organising programmes of educational and social events. There could be many reasons for this, including the isolation of being in a small branch which did not hold regular meetings, an absence of willing, capable volunteers able to co-ordinate activities and the peculiarities of regional economic characteristics. Reports comment on falling membership being the result of trade slackness or shortage of work, reflecting the insecurity and enforced temporary nature of employment for many women. In a Whitechapel factory in 1913, women's membership had contracted because 'as the women leave to get married, new machinery is introduced which does away with the necessity of taking on new members'.[57] Poor attendance at branch meetings, which were often held in the evening, was another problem; in Newcastle girls were struggling to come to meetings because of a 'lack of energy and vitality after the day's work' and because of 'cold and excessively wet weather'.[58] The Federation was aware of the obstacles women faced in turning out to evening union meetings and responded by making it easier and more appealing to attend union events. Meetings were held during lunch breaks where possible and in Coventry organisers moved its branch out of a coffee tavern used by trade union and socialist groups into a local vicarage.[59] However, whilst this move might have been calculated to reassure parents and husbands that their womenfolk were meeting in genteel surroundings, the perceived middle class-ness of a venue that was also home to the local Fabian Society and its productions of Shakespeare and Dickens on the vicarage lawns, may have deterred others from attending.

The importance of spending time with women explaining the benefits of unionisation is a recurring theme in Federation reports. Mary Macarthur recalled an occasion early in her career when she realised that she had mistakenly given girls the impression that the union was 'an automatic machine' for wage increases, after which she warned against making claims that gave false hope and an unrealistic image of trade unionism.[60] Despite fluctuating membership, the Coventry branch existed without interruption from 1907 and its success may have been due in part to the fact that its local organisers recognised from the beginning the struggle that lay ahead. Early on they emphasised their determination to grow despite the fact that 'the working girls here are most of them content with low wages for long hours. They prefer having that to nothing so we want to show them the advantages of unity.'[61] And yet, even when social events were organised, the chances that the picnics in the woods[62] and the garden parties in the grounds of stately homes[63] would actually add permanent strength to Federation branches is debatable. Evenings of songs, recitations, whist drives and refreshments, even if well attended, could result in no more than a few promises of membership.

The Federation also struggled to get women to continue to pay their subscriptions. The problem was exacerbated by the passing of the National Insurance Act in 1911. Boston has attributed at least some of the rise in trade union membership from this date to the introduction of National Insurance because of the government decision to allow its administration through friendly societies and trade unions in order to ensure the smooth running of the new system.[64] Yet despite the WTUL's exhausting country wide campaign, in the face of competition from the large, long-established insurance companies, to persuade women to become trade union members of the Federation rather than just paying into its Insurance section, by 1913 there was 'an unusually heavy' percentage of lapsed members amidst a realisation that the 'necessity of paying contributions under the Insurance Act has deflected many women from the trade union'.[65] This suggests that, despite the enormous efforts of the Federation, many women, even though the very lowest paid were exempted from contributing to National Insurance, could not afford to prioritise union membership in their weekly budget whilst also having to pay in to the new state insurance scheme.[66] It is possible that the introduction of the Trade Board Act in 1909, which established minimum pay rates in four areas of sweated home working, may have had a similar effect on women. Macarthur believed that the establishment of trade boards would stimulate growth in women's trade unionism and certainly the Federation and the WTUL did have considerable success in organising women whose trades were covered by the boards. In 1912, for example, the Federation claimed it had recruited a thousand women into a branch of Nottingham lace workers after two organisers spent several months in the district. However, in 1913 it reported that there had been a big decrease in membership 'in spite of minimum rates fixed by the Trade Board' covering the lace industry.[67] The Federation implied that this was in part due to victimisation of union members but it is possible that many women remained unconvinced of a need for a continued association with the union once it appeared that minimum rates had been established. Lewenhak suggests that there was a tendency among women workers to believe that the increased earnings guaranteed by the trade boards (although of course there were no guarantees that employers would adhere to the rates) were in fact 'decreed by paternalistic governments' rather than having been won as a result of campaigning.[68]

To focus, however, on perceptions of women's ambivalent attitudes towards trade unionism or their inability or unwillingness to pay subscriptions, implies that either women workers or their trade union organisers (in failing to educate them) were to blame for failed branches and a lack of consistency in membership. Such a view misses another of the hurdles faced by the Federation - that of the intimidation of its women members by employers. Although alleged victimisation of Federation members did spark off wildcat strikes, evidence that employers targeted women working either alone as home workers or in small establishments is much harder to uncover. As already noted, the Federation reported complaints of victimisation of members in the lace industry in Nottingham in 1913. Members were being lost in Cradley Heath, after the success of the strike in 1910 where intimidation of isolated workers could undermine women's resolve to stay in the union. Defying an employer without the presence of co-workers would have been a daunting prospect for a home worker who was likely to have far more regular contact with her employer than with the organisers and other active members of the Federation. It was difficult enough for women factory workers to deal with this issue, as letters to Federation headquarters from the Banbury branch indicate in 1908. Miss Harper reported that two women had already left the union 'as their position [has] become so intolerable' due to harassment and 'annoyance' from the manageress. The rest of the members were 'being watched to such an extent that we cannot properly get on with our work' and 'I am afraid that more will follow the two girls who are leaving'.[69]

The evidence suggests that Federation branches, in the years before the First World War, relied on a combination of factors to be able to establish, and then retain, membership. In times of dispute, immediate and intensive assistance from the Federation's national leadership was essential. This then had to be supported by local activists who were able to work in the women's best interests in order to build a strong and enthusiastic branch and to persuade women in the advantages of trade unionism. The Federation saw strikes as opportunities, using them to strengthen existing branches and establish new ones. Its reports prove that women workers were militant and prepared to address all manner of grievances at work; walk outs, spontaneous demonstrations and picket duty were undertaken with enthusiasm but, as the Federation knew, this could not always be translated into union activism or even stable membership. Amongst women who had no familial background in trade unionism or who worked in isolated trades without the constant presence of enthusiastic, persuasive local organisers, maintaining interest in the union once the dispute was over was not easy. The larger textile unions appear to have had greater success than the Federation in recruiting and retaining women members but, as Bornat found, women who joined the General Union of Textile Workers in Yorkshire often did so because it was an expected part of their working lives. Once recruited, however, they were not educated in the benefits of being a union member and were very rarely involved in the union's leadership. [70]

It was clearly much more difficult to sustain membership of a trade union where there was no history of organisation within a trade. If, in addition, the local employer was smarting from concessions wrung from him by the Federation, it could take considerable courage for a woman worker to retain her membership and indeed, many women doubtless thought it too risky to do so. If being a union member posed a risk, committed activism was positively dangerous, time-consuming and immensely difficult for women who had neither family support nor political experience. Gordon suggests that the Federation, whilst recognising the specific difficulties that women faced in becoming trade union members, did little to address the conditions that created these, such as women's lack of birth control, maternity rights and child care arrangements.[71] Whilst I agree with Gordon's assessment, I would also draw attention to those Federation organisers who invested time making sure that they understood the conditions faced by women in different trades, attempting to ensure that all efforts to work on their behalf were realistic and enduring. At a local level the Federation remained aware of women's vulnerabilities as workers but was not always strong enough to ensure that enough was done to protect women from ruthless employers, or paternalistic ones who persuaded female workforces that they could look after them far better than the union could.

The Federation organisers worked incessantly to gain recognition for women's trade unionism among workers, employers and local labour movements. They fought constant battles to keep women paying their subscriptions and encouraging local activism in order to ensure that their efforts endured. Organisers, rather than trying to retain overall control, sought ways to make their roles less central to the long term success of local branches so that they would not spend weeks campaigning in a district only to leave and find that the branch did not long survive their departure. But this of course was not always within their control; a national organiser, accompanied by the local Trades Council and British Socialist Party, conducted a 'vigorous campaign' in Worcester during 1913; dozens of meetings were held at factory gates and street corners.[72] There were several winter social gatherings and a branch of over one hundred members was formed from the potteries, textile businesses, glove factories, sauce and confectionery firms. Despite such effort, in the following year's Annual Report the branch is not even listed.[73] Sometimes, Federation campaigns were deliberately targeted by other unions; in Coventry considerable friction developed between the Federation and the mixed sex Workers' Union 'whose local officials have persistently canvassed our members with the result that organisation has been hindered and our membership has been depleted without any corresponding gain to the other Union'.[74] In other areas, lack of support from male workers could weaken the position of women members. During the strike at Hart and Levy's in Nuneaton in 1914, male colleagues in the factory tried to undermine the women's action because, the Federation claimed, they objected to the idea that 'girls' (referred to as 'children' by the male pressers) were taking the initiative and trying to tell the men what to do.[75]

Before the First World War, the small branches and unsteady membership that characterised the Federation contributed to its marginalisation within labour history and the considerable amount of organisation that was done by the Federation on behalf of other trade unions has not been recognised. During the strike at Hart and Levy's the Federation recruited well over a hundred women. It then took the decision that these women would be more appropriately recruited into the local branch of the Amalgamated Union of Clothiers and although Isabel Sloan, Federation organiser, remained in the town in an attempt to revitalise the local branch, it was the Clothiers Union that picked up the bulk of new membership subscriptions resulting from the dispute. Unlike so many of the men's unions, the Federation – at least before the War – was not seeking to increase its status by boasting huge membership numbers. Its aim, along with the WTUL, was simply to strengthen women's organisation. In order to more fully understand the work of the Federation, we have to continue to look closely at the social, political and economic climate in which its personnel operated and at the obstacles in its way, but most importantly, wherever possible, we have to examine the lives of the women workers who became its members and how the Federation motto, 'to fight, to struggle, to right the wrong' touched their lives.

Notes

1. Drake, B. *Women in Trade Unions*, London: Virago, 1920 (1984 edition) Table 1.
2. The Women's Trade Union League was founded in 1874 by Emma Paterson

as the Women's Protective and Provident League with the aim of helping to set up trade unions in every trade in which women were employed and were excluded from men's unions.

3   National Federation of Women Workers Annual Report 1912, TUC Library, London Metropolitan University.
4   Thom, D. 'The Bundle of Sticks': Women Trade Unionists and Collective Organisation Before 1918 in John, A. V. (ed.) *Unequal Opportunities: Women's Employment in England 1800-1918*, Oxford: Blackwell, 1986 p. 285.
5   '"A little too nice?" The National Federation of Women Workers in Coventry 1907-1918', presented at the South West and South Wales Women's History Network Conference, 2002, University of Glamorgan.
6   Thom, D. 'Women at the Woolwich Arsenal 1915-19', *Oral History Journal*, volume 6, no. 2, 1978, pp. 58-74.
7   Bornat, J. 'Home and Work: A New Context for Trade Union History', *Oral History*, vol. 5, 1977. See also Bornat 'What About That Lass of Yours Being in the Union?': Textile Workers and Their Union in Yorkshire 1888-1922 in Davidoff, L. & Westover, B. (eds.) *Our Work, Our Lives, Our Words: Women's History and Women's Work*, Hampshire: Macmillan, 1986.
8   Liddington, J. *Rebel Girls: Their Fight For the Vote*, London: Virago, 2006, p. xiii.
9   This point is discussed by Davis, M. *Comrade or Brother? The History of the British Labour Movement 1789-1951*, London: Pluto Press, 1993.
10 See, for example, Pelling, H.A. *A History of British Trade Unionism*, Middlesex: Penguin, 1987; Laybourn, K. *A History of British Trade Unionism*, Great Britain: Edward Arnold, 1997.
11 The records of the Federation were lost when it amalgamated with the General and Municipal Workers Union. The TUC Library at London Metropolitan University holds the Annual Reports of the National Federation of Women Workers and the Women's Trade Union League.
12 Davin, A. 'Feminism and Labour History' in R. Samuel (ed) *People's History and Socialist Theory*, London: Routledge and Kegan Paul, 1981, p. 176.
13 Founded in 1906, the National Federation of Women Workers was amalgamated into the General and Municipal Workers' Union in 1921.
14 Drake, B. *Women in Trade Unions*.
15 Lewenhak, S. *Women and Trade Unions: an Outline History of Women in the British Trade Union Movement*, London: Ernest Benn Ltd, 1977; Boston, S. *Women Workers and the Trade Union Movement*, London: Davis-Poynter, 1980.
16 Thom, The Bundle of Sticks, p. 261.
17 Gordon, E. *Women and the Labour Movement in Scotland, 1850-1914*, Oxford: Clarendon Press, 1991.
18 For an excellent discussion of what makes feminist history, see Davin, A. 'Feminism and Labour History' in Samuel, R. (ed) *People's History and Socialist Theory*, Routledge and Kegan & Paul: London, 1981
19 For example, *Midland Daily Telegraph, Coventry Herald, Coventry Standard, Coventry Times*

20 Coventry Trades Council Annual Reports, 1900–1906 (Board of Trade Library); 1914, Modern Records Centre, University of Warwick, MSS. 5/2/2.
21 Richardson Collection of Tapes at Coventry University Frederick Lanchester Library, research for Richardson, K. *Twentieth Century Coventry*, City of Coventry, 1972.
22 With grateful thanks to Mrs E. Trent for the interview and correspondence and also for the great interest she has shown in this research.
23 *Woman Worker*, published between September 1907 and June 1910 and then from 1916.
24 Gertrude Tuckwell Collection, TUC Collections at London Metropolitan University. The collection includes newspaper cuttings and material relating to issues of women's trade unionism and labour 1890-1921 with an emphasis on the WTUL and the Federation.
25 Federation Annual Report 1911.
26 *Woman Worker*, October 1907.
27 Ibid.
28 Ibid.
29 Federation Annual Report 1914.
30 Federation Annual Report 1911.
31 Federation Annual Report 1913.
32 Federation Annual Report 1913.
33 Gordon, *Women in the Labour Movement in Scotland*, p. 225.
34 Federation Annual Report 1911.
35 Chew, D. N. *Ada Nield Chew: the Life and Writings of a Working Woman*, London: Virago Press, 1982, p. 28.
36 Richardson Collection of Audiotapes, Edith Mayell, no. 74
37 Gordon, *Women and the Labour Movement in Scotland*, p. 240.
38 *Daily Citizen*, 17 January 1914, Gertrude Tuckwell Collection, File 13.
39 Correspondence between Oxford and Banbury branches of the Federation and the National Federation 1907-8, Gertrude Tuckwell Papers 216/m/7.
40 Ibid.
41 Federation Annual Report 1912.
42 Richardson Collection of Audiotapes, Mayell, no. 74.
43 *Woman Worker*, October 1907.
44 Federation Annual Report 1912.
45 *Woman Worker*, November 1907.
46 *Woman Worker*, December 1907.
47 Boston, *Women Workers*, pp. 70-1.
48 Trade union figures from Boston, *Women Workers*, p. 71.
49 Federation Annual Report 1914.
50 *Nuneaton Observer*, 23 January 1914.
51 Thom, 'The Bundle of Sticks', p. 269.
52 Fraser, W.H. *A History of British Trade Unionism*, Basingstoke, Palgrave Macmillan, 1999, p. 120.
53 Federation Annual Report 1912.
54 Federation Annual Report 1913.

55 Ibid.
56 Ibid.
57 Ibid.
58 Ibid.
59 *Midland Daily Telegraph* 8 February 1908.
60 Hamilton, M. *Mary Macarthur – a Biographical Sketch*, New York: Thomas Seltzer, 1926, p. 35.
61 *Woman Worker*, November 1907.
62 Federation Annual Report 1912.
63 *Woman Worker*, October 1907.
64 Boston, *Women Workers and the Trade Union Movement*, pp. 71-2.
65 Federation Annual Report 1911.
66 The Federation (Annual Report 1912) negotiated with the Government to secure exemption from contribution for women who were paid less than 9 shillings a week and a reduced rate of contribution for those paid less than 12 shillings a week. Many women remained uncovered by the National Insurance Act because of the casual nature of their employment.
67 Federation Annual Reports 1912 and 1913.
68 Lewenhak, *Women and Trade Unions* p. 126.
69 Gertrude Tuckwell Papers 216/7.
70 Bornat, 1986.
71 Gordon, *Women in the Labour Movement in Scotland*, p. 234.
72 Federation Annual Report 1913.
73 Federation Annual Report 1914.
74 Ibid.
75 *Nuneaton Observer*, 23 January 1914.

Alice Wheeldon revisited

Sheila Rowbotham

Alice Wheeldon was a suffragette in the Women's Social and Political Union and a left winger in the socialist Independent Labour Party in the Midlands town of Derby. During the First World War the Women's Social and Political Union, along with other feminist and socialist organisations split. Alice Wheeldon joined the anti-war group founded by ILP members, the No Conscription Fellowship, and also became part of an underground network which helped conscientious objectors to evade internment. On evidence from a spy employed by the Ministry of Munitions, she was accused of conspiring to assassinate the Prime Minister, Lloyd George, while he played golf, by obtaining the poison curare from her son-in-law, Alfred Mason. She insisted that she had sent for the poison to kill guard dogs guarding the young men who refused to fight in internment camps. The original charge had included King George V and Arthur Henderson , the Labour Party leader who was pro-war. But these latter two accusations were dropped, presumably because it made the case look incredible even amidst the paranoia of the war. Alice Wheeldon was imprisoned, along with Alfred Mason and her daughter Winnie Mason, though her other daughter Hettie was not convicted. After the war Alice Wheeldon was released on an amnesty from Lloyd George but, weakened by hunger striking while in prison, died in the influenza epidemic.

   It was the drama of her case which initially captured my imagination and I wrote a play called *Friends of Alice Wheeldon* which was performed by a radical theatre group in London and several Northern cities in Britain in 1980. However, as I researched the background I had become fascinated by the broader historical questions associated with her story and explored these in a long essay, 'Rebel Networks in the First World War' published with the play by Pluto Press in a book called *Friends of Alice Wheeldon*. Even after this was published in 1986, Alice Wheeldon's history refused to lie still. Contact with descendants of the radical group in Derby demonstrated how history does not stop. It continues to move in two senses: firstly by keeping on coming to light and secondly by the repercussions of memory. So the process of discovery is never finite. Revisiting Alice Wheeldon has raised many broader questions about traditions of radical politics and how these can be seen both historically and in the here and now.

In 1986, in *Friends of Alice Wheeldon*, I wrote,

> In returning to the interconnections of socialism and feminism in the early years of this century, I sometimes have to shake myself back into the present. I have a recurring dream of discovering a new set of rooms in a familiar house. Each time I return to the dream, I am puzzled. How could I live so long without realizing that just through a door and round the corner and down a passage there were unvisited rooms, waiting, neglected, commodious- new sketchily defined possibilities.'[1]

Because Alice Wheeldon and her family were brought into conflict with the legal machinery of the state in wartime, daily, personal life was exposed to public view. The sphere of the state had extended beyond what would have been acceptable in peacetime to monitor opinions and ways of living which would normally have remained private concerns. As a result, the source material available provided a unique insight into the connections between differing strands on the left which are not observed by studying specific organisations. It also gave a rare glimpse into that interior world of radical politics which usually escapes the minute books and thus vanishes from history – the emotions of hope and despair which people carry home with them.

Documentation had been gathered as a result of the trial and deposited in the Public Record Office (PRO). While politically sensitive material is sifted from the PRO, the material on the Wheeldon case could be complemented by reports from the intelligence agents investigating subversion in industry employed by the Ministry of Munitions in the private collection of the Conservative politician Lord Milner at the Bodleian Library in Oxford.

From these, as well as from press reports of the trial, I was able to piece together the world of a group of socialist feminists in a provincial town. Alice Wheeldon, who ran a second hand clothes shop, would speak and sell newspapers in the local market place. She belonged to the left of the ILP which was sympathetic to revolutionary socialism and syndicalism. Her daughter Hettie, who was a teacher, was also a socialist and held what were considered to be 'advanced views' on women and marriage. The other daughter, Winnie Mason, lived in Southampton, married to the left-wing chemist, Alfred Mason. The Wheeldons and the Masons belonged to a radical lower-middle-class milieu, reading left and feminist publications and books such as Bernard Shaw's *Mrs Warren's Profession* and Voynick's *The Gadfly*. They were scornful of what later came to be called 'the establishment', despising upper-middle-class hypocrisy and rejecting religion. I knew of similar groupings in London, Leeds, Sheffield, Glasgow and Eastwood, the village near Nottingham where D.H. Lawrence lived. The Wheeldon case thus provided a means of entering the hidden history of the suffrage movement – the personal cultural rebellion which accompanied the movement for the vote .

The publicity and material on the trial meant that there was more detail than is usually available about grassroots leftists. Moreover, after an appeal on a local radio programme Norah Romer sent me a copy of her father's diary. Reuben Farrow, a railway clerk was a pacifist and active with Alice Wheeldon in the Derby Independent Labour Party (ILP) but opposed to the extreme left tendency to which Alice Wheeldon and her daughter Hettie belonged. His diary revealed not only the public face of politics, the emotional toll of the disputes dividing the local ILP branch, but more of that interior world of the ethical socialism of the Independent Labour Party – vegetarianism and the effort towards personal democracy between the sexes by organising a baby-sitting rota.[2]

The material in the PRO and in the press reports of the trial which related to their anti-war activities showed the Wheeldon household to have been a linkage point between the opponents of the First World War and the left leadership of the shop stewards movement which was resisting the loss of control which resulted from the deskilling of wartime production methods. Employers were restructuring industry, not only to produce more, but also to break craft power. The shop stewards movement was contradictory – both a defence of the privilege of skill and an assertion of a more democratic and meaningful relation to work. However, the consciousness generated by the massive strikes and the organisational lessons of the rank-and-file networks were not simply work bound. The Wheeldon case led me to discover aspects of the shop stewards movement which had been missed in both the emphasis among labour historians on industrial action and the over simple dismissal of the shop stewards' movement among feminists as a movement defending male skills. I had already realised through the local and oral history work I and other socialist and feminist historians had done in the 1970s that there had been many more interconnections than has been supposed between feminism and syndicalism, for instance in Glasgow and London as well as Ireland, France and the US, so the Derby links fitted into the broader picture.[3] The left wing leadership of the shop stewards were not only generally involved in radical politics locally and in left organisations nationally, some of them supported the suffrage militants despite their scepticism about the efficacy of parliament. There were also efforts in Sheffield to break down the divisions between skilled and unskilled workers and between men and women in the workplace. Recognition of the limits of an exclusively workplace based politics was also present within the shop stewards movement at the end of the war. Indeed this awareness led some of them to the Communist Party when it was formed and into the left of the Labour Party.[4]

I managed to collect information on the revolutionaries from oral and written sources.[5] A key figure was the marxist philosopher, Willie Paul who wrote a book on the state and was later to be active in the Coventry shop stewards movement, lying low and producing the marxist paper *The Socialist* from a village near Derby in 1916. This was the organ of the Socialist Labour Party, a small marxist sect influenced by the American followers of Daniel de Leon, which stressed industrial direct action and had its main base in Glasgow. Willie Paul supported himself by running a clothes stall in Derby market and conferred with Alice Wheeldon on the second hand clothes business. An old socialist who had been leader of the Young Communist League, Harry Young, told me Paul, the political theorist and socialist business man, was 'personable'.[6]

I soon came to realise that, like the suffrage movement, the austere seeming Socialist Labour Party (SLP) had a hidden history too. Nothing is quite as it might appear in this proto-Leninist organisation. For example, Paul's friend from Glasgow, called John S. Clarke, who was in the SLP, was a poet and a lion tamer! Clarke had been influenced by a Scottish feminist and advocate of free love and birth control since the 1880s called Jane Clapperton.[7]

Another friend of Paul and Clarke and fellow member of the SLP, the militant shop steward Arthur MacManus, had been banned from Glasgow because of his industrial activity and sent to work at Cunards in Liverpool during 1916. However, he kept giving the authorities the slip and was secretly visiting Derby not only to see Paul, but also because it was a munitions centre. MacManus, who had supported the militant wing of the suffrage movement before the First World War when *The Suffragette* could not find a printer, met the Wheeldons in this period. He married Hettie in 1919. Arthur MacManus combined militancy as a shop steward with support for the Irish Nationalist cause. His political mentor was James Connolly, the leader of the disastrous 1916 Easter Rising,. MacManus' revolutionary politics were hardened when Connolly was executed by the British.

When the Communist Party was formed after the First World War he was made its chairman. MacManus was to be sent, under pressure from Lenin, to negotiate with the Labour Party leader Arthur Henderson for affiliation. This was rejected. A personal dimension to this historic encounter was that only a few years before these two political opponents met, MacManus' late mother-in-law, Alice Wheeldon, had been accused of conspiring to murder the same Arthur Henderson. Lenin seems to have been unaware of this local detail!

MacManus visited the Soviet Union and served on the Communist International's executive committee. In February 1922 Lenin wheeled him out to condemn the Workers' Opposition – the left Communists agitating for workers' control. Only two years before MacManus himself had chaired the British Shop Stewards' Conference demanding workers' control over production and distribution. Cruelly, destiny had turned the tables. He found himself rubber stamping the suppression of workplace democracy in the name of socialism.[8] Harry Young remembered him drinking heavily in Moscow and his memory is supported by an account in the autobiography of the Jamaican socialist writer Claude McKay, who saw MacManus at a party, '..swaying like a tipsy little imp' and accusing a clerk in the Department of Investigations and Arrests of being a spy. 'Spy ! Spy! I am not going to stay here I am going home. Spy!' When he was told to stop insulting real Communists and go back home, MacManus shouted, 'I am not a Communist. I am an Anarchist', whereupon a comrade clapped his hand over his mouth and 'lifting him up like a kid, carried him from the room.'[9]

The material on the Wheeldon case thus revealed a rebellious anti-war network which came into being during the First World War and spanned left-wing socialist feminists, militant shop stewards, revolutionary socialists and supporters of Irish freedom. The extreme circumstances of opposing the First World War as an embattled minority meant that this anti-war underground overcame some of the pre-war sectarian divisions between differing strands of the left. Left shop stewards, such as MacManus from Scotland and J.T. Murphy from Sheffield, found themselves working with the syndicalists in the North London Herald League and with Marxist opponents of the war in Hackney, North-East London, who were in the British Socialist Party. The Herald League also worked with Sylvia Pankhurst's Workers' Socialist Federation in East London, and were in contact with James Connolly in Ireland.

These networks extended beyond national boundaries. While in the US James Connolly had made contact with the syndicalist organisation Industrial Workers of the World, known as the IWW or the Wobblies, and IWW seamen were to help smuggle conscientious objectors across the Atlantic during the First World War. The IWW also had a branch in London.

Through the anti-war movement the left within the Independent Labour Party increasingly overlapped with the revolutionary left. Even the democratic liberals who joined an organisation to make diplomacy more open and answerable – the Union of Democratic Control – found themselves defined as subversive. The extreme circumstances of resistance created a sense of flux. Despite their political differences, these anti-war left wingers and feminists shared a disillusionment with the record of Labour in Parliament which was to be strengthened by their contempt for the Labour leadership who supported the war. The war also contributed to their hostility to the state, which curtailed many of the normal peace time civil liberties. Both experiences fostered an interest in direct forms of democracy.[10]

It was this combination of influences, connections and circumstances which transformed Alice Wheeldon's life with such tragic consequences. Scurrying around after the left-wing rebels, and treading acrimoniously on each others' toes, were several intelligence agencies, busily collecting information on everyone from liberal suffrage supporters to the SLP. It was to be this third area, through the state's intervention in the lives of the Wheeldon family, which was to take me into aspects of history unfamiliar to me. Up until this point my focus had been on power from below rather than power at the top.

In 1916, the Sheffield shop stewards, led by the young Marxist J.T. Murphy, went on strike when a skilled worker, a fitter, was conscripted into the army. They feared industrial conscription when the firm Vickers withheld papers which would have secured his discharge. In a determined effort to overcome the weakness of isolated acts of local resistance, the stewards set off on a fleet of motor cycles to take the news of the dispute to all the munitions centres in the country – including, of course, Derby.[11]

There was an acute shortage of munitions in 1916. The intelligence unit connected to the Ministry of Munitions feared a general strike was imminent. Fortunately for historians, who wish in turn to spy on them, they have left have an excellent collection of documents describing the workers' meetings in the private collection of Lord Milner. Among these is a panicky document about the danger of a general strike, *Notes on the Shop Stewards Movement Developing in the North and West of England*. 'All the disintegrating and reactionary elements in the State such as the Pacifists, the SLP, the Syndicalists, the IWW, the No Conscription Fellowship (NCF), the Sinn Feiners, the Union of Democratic Control (UDC), and the militant section of the ILP, flock to serve under the same banner.'[12]

The most sinister figures were considered to be J.T. Murphy, Arthur MacManus, Willie Paul, Walter Hill – a gay shop steward from Sheffield and friend of the socialist Edward Carpenter – and David Ramsey, a steward from Leicester. The leader of the unit, a rather dim right-wing Tory, William Melville Lee, added to this list the British Socialist Party, the Women's Social and Political Union, the Clyde Workers' Committee, the Central Labour College and the Plebeians (Plebs, an educational group). Under Lee was a John Buchan style adventurer called Lieutenant de Valda, who was well entertained by Douglas Vickers and other munitions employers. His equivalent to an NCO was a burly macho figure called Herbert Booth, who was known as Comrade Bert. He employed a former socialist and spiritualist with long black greasy hair and the pseudonym 'Alex Gordon'.

The unit, of course, was in the business of finding conspiracies and plots, and Alex Gordon, who was desperate for money and at the very bottom rung of the hierarchy, was particularly keen. That November he hung around the Sheffield meetings and got to know Walter Hill and Arthur MacManus. Gordon arrived at Alice Wheeldon's house in Pear Tree Lane, Derby on 27th December, claiming he was on the run as a conscientious objector. He introduced her to Booth and they persuaded her to write to her son in law Alf Mason for curare. Alice Wheeldon said in the subsequent trial that she understood this was to poison the dogs guarding young men in the internment camps; the prosecution claimed she planned to shoot a poison dart at Lloyd George while he played golf.

The letters and parcels were intercepted and Alice, Hettie, Winnie and Alf were arrested early in 1917. The Attorney General was F.E.Smith, friend and associate of that notorious right winger Sir Edward Carson, who had threatened an armed uprising against Irish Home Rule before the war. F.E. Smith, a brilliant lawyer, acted for the prosecution. Herbert Booth gave evidence in the trial. When I showed a copy of his evidence to a solicitor friend, he immediately pointed out how it had been doctored to appear more convincing. Gordon however was regarded as too tacky. He was shipped out to South Africa, out of the way. War panic was at its height; Alice got ten years penal servitude, Winnie five, Alf seven. Only Hettie was found not guilty. The unit however had received so much publicity that its cover was blown and its rival MI5 won out. Lloyd George had got into power with the support of the extreme right in 1916, but by 1918 he no longer needed Carson, Smith or their protégé Lee. They were embarrassing and he dumped his former allies.[13]

Alice Wheeldon was in her fifties and her health suffered in prison. She died, impoverished and ostracised by neighbours, in Derby in February 1919. The local press reported the funeral in considerable detail, listing the names of friends from the socialist, anti- war and suffrage movements who attended – among them David Ramsey's mother. The *Derby Mercury* described how the mourners stood in an oppressive silence as Alice's son William Wheeldon, who had been in hiding for refusing to fight, pulled a red flag about three and a half foot square out of his pocket. It fluttered in the wind as he placed it over his mother's coffin.[14] Then John S. Clarke, also on the run, struggled up the slippery earth and, looking down into her grave, delivered a funeral address in which he insisted that she had been killed by a 'judicial murder'.[15]

In 1919, shortly after Alice Wheeldon's death, a terrified Alex Gordon, carrying a rifle and broke as ever, returned from South Africa and told his story to the left paper *The Daily Herald*.[16] John S. Clarke wrote a bitter *Epitaph of Alex Gordon*.

Maggot -worms in swarms below
Compete with one another
In shedding tears of bitter woe
To mourn- not eat a brother.[17]

After *Friends of Alice Wheeldon*, was performed in London in 1980 an old socialist, Harry Young, who had been with Arthur MacManus in Moscow in the early twenties, asked me, 'How did you know all those things about Arthur?' I was, of course, delighted because I had been guessing in my portrayal of his personal character. The problem was that some people assumed I had made up the historically based material in the play such as the links between feminists and socialists. For instance, the assistant to a BBC producer who wanted to put the play on the radio told him it was all too far fetched! It was partly exasperation with this unthinking ideological resistance to recognising the connections between feminism and socialism in the past which made my introduction to the play much longer than I had intended.

After the book was published I was to find that the truth was actually much *more* extraordinary than I had thought. I had, however, made an error about William Wheeldon. An old man called Albert Chapman, who made contact after I went on the local radio programme asking for information, claimed William worked for the Burton-on-Trent Cooperative Society and that he knew his son. This turned out to be a false trail. Nicholas Hiley, an historian who studies the intelligence groups, and had become convinced that the Wheeldons had suffered a grave injustice, found that in fact William, unable to get his teaching job back even in 1920 because he had been in prison, tried to run a dairy in Croydon.

Tragedy and vilification continued to follow the family. In 1920 Hettie died after giving birth to a still born baby. The following year William went to live in the Soviet Union and took Soviet citizenship. At this point the trail was lost. Then, in 1992, the KGB revealed that a British Communist sympathiser called 'William Wileden' had been arrested and shot in one of Stalin's labour camps. Nicholas Hiley has established that this was William Wheeldon, last heard of in a Russian city called Samara (now Kuybyshev) in 1928.[18]

Nicholas Hiley and I went to Derby, on June 6 1986, after *Friends of Alice Wheeldon* was published, where I spoke to a meeting which included older women members of the Labour Party who could remember hearing adults whispering about the scandal. I also met the granddaughters of Alice's suffrage friend, Mrs Robinson, who up until then had been simply a name in the newspaper accounts of the funeral. From Mrs Kidger and Mrs Keeling I learned more about the local background. There had already been an attempt to link Mrs Robinson with the burning of a local church. The suffragettes were suspected but she always maintained it had been done by the police to discredit them and that the policeman who came to see her still stank of petrol. Mrs Robinson cut her hair short, ran a health food shop and used to ride a motor bike and side car in which she had smuggled young men out of the internment camps. I had erred on the side of conservatism. Hettie, who had had affairs with several men in the socialist movement, declared that no man was going to tie her down, when she became pregnant in 1917. She was in fact having an abortion from another socialist man when I had portrayed her in my play courting Arthur MacManus. Betty Keeling and the Kidgers confirmed how the memory of the Wheeldon case lived on. Frank Kidger had been warned off from courting his wife as late as the 1950s because her grandmother had been Alice Wheeldon's friend.

Most exciting was a visit from Chloe Mason, a socialist and feminist from Australia who had read my book and realised Alice was her great grandmother. Her father, Peter Mason, was the son of Alf and Winnie Mason. He had gone to Australia to start a new life still haunted by the trial. The uncanny thing was that Chloe looked just like Alice! She too made contact with Nicholas Hiley and began visiting people who had known Winnie and Alf, including Mrs King the daughter of a student friend of Winnie's. Mrs King, who had corresponded with Nicholas Hiley, was still distressed by the way in which the trial and imprisonment had caricatured and defamed Alice Wheeldon and her family.

I had begun writing about Alice Wheeldon amidst the co-operative culture of early feminist history and had been greatly helped by discussions with the late Gloden Dallas and with Theresa Moriarty. As I was drawn into the history of the left and intelligence, Raymond Challinor, Ken Weller, Julian Puttcowski and Nicholas Hiley were generous with references and ideas. After writing the play and publishing *Friends of Alice Wheeldon*, meeting Chloe Mason and the descendants of her friend Mrs Robinson, taught me how history continues. It is never ultimately 'known' simply because you catch aspects of the past between two book covers. Meeting the little band of people who still cared that an injustice had been done to Alice Wheeldon was immensely important to me, not only for what it revealed, but also because it was going against the grain of an increasingly competitive and individualistic ethos in scholarship in Britain.

Investigating the case of Alice Wheeldon enabled me to discover how memories are passed down through families; hidden threads of defiance against the official version of events along with fear is transmitted through generations. For instance, Chloe Mason told me that the power and cruelty of 'the system' could still make Peter Mason, himself a radical scientist, terrified of his daughter protesting on any issue likely to bring her to the attention of the state. Chloe knew that William Wheeldon's letters to her family had become sadder and sadder and had stopped in 1928. But the family thought he had caught typhus and died. The news from the KGB refuted this.

In November 1997 the MI5 files were released to the Public Record Office finally confirming that Alice Wheeldon had been set up by 'Alex Gordon' a pseudonym for a man called Vivian Rickard. The journal *Statewatch* commented on the material in an article headed, 'MI5: historical files being destroyed' which observed, '.. the release of MI5 files more than justifies the interest of historians in questioning the perceived wisdom of mainstream contemporary accounts.'[19]

I have continued to be fascinated by the people in the Wheeldon circle. My interest is partly in them as individuals and Fiona Cameron has uncovered new and intriguing information by researching into her family's history. In 2007 she sent me an account describing how William Marshall, Alice's father, was an engine tenter when she was born in 1866. Fiona Cameron's account also shows how Alice married William Wheeldon when she was only 19 and he was 32 – perhaps part of the attraction was the escape he offered her from domestic service.[20]

Alice Wheeldon's story resonates with me too as part of a more general historical preoccupation with uncovering hidden personal networks and understanding how these interact with the public realm of politics. The process of discovering those unvisited rooms in my dream goes on. In a memoir, *Molly Murphy: Suffragette and Socialist*, published in 1998 by Salford University, Molly Murphy recounts selling the WSPU paper *The Suffragette* in Sheffield in 1912, to a shy, serious young man. This was of course J.T. Murphy, the shop steward who had upset the spies reporting to the Ministry of Munitions by seeking to involve the women workers in the 1916 strike in Sheffield. 'He always swears he fell in love with me that night. Of course he didn't tell me so then. Indeed I think he became too interested in listening to the speaker to make any conversation at all'. She adds that Murphy joined

> the list of young men who regularly found their way to our shop in Chapel Walk, most of them socialist working men who were active in one or other phase of the Labour Movement. That they were interested in "Votes for Women" I have no doubt and that they were interested in our movement was evident from the way in which they could always be relied on without asking to act as our body guards whenever they knew some of us had decided to do some heckling at an opponent's meeting.[21]

The body guards were certainly there too in Glasgow and East London – perhaps there were other unrecorded love affairs as well. Radical movements spill over the edges and are inclined to intermingle. This has frequently been lost in the histories.

There is another reason for my interest in revisiting the case of Alice Wheeldon, for it occurred just at that fluid moment in socialism, before bolshevisation and before the top down traditions of labourism were established. Before the First World War, there had been a lively radical culture suspicious of leaders, passionate about democracy, wary of the state, imagining a 'new age' at work and in communities. This was to persist in the beleaguered anti-war movement, despite being battered and badly shaken by the war-time state. The tragic personal story of Alice Wheeldon unfolded when the left was in transition. 'Lenin is no pope or god,'[22] declared Willie Paul in 1920. The pressure of ensuing events was to make this a difficult position to hold onto over the years. The formation of the Communist Party and the ascendency of the Labour Party was to divide this anti-authoritarian left and bury the more libertarian strands from view.

Stuart Hall has remarked, 'One of the many tricks which the retrospective construction of tradition on the left has performed is to make the triumph of Labourism over these other socialist currents – the result of a massive political struggle in which the ruling class played a key role – appear as an act of natural and inevitable succession.' [23] We are still living with the consequences of the perspective which resulted from this partial eclipse. Indeed the trial of Alice Wheeldon has assumed a new relevance, as John Jackson, the Director of open Democracy, pointed out in *History Today* in 2007, for the role of the intelligence services in wartime and the power of the state to influence the judiciary are once again being contested.[24]

GLOSSARY

British Socialist Party (BSP): Formed in 1911 by the fusion of the marxist Social Democratic Federation and various left groups; it split over the First World War, the pro- war group joining the Labour Party in 1916.

Edward Carpenter: English socialist who settled outside Sheffield in the 1880s, writing on socialism, women's emancipation and homosexuality.

Lord Edward Henry Carson: Conservative politician and opponent of Home Rule for Ireland.

Central Labour College: Marxist workers college in London.

Jane Clapperton: Campaigner for women's sexual freedom and birth conrol from the 1880s, active in the anarchist and socialist left.

Clyde Workers Committee(CWC): Formed in 1915 on the River Clyde, Scotland to unify workers' struggles against the conditions of wartime production.

Communist Party of Great Britain (CPGB): Founded in 1920 from several socialist groupings, it was repeatedly refused affiliation to the Labour Party and developed as a separate party.

James Connolly: Active in the socialist movement in Ireland and the US where he was involved with the Socialist Labour Party and the Industrial Workers of the World. Returned to Ireland and became active in the nationalist movement. Led the Easter Rising in 1916. Executed by the British.

Daniel de Leon: Leader of the American Socialist Labour Party, renowned for his sectarianism.

Reuben Farrow: A Christian socialist and member of the Derby Independent Labour Party

Arthur Henderson: Labour Party chairman during the First World War. He served in the Coalition Cabinet 1915-1917, earning the hatred of the left in the anti-war movement.

Herald League: Formed before the First World War to sell the left paper *The Daily Herald*, many of the local groups became centres of resistance to the war.

Independent Labour Party (ILP): A socialist party formed in 1893, it contained, ethical, reformist and ethical elements. It looked forward to the creation of a socialist commonwealth by gradualist means and was affiliated to the Labour Party.

Industrial Workers of the World (IWW, the Wobblies): An organisation active among workers in the US, it emphasised democratic control at the workplace and recruited among unskilled and immigrant labour.

David Lloyd George: A prominent figure in the Liberal Party who became Prime Minister in 1916.

Jack (J.T.) Murphy: leader of the Sheffield shop stewards and supporter of women's rights.

No Conscription Fellowship: Formed during the First World War by ILP members to oppose conscription, it supported conscientious objectors and put out a newspaper *The Tribunal*.

Plebs: Marxist educational group emphasising the need for autonomous working-class education.

FE Smith (First Earl of Birkenhead): Conservative lawyer and politician. Opposed Irish Home Rule and appeared for the Crown in the trial of Roger Casement. Became attorney-general in 1915.

Socialist Labour Party (SLP): Small Marxist group led by Daniel de Leon in the US. It emphasised industrial action but was not completely syndicalist, accepting the need for political action. Its paper was *The Socialist*.

Syndicalism: Used loosely, this term meant an approach to rank-and-file industrial organising which stressed direct action at the workplace. It was anti-bureaucratic and anti-statist. More narrowly it referred to the group around *The Syndicalist* which opposed using parliament to forward the cause of the working class.

Union of Democratic Control (UDC): Established in 1914 to try and make diplomacy more open and democratic.

Women's Social and Political Union (WSPU): Grew out of the Independent Labour Party and formed by the Pankhursts to campaign for votes for women.

Workers' Socialist Federation: Formed in 1916 by Sylvia Pankhurst in East London from her socialist suffrage organising. Produced a newspaper called *The Workers' Dreadnought*.

A shorter version of this chapter appeared as 'A la redecouverte d'Alice Wheeldon' in ed. Martine Spensky, *Les femmes a la Conqueste du Pouvoir Politique*, Centre de Recherches sur le Commonwealth et les Iles Britanniques de Universite de Paris V11, l'Harmatton, Paris 2001.

Notes

1. Rowbotham, S. *Friends of Alice Wheeldon: Rebel networks in the First World War* London: Pluto Press, 1986, pp. 120-121.
2. Ibid. Pp. 4-11.
3. On France see Bouchardeau, H. *Helene Brion: La Voie Feministe*, Editions Syros, Paris, 1978. On the US see Gordon,L. *Woman's Body, Woman's Right: A Social History of Birth Control in America*, New York: Grossman, 1976; Baxandall, R. *Words on Fire: The Life and Writing of Elizabeth Gurley Flynn*, New Brunswick: Rutgers University Press, 1987.
4. See Rowbotham, S. *Friends of Alice Wheeldon*, pp. 25-33, 40-48, 87-94.
5. Challinor, R. *The Origins of British Bolshevism*, London: Croom Helm, 1977 is particularly useful. I am grateful to Raymond Challinor for allowing me to look at the manuscript notes of the socialist Lester Hutchinson.
6. Sheila Rowbotham, interview with Harry Young, February 1980.
7. See Challinor, R. *John S.Clarke, Parliamentarian, Poet, Lion-Tamer*, London: Pluto Press, 1977 and on Jane Clapperton, Lucy Bland, *Banishing The Beast: English Feminists and Sexual Morality*, London: Penguin, pp. 6, 78, 172, 211.
8. On Arthur MacManus see Rowbotham, *Friends of Alice Wheeldon*, pp. 11-14, 19-21, 27-33, 44-51, 87-97.
9. McKay, C. *A Long Way from Home*, London: Pluto Press, 1985, pp. 200-201.
10. See Rowbotham, *Friends of Alice Wheeldon*, pp. 33-40.
11. See ibid .pp. 40-48 and Murphy, J.T., *Preparing for Power*, London: Pluto Press, 1972, pp. 129-30.
12. Notes on the Strike Movement now Developing in the North and West of England, Milner Papers.
13. See Rowbotham, *Friends of Alice Wheeldon*, pp. 44-80.
14. *Derby Mercury*, 28 February 1919. See also *Derby and Chesterfield Reporter*, 28 February 1919 and *Derby Daily Express*, 22 February 1919.
15. *The Socialist*, 6 March 1919.
16. William Mellor, *Daily Herald*, 20 December 1919.
17. Clarke, J.S., 'Epitaph of Alex Gordon', quoted in Challinor, *Origins of British Bolshevism*, p. 146.
18. Michael Durham, 'Russians wrong about Briton who died in Stalin camp', *Independent on Sunday*, 6 September 1992 and 'Death of an English Socialist', *Independent on Sunday*, 13 September 1992.
19. Anonymous, 'MI5: historical files being destroyed', *Statewatch*, January-February 1998.
20. I am grateful to Fiona Cameron for sending me her unpublished manuscript on William Marshall and his children (July 2007).
21. Molly Murphy, in *Molly Murphy: Suffragette and Socialist*, Institute of Social

research, University of Salford, 1998. I am grateful to the late Gloden Dallas and to Ken Weller for information on Glasgow and London.
22. William Paul, quoted in Challinor, *Origins of British Bolshevism*, p. 232.
23. Hall, S. 'The State: Socialism's Old Caretaker', *Marxism Today*, November, 1984, p. 24.
24. Jackson, J., 'Losing the Plot: Lloyd George, F.E. Smith and the trial of Alice Wheeldon', *History Today*, May 2007, p. 47.

Scottish socialist women in the inter-war years

Annmarie Hughes

Little has been written about Scottish women's involvement in the labour movement or their political agency in the interwar years. However, it has been argued that in contrast to the years before the First World War, the interwar years were a barren period for British, or rather English, women of the labour movement.[1] The challenges women had mounted against the sexual division of labour and the male-dominance of their movement were apparently sidelined, constrained by the reassertion of traditional gender ideals, the economic climate and the need for class unity in the face of the reactionary governments. In addition, because women's political agency was largely confined to the sphere of local government it is implied that their contribution to labour politics was less significant than that of their male counterparts operating in national politics.[2] Regardless of these constraints a significant number of Scottish women proved capable of advancing the interests of what were identified and accepted as their constituents, working-class women, and often, in feminist ways, developing strategies which challenged the sexual division of labour and the male-dominance of their movement. These women were at one and the same time reactionary, revolutionary and prudent in their protests on behalf of working-class women.[3]

Graves argues that Labour Party women were unable to forward feminist demands between the wars due to the domination of men in British politics and the adverse economic climate of these years. The economic climate resulted in declining membership of Labour women's organisations in depressed areas and corresponded with a rise of young, better educated, female members in the more affluent areas of Britain. Seemingly, these young women had no direct experience of poverty and disliked feminism. Graves also maintains that Labour women underestimated the power of the female vote and this was aggravated because activists were torn between their loyalties to their class and their gender, more so after the Conservative government 'set out to punish the unions for their temerity in calling the

General Strike'. Gender concerns were further sidelined when both sexes were compelled to support their class in the struggle against 'reactionary government and fascism in the later 1930s'. Thus after a rare period of unity, strength and optimism between 1917 and 1920, women were unable to mount a challenge against the male dominance of the labour movement.[4]

Scott also argues that the Co-operative Women's Guild lost its radical and feminist approach by the 1930s, attributing this to socio-political changes and transformations in leadership, which ensured that the Guild's independence and autonomy were eroded. By the 1930s, under the new secretary Eleanor Barton, women who did not sympathise with the Labour Party, including Communist Party members, were ousted. Correspondingly, following the Labour Party line, seemingly the Guild began to subscribe to traditional notions of womanhood rather than promoting women as citizens as they had done until the 1930s.[5]

These historians highlight the impediments faced by 'socialist' women as female members of the Independent Labour Party [ILP], Labour Party, Communist Party and Co-operative Women's Guild identified themselves in Scotland. To concentrate on the obstacles they faced, however, neglects the significance of women's political agency, especially in local government, in the areas of health, housing, education, public assistance relief and other welfare services. From the 1920s public services were transferred to local authority control and were supported by Exchequer grants. In 1929 Patrick Dollan, leader of the Labour group on Glasgow City Council, acknowledged that it was local governments who made legislation effective.[6] At this time, much of the legislation pertaining to welfare services and the provision of council housing was permissive rather than compulsory in nature. Therefore the provision and quality of welfare and housing was susceptible to the pressure of local protests. In addition, these services were of fundamental importance in Scotland, which had some of the worst housing in Britain and high levels of social deprivation. Women may have been largely confined to local politics but they were operating in a political space with the capacity to allow them to considerably improve the everyday lives of their constituents. As the Labour Party activist Marion Phillips pointed out that male members of the party were only 'sympathetic to feminine questions', by which she meant welfare, when women brought them to their notice, but that it was women who most affected public opinion.[7]

Thane highlights the importance of Labour women's political agency which she maintains contributed to improvements in welfare because it was women who were responsible for placing this on the party's agenda. Simultaneously these activists developed an implicit 'critique of the sexual division of labour, and of the role of the state and the labour market in constructing and reinforcing the sexual division of labour'. They did so by promoting 'a politics which valued, rather than devalued, the home' and women's experiences within it and without simultaneously devaluing women's paid work. Thane states that these women 'sought to develop a state and a society in which the marriage relationship and male earnings need not necessarily subordinate and silence women'. As they had done before the First World War, labour women continued to seek ways to achieve 'compatibility between gender equality and gender difference', what Gordon claims was not 'incompatible but difficult: complementary gender roles along with equality of the sexes'.[8]

In Scotland socialist women also challenged the sexual division of labour, uniting across parties and place in protests which ranged from demands to have information on birth control made available to working-class women and family endowments established, to calls for separation allowances. They also sought training schemes for unemployed women, opposed marriage bars and promoted equal pay for equal work.[9] They may not always have enjoyed success, but they did not lose their 'radical and feminist edge'. However, Scottish activists were hampered by the peripheralisation of the movement from the centre of power and the male-dominance of their movement.[10] Helen Gault, a feminist and ILP councillor, was not alone in the view that 'among socialists the belief in equality is only skin deep'.[11] Female activists were also constrained by the severe economic conditions which beset interwar Scotland and which resulted in membership losses. In 1921 the Co-operative Women's Guild had 230 members in its Greenock Central branch; in Glasgow's Gorbals branch there were 302 members, Govan had 310 and Paisley 460 members. By 1927 there were 105, 82, 135 and 286 respectively.[12] Indeed, economic impediments ensured that the Scottish Women's Sections of the Labour Party were unable to send delegates to the national conference in 1932.[13]

Although these activists shared many of the impediments endured by females of the labour movement across Britain, women's experiences differed over time and across parties and place.[14] In Scotland the ILP was the dominant political force until its disaffiliation from the Labour Party in 1932. The ILP has been identified as the 'social conscience' of the Labour Party and the more women-friendly branch of the movement.[15] In 1925 when the ILP was at its most powerful in Scotland, 24 per cent of Glasgow City Council's 'socialist' representatives were women. Yet by the time the Labour Party gained control of the Council in 1933 women made up less than 10 per cent of 'socialist' representatives.[16] It was also 'under the auspices of the ILP', who identified themselves as 'the real women's party', that most of the women's political activity took place. The ILP was the think tank and propaganda body of the Labour Party, linking the social to the political through its aims to effect municipal socialism.[17] This facilitated a space for women to advance their 'special interests' in housing and welfare, ensuring that they could make a marked difference to the lives of their constituents. The ILPer Agnes Paterson Hardie, eldest daughter of Kier Hardie, in her role as Provost of Cumnock challenged and defeated the landowner, Lord Bute of Cumnock, to ensure the removal of slum dwellings from his land and their replacement with council housing. By 1945 three-quarters of Cumnock's population had been re-housed in council houses which were supplied with extra amenities.[18]

Housing was regarded by many women of the labour movement as a feminist issue because the home was the 'workshop' of the housewife and amongst those activists who did not regard this as a feminist issue it was nevertheless a class concern – gender and class were not mutually exclusive. Many Scottish socialist women came from working-class backgrounds, including Agnes Dollan, who was one of eleven children brought up in poverty. She began work in a factory and then became a telephone operator. Indeed, her experiences of poverty and the low wages, long hours and lack of promotional opportunities women endured prompted her to get involved in trade unionism, feminism and ILP politics.[19]

Thus socialist women recognised the issues that affected working-class women and sought to improve their lives by campaigning for improved housing, access to welfare services and a reduction in the price of rents and food as they had done before the First World War. In 1926 the Glasgow Property Owners and Factors Association 'dubbed' Clydebank the 'spiritual home of anarchy'.[20] They had good cause due to the rent strikes orchestrated by the ILPer Jane Rae during the First World War and throughout the 1920s.[21] In 1929 Mary Barbour, an ILP councillor for Govan, Glasgow's first female ballie and a prominent member of the Glasgow Labour Housing Association, [GLHA], along with Christine Moodie, another ILP councillor and president of the GLHA, took a deputation to the Secretary of State for Scotland. On behalf of Glasgow tenants these women charged Glasgow's property owners with harsh and unfair treatment of their tenants due to the increased number of evictions being enforced in this city. Between 1928 and 1929, 20,000 families were evicted. Under pressure from socialist women, the Secretary of State for Scotland requested that the Property Owners and House Factors Association meet with him to try to resolve the situation.[22] This did not resolve the situation, but women's protests did have an impact.

In 1932, the National Federation of Property Owners' and Factors of Scotland, and the Factors' Association of Glasgow, presented a memorial to the Prime Minister, the Chancellor of the Exchequer and the Secretary of State for Scotland. They asked for the adoption of the English rating and valuation system which they hoped would reduce rents and thereby diminish friction between factor and tenant.[23] This request followed a mass meeting in Govan organised by Mary Barbour to arrange further rent strikes in Glasgow. 'Thousands rushed the doors' at the meeting and 'hundreds had to remain outside'.[24] Women's protests to have the cost of rents reduced continued and were increasingly directed at the cost of council housing and their demands were eventually conceded.[25] These protests may have been reduced to insignificance by a male-centred historiography, which has given priority to men of the labour movement and national politics, but they were vital, unrelenting and often successful and where they were not, they kept welfare issues at the centre of public attention.

Hannam and Hunt argue that the social, economic and political environment that emerged during the First World War ensured that consumption, and in particular the cost of rent and food, were submerged within the party's wider political concerns over standards of living so that after the war there was a shift from concerns over the cost of housing to one about the conditions of housing and food. Thus, 'at the end of the 1920s', although some women 'imagined a socialism' which included a politics of consumption, it remained a possibility rather than a reality.[26] Socialist women may have been impeded from developing a politics of consumption, but they continued to promote 'a domesticated version of socialism' that challenged the ways in which the ILP 'privileged production over consumption'. From 1915 Scottish socialist women contesting rent prices and the cost of food and fuel involving themselves in demonstrations and protests. In 1920 at the Labour Women's Conference held in London 400 delegates discussed 'The Question of Bread Prices' and by 1924 the Labour government had adopted this issue, setting up a Royal Commission on Food Prices because it was estimated that they had increased by 79 per cent between 1914 and 1924. In 1925 the Committee's report recommended that a 'Food Council' be established to 'harmonise the interests of producers, distributors and the consumers of food'. The Council was to act as an advisory body and watchdog which could intervene in the interests of the consumer and would report directly to the Board of Trade. The Council was to consist of 12 members, including two 'practical housewives' two trade unionist and the director of the Co-operative Wholesale Society who was seen to have wide business experience. Opposition to the establishment of the Council argued that this was 'a definite advance in the direction of state socialism', but Scottish socialist women were aggrieved that it did not go further in this direction. Under the auspices of the Women's Advisory Council of the Glasgow ILP in 1925, Mrs McLean, the presiding officer, informed delegates that they were there to discuss the 'high price of food' and the 'breadbasket of the housewife'. ILPers, Mary Shennan, Mary Laird and Helen Gault accused the government of 'not dealing with the high price of food and profiteering' and condemned the Food Commission's inquiry for not going further along the road of 'state socialism'. Gault put forward a motion that,

> This conference deems it advisable that all working-class women should rouse an intense agitation in all districts and adopt all means in their power to combat the high price of foodstuffs, and, if necessary, organise boycotts against the buying of such commodities that can be easily dispensed with, and by this means start a movement which, if sufficiently supported, can be the direct means of reducing the high cost of living.[27]

Furthermore, Gault and Laird were not just ILP councillors, they were prominent figures in the Co-operative Women' Guild and Laird was president of the Glasgow Women's Housing Association. Socialist women united across parties to advance 'bread and butter' politics. In 1929 they maintained that the test of a government was 'whether or not it has put more food on the plates of the people'. They also claimed responsibility for bringing 'housing, unemployment, child welfare and rents' into the world of politics.[28] For socialist women standards of living, consumption and social policy overlapped.[29]

Socialist women forged links with each other across the various parties of the labour movement to enhance their potential to promote a gendered policy agenda. Mrs Glover from Glasgow was a member of the Communist Party, the Co-operative Women's Guild, and through this, affiliated to the Labour Party. Indeed a communist member of the Guild introduced her to the organisation and she expressed the view that activists from different ideological strains within the labour movement worked together, because 'we all had the same aims'. Family networks also cemented alliances. Greenock's first female Labour Councillor, Mrs McLeod, was related to a noted Communist Party activist.[30] The capacity to forge links was not limited to Scotland. Selina Cooper, an English Labour Party activist, found herself working with members of the ILP and the Communist Party, sympathising with some of their criticisms of her own party.[31] In local politics many women shared aims and ideals designed to improve the everyday lives of working-class women and enhance the status of womanhood. The ILP's vision of womanhood which mirrored the existing sexual division of labour promoted women as 'guardians of the race' and 'shrines of human life', was also exploited by socialist women.[32] Although this worldview was a constraint, it provided a platform that allowed women to extend their political profiles and promote their 'special interests' without facing male antagonism. The ILP noted that, 'women suffer most in unemployment in the unequal combat between poverty and necessity'.[33] Whilst acknowledging this, unemployment was seen as a male affliction. The ILP hoped to alleviate unemployment by introducing direct labour schemes, mainly house-building.[34] As a political issue, however, housing provided a space for women to exercise their political agency. Women's committees were formed to oversee housing issues, seen as an area of women's 'specialism', and the ILP conceded that they had proved themselves 'capable', effecting domestic reform, and notably that improvements in the housing situation were 'indebted to them'.[35] Hence it was a political rhetoric accommodating many signifiers, some of which women could take advantage of.

Socialist women also advocated the elimination of household drudgery through the provision of labour-saving devices in all new houses. In addition they sought to establish direct labour schemes for women in the form of communal restaurants, laundries, bakeries and nurseries to create work for unemployed women and release housewives from the burdens of housewifery and mothering, enabling them to take their 'proper share of the duties of citizenship'.[36] This was a direct challenge to men's dominance of citizenship and a confrontation of the signification that unemployment was a masculine problem. Thus although the proposed work would entrench the sexual division of labour, men were unlikely to oust women from these sex typed occupations, as they were endeavouring to do in jobs that had fluid labels.[37] However, these proposals were met with male derision.[38]

Nevertheless, socialist women continued to challenge the sexual division of labour. They protested against the sex-typing of employment training, challenging the Glasgow Trades Council's policy regarding the unemployed. Instead of having domestic service training, activists maintained that women should be able to choose whatever employment training they felt to be appropriate rather than having training foisted upon them.[39] Socialist women also contested the unfair treatment of unemployed women. In 1932, Mrs Brand of the Transport and General Workers' Union catalogued how the government was 'penalising the women worker'. Married women were being denied the right to benefits through the Anomalies Act, while unmarried women's benefits were being substantially reduced.[40] Women put forward a gendered critique of unemployment, but their criticism did little to effectively alleviate the problem, which was essentially conceptualised as masculine.[41]

Socialist women challenged this perspective through their involvement in protests against the effects of the means test on housewives. They orchestrated demonstrations and deputations and exploited the discourse which promoted women as the guardians of the family, which proved more productive than utilising an oppositional class or feminist rhetoric. Glasgow Council allowed deputations from representatives of working-class wives and mothers who demanded the abolition of the means test, but frequently refused deputations from 'socialist' organisations demanding this.[42] Women knew how to influence public opinion on matters relating to social welfare. Socialist women also used this strategy, exploiting interwar concerns about the quality and quantity of the British race, to forward policies that would benefit women. Protesting in pragmatic and 'prudent' ways, these women avoided the appearance of subverting the 'breadwinner' ideal. Thus when they demanded improvements to the Widows' Pension Act 1925, they maintained that the benefit would ensure that men's wages were not undercut by women seeking work because they were desperate to feed and maintain their families.[43] In 1929 the Labour Party extended the scope of the 1925 Old Age and Widows' Pensions.[44]

Cairns believes that Scottish socialist women were accommodative of policies designed to shore up the male breadwinner ideal as evidenced by their support of the 'living wage' as espoused by the ILP in the document *Socialism For Our Time*,, which he claims 'had utterly no relevance for women'.[45] This is true of working women because it was designed to provide a breadwinner wage sufficient to support a family. However, the 'living wage' promoted by the ILP embodied a family endowment for married women.[46] Many female activists believed that a family endowment[1] would enhance the status of women who desired marriage and motherhood as an occupation because it acknowledged a woman's right to economic independence within marriage. Thus women of the ILP and the Women's Co-operative Guild supported this policy because it provided concessions to feminist demands.[47] Simultaneously they contested the marriage bar, demanded better wages for women's trades and equal pay for equal work.[48] The ILPer Annie Maxton felt that men's low wages drove married women into the workplace. She understood the hardship of the double burden but

---

1 Better known today by its nearest equivalent - family allowance

also recognised and supported women who chose to work in the formal labour market, arguing that they deserved equal pay for equal work.[49]

Jane Lewis argues that when labour women demanded family endowments they emphasised the link between the welfare of the child and the future of the race. Intervention by the state on the part of the child had a longer tradition and raised fewer fears of subverting the male breadwinner's responsibility than intervention on behalf of wives.[50] Although Scottish female activists also used this strategy, they additionally protested against the unequal economic relations of married couples, openly challenged the sexual division of labour.[51] Nor were they averse to framing their demands for endowments within a class-based rhetoric to accommodate any hostility they might encounter from the male-dominated labour movement, arguing that an endowment would 'combat the exploitation of women by capitalism'.[52] Subverting the breadwinner's economic responsibility for the family was far from the dominant perspective in the labour movement. Trade unions were hostile to family allowances, regarding them as wage subsidies with the potential to push down wages.[53] By contrast, *Forward* reported in 1929 that the Scottish Advisory Council of the ILP had already adopted a resolution in favour of Family Allowance for school children, to be given to mothers or guardians and to be paid for through the taxation of the wealthy.[54] Socialist women added that all other demands should be set aside until endowments were conceded and that 'the Labour Government would be judged by the amount of happiness it brought to the home of the people'.[55] By 1930, under pressure from the ILP, the Labour Party added family endowment to their programme.[56]

The Co-operative Women's Guild and ILP women also demanded that working-class women should have access to birth control and maternity care as ways in which the conditions of the 'trades of motherhood and housewifery' could be addressed.[57] These activists recognised that large families and constant childbearing inhibited women by absorbing their time and energy and detrimentally affecting their health. This undermined working-class women's ability to participate in active citizenship. Hence by challenging these constraints socialist women implicitly contested the gendered nature of citizenship. Socialist women's demands that working-class women should have access to information about birth control proved to be extremely contentious in Scotland. The Scottish labour movement was more hostile to birth control than its English counterpart, but this was not a united hostility. In 1924 a number of prominent ILP women sent a deputation to the ILPer John Wheatley, then Labour Minister for Health, to state the case for information on birth control to be made accessible to working-class women at clinics set up by local authorities. Wheatley rejected birth control on religious grounds and argued that to provide such information was far too revolutionary.[58] He was not unique in his hostility towards birth control.[59] In 1926 an article by ILPer Walton Newbold was published in *Forward* attacking the Motherwell ILP MP, Rev. James Barr, for his,

> superstitious and obscure speech on birth control, which, deliberately closed the book of knowledge and forbade its opening by appealing to religious prejudices, even though the women of the labour movement had by majorities more overwhelming than they had shown on any other issue of a controversial character declared time and again in their conferences for legislation.[60]

Not one of the Scottish ILP MPs who had gained 'revolutionary' reputations for their militant activities between 1910 and 1922 and for their condemnation of capitalism in Parliament voted for the Birth Control Enabling Bill to permit the dissemination of information about contraception.[61] There were various reasons for this. Cairns determined that male animosity to birth control was to accommodate the Catholic Church and Catholic voters. Yet, opposition to contraception was not the preserve of the Catholic clergy. Barr, a United Free Church minister, was one of its most hostile critics. Indeed, Church of Scotland ministers, unlike Church of England ministers, proposed to 'repudiate the countenance of methods of birth control' because they felt it to be a 'mortal sin'.[62] In 1926 the socialist Dora Russell of the Women's Birth Control Group expressed the view in *Forward* that 'the shadow of threatened religious opposition blinds many Scottish members and organisers to the reality of possible support – great in numbers – passionate in belief' for birth control.[63] Seemingly opposition also stemmed from the socialist movement's adherence to 'Knoxian theology and obsessive Puritanism'.[64] However, the ILP, when promoting municipalisation, consistently argued that poverty, poor living conditions, infant mortality and disease were by-products of the capitalist system. Large families were not the problem, capitalism was. Birth control and smaller families threatened the ILP propaganda and divided the party. Although in the minority, there were women who held the view that birth control was not a 'political question' which should be 'tacked' on to the ILP's programme. Female activists were also concerned that if contraceptives did not avert pregnancy then women would be held accountable or accused of adultery.[65] Most socialist women, however, argued that the fight for knowledge which would allow women to control their fertility would unite and politicise significant numbers of women. Thus they orchestrated protests against the male dominant leadership stance. In 1926 a meeting of 600 female voters was held in Motherwell. Only two people dissented from the resolution passed to protest against Barr's decision not to support the Birth Control Enabling Act and to request that he 'reconsider his decision'.[66] A further three hundred people in Wishaw and four hundred women from Motherwell endorsed the cause of socialist women by signing petitions demanding information on birth control.[67] Dora Russell also challenged the prominent ILP men subverting their reactionary and class conscious reputations when she stated,

> Women find our reactionary leaders shirking this opposing it in defiance of decisions of the Women's conference. Our champions, profiting by women's votes condemn women to suffering and ignorance as if they were a slave class.[68]

The Birth Control Enabling Act was passed in 1930, making it permissible for married women, whose lives, or the life or their unborn child, would be endangered by pregnancy, to receive information about birth control in local authority clinics. However, the Act was not extended to Scotland until 1934. By 1936 Scotland lagged significantly behind England in the provision of municipal birth control clinics: there were 118 municipal clinics in England providing information on birth control and only two in Scotland, one in Aberdeen and one in Greenock.[69]

The ILP considered the issue of birth control to have no 'economic or social value, whatever its individual and family virtues!'[70] Thus the ILP persisted in promoting socialism in archaic ideological terms, a politics that was intended to emancipate the housewife from the evils of capitalism, within the existing sexual division of labour. For the majority of women, the home was to be their 'workshop' and 'the centre and pivot of human life, the nursery of the child and the training ground of tomorrow's men and women'.[71] And Patrick Dollan could state with comparative impunity that it was a 'terrible reflection on Glasgow politics that birth control was more important in the 1927 municipal elections than the introduction of direct labour'.[72]

Dollan's assertion was a strategy to undermine any possibility that the issue of birth control would displace, or detract from, the question of unemployment, deemed a 'public' political concern, unlike birth control, which was identified as a 'personal' issue. Women's concerns were frequently conceptualised as 'personal', subservient to the 'public' and thus sidelined. These impediments ensured that women faced difficulties when expressing an alternative vision of society which undermined that of the male-dominated labour movement, but they were subversive. Some socialist women used a class-based critique, arguing that working-class women should have the same privileges as the 'rich': the right to control their fertility. Others exploited concerns over the British race. Birth control and improved maternity care were identified as measures that would help reduce Scotland's relatively high levels of maternal and infant mortality. In 1931 the Scottish Women's Co-operative Guild established a Committee to investigate the extent and causes of maternal mortality. After the Committee's report, the majority of the Guild's members voted in favour of supporting the dissemination of the 'instruction of constructive' birth control methods because they believed that the use of contraception would contribute to a falling incidence in maternal mortality.[73] Certainly this was not the dominant Labour Party line or a reflection of the Labour Party's vision of womanhood.

Maternity care and child welfare were major concerns of socialist women. In the face of government cuts in public expenditure and attempts to claw back services, by 1931 they had helped to establish fifty day nurseries and child gardens which were maintained under the maternal and child welfare schemes which they also promoted actively.[74] In 1926 Glasgow Corporation built new premises for the West Govan Child Welfare Association, agreeing to contribute 50 per cent of the maintenance cost. At its opening it was acknowledged that the ILP councillor Mary Barbour's influence on the Corporation had been instrumental in the decision to support the extension of child welfare.[75] She also challenged traditional gender ideals. At the opening of the Govan Child Welfare Clinic, Barbour stated that the new clinic, 'was not merely a child welfare clinic, but an institution for mother-craft and father-craft too'. She let it be known that the clinic, 'would see its first meeting for fathers', asking 'health visitors to turn out' to make sure that the meeting was a success.[76] Barbour was also linked to the Govan's Welfare and Advisory Clinic which provided information and access to contraception and which maintained that 'it is of the utmost importance that this knowledge which has been in the hands of the rich should be given to the poor for their benefit and well being'.[77] Marion Henery, a member of the Lanarkshire Communist Party, recalled how she was aware of the Glasgow birth control clinic, referring to it as 'very unusual' and a 'kind of keep quiet thing'. However, she also diffused knowledge about the clinic to other Communist Party members in Lanarkshire.[78] Although relative ignorance of birth control persisted and limited incomes inhibited the use of contraceptives, women's political networks disseminated knowledge of the availability of birth control and gradually spread the message that the 'poor should be no different to the rich' in their ability to reduce family size. In turn, the idea that greater freedom, better lifestyles and improved health would be amongst the benefits of using birth control took root.[79]

Socialist women also defied the party line to promote the right of working-class women to control their fertility. The ILP activist Mrs Auld presided over the public opening of Govan's branch of the Glasgow Women's Welfare and Advisory Clinic and Barbour was one of the main speakers. She wished the organisers every success, and referred to the involvement of socialist women in obtaining the objective for the establishment of the clinic. She was also happy to work with the Moderate councillor Mrs Bell to establish these objectives.[80] By the late 1930s the Glasgow branch of the Scottish Federation of Mothers' Welfare Clinics were having to turn women away, gaining as many as thirty new members each week. Attendance was also increasing in Paisley. Many of these private clinics throughout Scotland were aided by donations from local councils. Branches of the Mothers' Welfare Clinics at Johnstone, Paisley and Renfrew all received council grants, whilst medical officers employed by the councils sent women to such clinics.[81] Local government was an arena of politics in which women were increasingly numerically and politically influential allowing them greater ease with which to promote their aims more successfully. At the Scottish Co-operative Women's Guild Annual Conference in May 1930 it was noted how 'women through their training in the Guild were making very efficient Town Council members'.[82]

Labour women educated women in politics, raised their awareness of class and gender, promoted public speaking and encouraged women to stand as candidates in political campaigns. Furthermore, they used a variety of means at their disposal to promote their aims of improving the lives of working-class women. In addition, implicitly and explicitly they challenged the sexual division of labour. At times they did so by manipulated concerns over the race and exploited the dominant language of interwar Britain to these ends. They also used the ILP's emphasis on municipal socialism in constructive and feminist ways. Overtly and covertly, and often in direct defiance of the attitudes of many of the men of the labour movement, feminist activists challenged the sexual division of labour. They also worked with other women's groups and other parties to these ends. Like their counterparts throughout Britain socialist women were most successful at the level of local government, but the permissive nature of welfare legislation ensured that this was an area of politics which was significant because it directly related to people's everyday lives. Thus women's political activity contributed immensely to the improvements in health, housing and welfare which took place between the wars, to the progress of the labour movement and to the foundations of the welfare state whilst weaving the threads of the first wave of the feminism movement into the Second World War era by continuing to challenge the sexual division of labour.

Notes

1   For Scottish women's neglect in British studies see, Breitenbach, E., Brown, A. & Myres, F. 'Understanding Women in Scotland', *Feminist Review*, pp. 44-65. A notable exception is, Hannam, J and Hunt, K. *Socialist Women Britain, 1880s to 1920s*, London: Routledge, 2002.
2   For a rejection of this implication see Digby, A. and Stewart, J [eds], *Gender, Health and Welfare*, London: Routledge, 1996.
3   See,. Harrison, B. *Prudent Revolutionaries: portraits of British feminists between the wars*, Oxford: Clarendon Press 1987.
4   Graves, P. *Labour Women, Women in British Working Class Politics 1918-1939*, Cambridge, CUP,1994, p.10 and 'An Experiment in Women-Centred Socialism: Labour Women in Britain', in Gruber, H. & Graves, P. [eds.], *Women and Socialism, Socialism and Women Europe Between Two World Wars*, Oxford: OUP, 1998, pp. 181-214.
5   Scott, G. *Feminism and the Politics of Working Women. The Women's Co-operative Guild 1880s To The Second World War*, London: UCL Press, 1997.
6   *Glasgow Herald*, 23 September 1929.
7   Ibid.
8   Thane, P. 'Visions of gender in the making of the British welfare state: the case of women in the British Labour Party and social policy 1906-1945, Bock, G. & Thane, P. [eds], *Maternity and Gender Policies Women and the Rise of the European States 1880s-1950s*, London: Routledge, 1991, pp. 95-97 and Gordon, E. 'Women and Working-class Politics in Scotland 1900-1914' in Corr, H. & Jamieson, L. [eds.] *State, Private Life and Political Change*, Basingstoke: Macmillan,1990, p. 234 respectively.
9   Thane, 'Visions of Gender' pp. 98-99.
10 See McKinlay, A. 'Doubtful wisdom and uncertain promise' in McKinlay, A. & Morrris, R. J. [eds.], *The ILP on Clydeside 1893-1932 from foundations to disintegration*, Manchester: MUP, 1991, pp. 123-153.
11 *Forward*, 28 February 1925.
12 Glasgow Regional Archive, [GRA], Scottish Co-operative Women' Guild, 29th Annual Report, 1921, p. 23 and 35th, 1927 p. 23, [SCWG].
13 *Labour Women*, June, 1932, p. 87.
14 See Hannam, J & Hunt, K. 'Gendering the Stories of Socialism: An essay in Historical Criticism', in Walsh, M.[ed.], *Working Out Gender Perspectives from Labour History*, Aldershot, Ashgate, 1999, pp. 102-118.

15 See, Sowerwine, C. 'Socialism, Feminism and the Socialist Women's Movement from the French Revolution to World War II ' in Bridenthal, E., Stuard, S. M. and Wiesner, M. E. [eds.], *Becoming Visible Women in European History*, Boston, Houghton Mifflin, 1998, pp. 357-388.
16 Cairns, D., 'Women and the Clydeside Labour Movement', University of Strathclyde M.Phil. Thesis, p. 106.
17 Ibid.
18 Knox, W. *Scottish Labour Leaders*, Edinburgh: Mainstream, 1984, pp. 137-139.
19 Oxford Dictionary of National Biography at http://www.oxforddnb.com; *Scotsman*, 8 September 1937 and Knox, *Labour Leaders*, p. 89.
20 *Govan Press*, 29 January 1926.
21 *Forward*, 17 August 1927.
22 *Glasgow Herald*, 10 September 1929.
23 *Govan Press*, 17 June 1932.
24 Ibid., 29 February 1932 and *Forward*, 14 May 1932.
25 See, Glasgow Regional Archive (GRA), Glasgow City Council Minutes, 16 March 1933
26 Ibid.
27 *Scotsman*, 13 April 1920, 11 December 1924 and 9 May 1925 and *Forward* 14 February 1925
28 *Glasgow Evening Times*, 16 November 1929.
29 *Forward*, 8 June 1929.
30 *Labour Women*, June, 1936, pp. 192-193.
31 Liddington, J. *The Life And Times Of A Respectable Rebel Selina Cooper 1884-1946*, London: Virago, 1984, p. 372.
32 *Forward*, 11 May 1922.
33 *Forward*, 11 March 1922.
34 *Govan Press*, 9 August 1929.
35 *Forward*, 19 March 1922.
36 See *Forward*, 1 July 1922 and GRA, Barhead ILP Women's Sections Manuscript Minutes, 6 September 1926.
37 See Lewis, J. 'In Search of a Real Equality: Women Between The Wars', in Gloversmith, F. [ed.], *Class, Culture and Social Change A New View of the 1930s*, Brighton: Harvester Press, 1980, and for Scotland see, Hughes, A. 'A Rough Kind of Feminism, The formation of working-class women's political identities, Clydeside 1919-1932', Unpublished Ph.D. Thesis, University of Strathclyde, 2001 chapter 2.
38 *Forward*, 21 June 1919 and *Govan Press*, 9 August 1929.
39 GRA, Glasgow Trades and Labour Council Executive Minutes, (GTLC), 4 February 1926.
40 *Forward*, 14 May 1932.
41 *Forward*, 5 March 1932.
42 See, *Govan Press*, 18 June 1930 and 1 July 1932 and Glasgow City Council Minutes, 2, 16 and especially 30 March 1933.
43 See SCWG 27th Annual Report, 1919, pp. 15-16 and 33rd Annual Report 1925,

p. 18.
44 Thane, P. *The Foundations of the Welfare State Social Policy in Modern Britain*, London: Longman, 1982, pp. 197-199.
45 Cairns, *Clydeside Labour Movement*, p. 115.
46 Graves, op. cit. 'Women-Centred Socialism', pp. 197-198.
47 SCWG 32nd Annual Report, March 1924, p. 16 and ILP Women's Section, 19 October 1925.
48 GTLC Minutes, 4 February 1926.
49 Ibid., 19 October 1925.
50 Lewis, J. *The Politics of Motherhood: Child and Maternal Welfare in England 1900-1939*, London, Croom Helm, 1980, pp. 165-190.
51 ILP Women's Section, 2 March 1925 and 6 September 1926.
52 Ibid., 2 March 1925.
53 STUC, 33rd Annual Report 1930 p. 87.
54 *Forward*, 12 April 1929.
55 *Glasgow Herald*, 23 September 1929.
56 Graves, Women-Centred Socialism', p. 196.
57 SCWG Central Council Minutes, 7 January and 4 February 1931. See also, ILP Women's Section, 8 February, 6 September and 6 November 1926.
58 *Forward*, 1 April 1926.
59 *Forward*, 29 March 1924 and April 17 1926.
60 *Forward*, 13 March 1926.
61 Ibid. For the ILPers see McKinlay & Morrris, [eds.], *The ILP on Clydeside*.
62 *Glasgow Herald*, 22 September 1930. For England see, Jane Lewis, 'Public Institutions and Private Relationship – Marriage and Marriage Guidance 1920-1968', *Twentieth Century British History*, Vol.1, No. 3, 1990, pp. 233-265.
63 *Forward*, 27 March, 1926.
64 Young, J. D. *Women and Popular Struggles: a History of British Working-Class Women, 1560-1984*. Edinburgh: Mainstream, 1985, pp. 161-164. See also, Knox, *Labour Leaders*, p. 26
65 *Forward*, 3 and 10 April 1926.
66 *Forward*, 27 March 1926.
67 Ibid.
68 *Forward*, 27 March 1926.
69 *Glasgow Herald*, 26 May 1936.
70 *Forward*, 1 October 1927.
71 *Forward*, 14 October 1922.
72 *Forward*, 5 November 1927.
73 Ibid.; SCWG, Central Council Minutes, 7 January and 4 February 1931; ILP Women's Section, 8 February, 6 September and 6 November 1926.
74 *Forward*, 21 February 1931 and 8 October 1932.
75 *Govan Press*, 26 November 1926.
76 Ibid.
77 Ibid., 13 August 1926.
78 Interview with Joe and Marion Henery, William Gallagher Memorial Library,

Tape 7.
79 GRA, Scottish Federation of Mother's Welfare Clinics Manuscript Minutes Book, [Mothers' Federation Minutes], 27 September 1927.
80 *Govan Press,* 13 August 1926.
81 Mother's Federation Minutes, 28 February 1938.
82 *Glasgow Herald,* 17 May 1930.